No Fire Next Time

No Fire Next Time

*Black-Korean Conflicts and
the Future of America's Cities*

PATRICK D. JOYCE

CORNELL UNIVERSITY PRESS
Ithaca & London

First published 2003 by Cornell University Press

First printing, Cornell Paperbacks, 2003

Printed in the United States of America

Library of Congress Cataloging-in-Publication Data

Joyce, Patrick D.
    No fire next time : Black-Korean conflicts and the future of America's cities / Patrick D. Joyce
        p. cm.
    Includes bibliographical references (p.   ) and index.
    ISBN 0-8014-3941-8 (cloth : alk. paper) — ISBN 0-8014-8890-7 (pbk. : alk. paper)
    1. African Americans—Relations with Korean Americans.
2. African Americans—New York (State)—New York—Social conditions. 3. Korean Americans—New York (State)—New York—Social conditions. 4. African Americans—California—Los Angeles—Social conditions. 5. Korean Americans—California—Los Angeles—Social conditions. 6. Social conflict—New York (State)—New York. 7. Social conflict—California—Los Angeles. 8. New York (N.Y.)—Race relations. 9. Los Angeles (Calif.)—Race relations. I. Title.
E185.615.J695   2003
305.895'7073'091732—dc21

                                                        2003002345

Cornell University Press strives to use environmentally responsible suppliers and materials to the fullest extent possible in the publishing of its books. Such materials include vegetable-based, low-VOC inks and acid-free papers that are recycled, totally chlorine-free, or partly composed of nonwood fibers. For further information, visit our website at www.cornellpress.cornell.edu.

Cloth printing   10 9 8 7 6 5 4 3 2 1

Paperback printing   10 9 8 7 6 5 4 3 2 1

Contents

Acknowledgments

I am grateful to the many people who offered me their talents and resources while I was writing this book. The Mellon Foundation and the International Migration Program of the Social Science Research Council gave me generous financial support while I conducted much of the research. Various organizations allowed me to present early drafts of my work at annual meetings or conferences, including the American Political Science Association, the New England Political Science Association, and the Russell Sage Foundation.

I owe a special debt to the individuals from New York City and Los Angeles who granted me interviews and graciously gave me their time and insight. My editor at Cornell University Press, Roger Haydon, contributed countless ideas for improving an imperfect manuscript, as did Cornell's anonymous reviewers and copyeditors. I received invaluable advice, inspiration, and wisdom from a number of academic colleagues, but none more than Paul Peterson, Theda Skocpol, Michael Jones-Correa, and Raphael Sonenshein. To Juliet Gainsborough, Srinivas Gandhi, and Eric Thun, my companions on the long journey through graduate school, I cannot express in words my thanks for the countless coffees and conversations that made the whole endeavor worthwhile, and for the lasting bond of friendship. Most important, I could not have completed any of this work without the love and patience of my wife, Rajee; my children, Arjun and Priya; my parents, Karen and Mike Joyce; and my parents-in-law, Ratna and Rao Kolagotla. I dedicate this book to my grandparents, Leona and Harold Nadle and Mable and William Joyce, whose instincts for fairness, tolerance of others, and love of learning continue to shape everything I do.

PATRICK D. JOYCE

Cambridge, Massachusetts

No Fire Next Time

Introduction

God gave Noah the rainbow sign,
No more water, the fire next time!
—Prophecy re-created from the Bible
in a song by a slave (Baldwin 1962, 106)

In 1962, James Baldwin invoked these words in a clarion call to the nation. As he saw it, America's resistance to racial equality threatened to provoke a terrible vengeance by blacks. White intransigence deepened black despair and fed the racial pride of black nationalism. As African Americans came to believe that only power, and not goodwill, could improve their position in American society, they would see little choice but to answer the sins of whites with violence.

Racial warfare would assume biblical proportions, and the fate of the nation hung in the balance.

Baldwin's words appeared prescient. In a few years, racial violence ripped across American cities, as blacks rioted in Los Angeles, Detroit, Newark, and scores of other places. By the end of the 1960s, the storm had subsided, only to return again in the 1980s and 1990s to cities like Miami, Los Angeles, and Cincinnati.

As Baldwin feared, racial violence did not alleviate the senselessness of America's oldest tragedy but compounded it. However, the violence did not come as warfare between blacks and whites, as Baldwin expected. Instead, it took its toll in ways he might have found puzzling. First, the flames devastated black communities more than white, leaving society's dominant institutions intact. Second, the flames touched newly arrived immigrants who were neither black nor white, further complicating American race relations.

The worst episode struck Los Angeles in 1992 and enveloped mostly black and Latino communities. Although the violence began with black rage at the implausible acquittals of four white police officers in the beating of Rodney King, it was fueled by tensions between African Americans and Korean Americans. A string of highly publicized shootings over the years had culminated in the senseless killing of a black teenager by a Korean merchant, and a court verdict upholding a reduced sentence for the merchant was handed down just a week before the riots, inflaming black opinion.

Then came the civil unrest; violence seemed to beget violence. Arson cut a wide swath through the City of Angels and left hundreds of Korean stores gutted in its wake. Korean merchants armed themselves and fired at looters from rooftops. To the nation, the media conveyed the powerful image of burning buildings.

But was violence the inevitable result of black-Korean tensions? Events in New York City two years earlier prove that it was not.

Instead of riots, the image conveyed from New York was of throngs of demonstrators with fists and picket signs thrust in the air as they marched outside a Korean grocery where a merchant had reportedly assaulted a black customer. Black activists led a boycott that mobilized hundreds of supporters in a year-long and highly contentious series of protests. Korean merchants and other opponents of the boycott responded in kind, rallying hundreds of their own supporters to counterdemonstrate.

Tensions between blacks and Koreans had emerged in the 1980s over the same issues in both Los Angeles and New York City, but in each city they reached a different climax: if the first was inexplicably violent, the second was remarkably restrained.

The contrast between these two images provides the central puzzle of this book: What makes groups engage in conflict violently in some situations but nonviolently in others? The implications go well beyond understanding black-Korean conflict or even racial and ethnic conflict in the United States more generally. World history is replete with cases of peaceful social movements, labor strikes, and political campaigns that inexplicably degenerate into violence.

Sociological theories of race and ethnic relations provide little help in solving this puzzle. Rounding up the usual suspects—such as poverty, unemployment, segregation, and racism—fails to account for the different outcomes in Los Angeles and New York. These factors existed in roughly equal measures in both cities. In highlighting these factors, sociologists may have correctly pinpointed the sources of injustice. However, they have neglected to identify the mechanisms that translate latent tensions into overt conflict.

In this book, I argue that the solution to the puzzle lies in politics—in particular, political institutions, which vary from place to place and have profound consequences for the way groups interact. Political scientists have had the tools at their disposal for explaining how tensions translate into conflict, but since they rarely look beyond the boundaries of conventional politics, they have largely neglected the task. This book takes up that challenge and demonstrates how political institutions shape social conflict by channeling tensions.

The puzzle of protest and violence in black-Korean conflicts also has important practical implications. What can we do to avoid intergroup violence? How can we encourage groups to build lasting bridges to one another instead? As we look to the future, these questions assume a particular urgency.

THE URGENCY: INEQUALITY, DIVERSITY, AND INSTITUTIONS

At this moment in time, we should be especially mindful to search out any lessons that can be learned from past episodes of conflict. The United States faces a contentious future, the likelihood of which is suggested by three trends: first, racial and ethnic diversity is increasing; second, economic inequality has widened; and third, our governing institutions have weakened. These trends originate in separate causes, but their coming together at the same point in history means that the potential for racial and ethnic tensions may be heightened just as our capacities to cope with them have diminished.

Increasing Diversity

Racial and ethnic diversity is on the rise, bringing radical demographic change in the United States. Today, about three-quarters of Americans are non-Hispanic white; by mid-century, however, that group will make up only 53 percent of the population, according to projections by the U.S. Census Bureau (2001). Urban areas are experiencing the changes most rapidly: already, a majority of the population living in the nation's one hundred largest cities is black, Latino, and Asian (Schmitt 2001).

The United States currently has more foreign-born residents than ever, and their proportion in the population, now above 10 percent, is approaching the historical peak of 1910, which was 15 percent (Gibson and Lennon 1999). Between 1990 and 2000, the number of immigrants grew by 57 percent, actually outpacing their growth earlier in the century (Kilborn and Clemetson 2002). Immigration from Latin America and Asia is a major factor producing the change: among first-generation immigrants counted in the 2000 census, 51 percent were born in Latin America and 27 percent in Asia (Brittingham 2000). By 2050, Latinos and Asians will double their proportions in the population, to 24 percent and 9 percent, respectively. Blacks, on the other hand, will increase their share of the population only slightly, from 13 percent to 15 percent (U.S. Census Bureau 2001).

If history is any guide, high levels of immigration promise greater intergroup conflict. Contrary to popular perception, the assimilation of immigrants has always been a conflictual process and has proceeded in fits and starts rather than in a smooth linear fashion (Skerry 2000). In the past, high rates of immigration—and ethnic diversity itself—propelled waves of ethnic conflict (Olzak 1992; Shanahan and Olzak 1999). In the wake of rapid population change, new immigrants and old minorities competed for scarce resources or fought for social and political inclusion in the racial hierarchy. In the nineteenth century, for instance, Irish immigrants at times allied politically with white supremacists and took part in violent attacks on blacks in order to evade nativist threats and become accepted as "white" by other groups (Ignatiev 1995). In the twentieth century, Jews and blacks developed a tortuous relationship, alternately clashing and cooperating. In the future, Americans have good reason to fear terrorism at home and to expect war abroad—developments that will breed further mistrust of new immigrant groups.

If past trends continue, the United States faces the danger of increased tensions among new and old groups. This is likely to be true especially for racial and ethnic minorities, whose common experiences with discrimination and disadvantage would otherwise suggest a solid basis for coalition.

Widening Inequality

Economic inequality has grown since the middle of the twentieth century. At a time when social ties have frayed, the chasm between rich and poor gives Americans even less reason to identify with one another. Just as important, it makes resources scarcer for the disadvantaged, generating competition among those who can least afford it.

From the late 1960s to the late 1990s, family income declined for the poorest Americans as it rose for the wealthiest (Wilson 1999, 25). In the final years of the century, the economic fortunes of the disadvantaged began to improve. Poverty levels declined for every racial and ethnic group, although the levels for blacks and Latinos remained about three times that of whites (Dalaker and Proctor 2000).

Despite some encouraging trends, there appears to be little cause for optimism. The fast paces of globalization and technological change, two of the chief causes of widening inequality, do not appear to be slowing. Although government has long played an important role in equalizing incomes (Wilson 1999, 2–3), the strength of conservative political forces at the national level will make it difficult for unions to achieve better wages for workers and will likely reduce the chances for significant job training programs to ease workers from traditional occupations into the increasingly hi-tech and service-driven economy. Moreover, the nation's longest period of economic expansion in recent history has ended (Hall et al. 2001), which could reverse recent trends and lead to the resumption of widening inequality.

The gap between rich and poor does not seem likely to narrow anytime soon, a dire portent in light of the first trend—increasing diversity—and the third—the weakening of political institutions.

Weakened Institutions

The nation's governing institutions have been undergoing changes that diminish their capacities for preventing and mediating racial and ethnic conflict. Two dynamics are especially important: the decay of political party organizations as mobilizing forces and the devolution of political power from the federal government to the states.

In recent decades, political parties in the United States have declined in significance in certain ways—such as the degree of loyalty given them by voters—and risen in significance in others—such as their role as campaign fundraisers. But the change in parties that has the most serious consequences for intergroup relations is their decay as electoral organizations—and the attendant decline in capacity to mobilize citizens for political action at the local level.

Compared to other nations, the United States has never had strong parties. Political reforms that began with the Progressive Movement of the 1920s, however, set in motion forces that redefined political parties, insulating them from their traditional roots in urban neighborhoods and stripping them of their ability to mobilize new groups in urban politics (Ginsberg and Shefter 1999).

Big cities experienced a resurgence in electoral mobilization during the postwar decades, as African Americans formed coalitions with liberal whites on the path to political incorporation (Browning, Marshall, and Tabb 1990). However, the broader trend toward an insulated, nonmobilizing politics has been reinforced more recently by another institutional development, the "new federalism," in which the federal government has reduced financial aid to cities and increasingly transferred decision-making authority to state governments.

Advocates of this devolution of power argue that it strengthens cities and empowers citizens at the local level (*Economist* 1998; Goodwin 1996). Devolution may have bolstered state legislatures, but recent research suggests it has not done the same for city governments (Cole, Hissong, and Arvidson 1999). Cities continue to occupy vulnerable positions in the competitive arena of federalism, where labor and capital flow freely across city lines (Peterson 1981). Unable to pursue redistribution effectively, local governments are generally powerless to influence many of the larger societal forces that generate tensions among groups.

As a result, when national policymakers changed social welfare from a federal to a state responsibility, they shifted the burden of redistributive policy to a level of government that lacks both the incentives and the resources to assist the poor (Peterson 1995). A prosperous economy during the 1990s allowed cities and states to reduce their welfare loads without visibly increasing poverty, but a reversal of economic fortunes could test their limits. In 2002, poverty increased for the first time in eight years (Pear 2002). By denying cities a safety net for the disadvantaged, devolution thus potentially exacerbates the impact of widening inequality on race and ethnic relations.

Moreover, as a result of declining federal aid to cities, urban political actors and institutions are becoming less oriented toward electoral mobilization and more oriented toward public management (Eisinger 1998). Some may see this type of reform as a positive development. However, every reform has its tradeoffs and its unintended consequences. In this case, the impact on cities echoes the worst tendencies of the Progressive Era, further stripping local governments of the incentive to promote an active citizenry.

Without a strong grounding in local communities, parties and politicians lack the resources and legitimacy to mediate effectively among groups in conflict. These changes reduce the capacity of political institutions to channel tensions, just as growing diversity and widening inequality make the future of intergroup relations increasingly uncertain.

OVERVIEW

I begin the book with an overview of the phenomenon of black-Korean conflicts, which have introduced a new phase in race relations in the United States. Drawing on original data that I collected for this book, the first chapter paints a portrait of black-Korean conflicts in cities across the nation: where they happened, how they began, how they ended, who their participants were, and what goals they had.

In chapter 2, I assess theories of race and ethnic relations that have been used to explain black-Korean conflicts and test their ability to explain actual patterns of conflict in a large number of cities across time. Most theories focus on cultural or political beliefs or on economic interests. However, none adequately accounts for the transformation of latent tensions into overt conflict. I develop the argument that urban political institutions help to configure the environment in which intergroup tensions emerge, thus affecting the likelihood that tensions are translated into organized, nonviolent protest.

Simply put, cities with strong traditions of machine-style politics—in which material incentives and neighborhood-level connections to politics long served as incentives for people to participate in politics—tend to promote grassroots political activity, which enables community activists to channel tensions by mobilizing supporters. On the other hand, cities with the insulated, reform-style political institutions that were the legacy of the Progressive Movement tend to leave tensions unorganized and more likely to result in violence. Black political representation also facilitates nonviolent forms of conflict. Analysis of the national data on black-Korean conflicts supports this explanation but also leaves gaps that require supplementing it with another approach—a closer examination of case studies—in order to refine a political-institutional theory of conflict.

Chapter 3 returns to the two cities that frame the original puzzle, New York City and Los Angeles. By contrasting the different forms of conflict and the different arrangements of political institutions in the two cities, it sets the stage for the next two chapters, which trace the development of black-Korean conflicts over time. Drawing on field interviews, press reports, and public documents, I demonstrate how the political contexts of each city—New York, a traditional machine city, and Los Angeles, a nonpartisan reform city—shaped the expression of tensions differently, generating protest in the former and allowing large-scale violence in the latter.

Together, the breadth of the national-level analysis and the depth of the case studies help to solve the theoretical puzzle of why groups engage in conflict violently in some contexts and nonviolently in others. In chapter 6, I tie these strands together with the argument that political institutions and conventional political processes influence the tenor of social discourse—on the streets, as well as in the halls of government. Politics shapes conflict by influencing the extent of community organizing and by contributing to different forms of black nationalism, different relationships between community organizations and police departments, and different patterns of conflict intervention by public officials and other parties. The experiences of cities with black-Korean conflict also offers lessons for the prevention and resolution of racial and ethnic conflicts in American cities, which I specify in this final chapter.

FROM THEORY TO RESOLUTION

My emphasis in this book is on factors within the realm of realistic change. The forces of unrestrained global capitalism and deeply embedded racial bias are ultimately responsible for the injustices that underlie intergroup conflict. But achieving direct, radical change in the structure of society is a distant, if not impossible, goal—especially for individuals and organizations at the local level, constrained as they are by the profound vulnerabilities of cities in the American federal system.

Furthermore, those seeking social change cannot rely on the goodwill of a majority that fails to understand the plight of the disadvantaged. Progressive policies are not achieved by the mere asking—they are won by hard-fought battles, and only sustained by durable political coalitions. The practical question, then, is not just how to change the world but how to facilitate the growth of coalitions that will find that goal more easily within their reach.

Durable, meaningful coalitions across group lines must be anchored locally: in cities and neighborhoods. Thus, my focus on local solutions is not meant to absolve national policymakers of their responsibility for pursuing egalitarian policies but to suggest parallel strategies that can help strengthen such efforts at the grassroots—and particularly, strategies that cities can ably pursue. On their own, cities lack the capacity to alleviate social and economic conditions stemming from national trends. If they learn the lessons from black-Korean conflicts, however, they may improve their chances of resolving conflicts and preventing future violence. To borrow James Baldwin's words, they may spare themselves the fire next time.

As astute observers of intergroup relations have increasingly noted, interest-based conflicts at the grass roots are among the greatest obstacles to progressive, multiracial coalitions (Sonenshein 1993; Wilson 1999). Overcoming these conflicts requires, first, that we acknowledge and investigate them. However, that task is complicated by their many forms and their wide dispersal. Thus, it is crucial to compare the experiences of similar conflicts in different cities.

While undertaking the research for this book, I noticed that activists and officials trying to end conflicts in one city were often unaware of the paths taken by conflicts in others, even though other cities' experiences held valuable lessons for their own efforts. So if my theoretical goal in this book is to contribute to scholars' understanding of racial and ethnic conflict by highlighting the role of political institutions, my practical goal is to assist concerned citizens in thinking about the task of preventing and resolving it.

Comparing conflicts between African Americans and Korean Americans in different cities yields a larger lesson for the new century: that groups need not embrace each other in violence. The images of black-Korean conflict from New York City and Los Angeles may serve as signposts to alternative futures: both contentious, but one of them devastating. The experiences from these two cities, however, also hold more than a promise of the bad against the worse. They contain the seeds of a better future—buried deeply, but there nonetheless.

If we read the signposts right, we might even find it possible to construct genuine and durable coalitions across racial and ethnic lines. If conflict is inevitable, as it appears to be, we can work to ensure that it is productive rather than destructive and builds bridges rather than burns them.

Chapter 1

Black-Korean Conflict in American Cities

The images broadcast nationwide from Los Angeles in 1992 led the American public to the conclusion that African Americans and Korean Americans were inextricably locked in violent struggle. The civil unrest seemed to prove that blacks and Koreans everywhere were doomed to this fate. This was not only a popular conception; scholars also saw relations between blacks and Koreans as inescapably violent, if tragically so. In the view of Reginald Robinson, the riots were evidence of "the violent reality of African American and Korean life in Los Angeles" (1993, 20). Blacks and Koreans, constrained by racial oppression to a "violent discourse," were unable to coexist peacefully in American cities.

Is this characterization of black-Korean relations accurate? Have conflicts between blacks and Koreans in American cities generally been marked by violence, or have they more often assumed peaceful forms? Even if Robinson is right about racial oppression playing a role in generating conflicts, is there perhaps something particular about the city of Los Angeles that made collective violence inevitable?

Generalizing about a set of social interactions from a single case always carries a risk: the case may be unrepresentative of the larger set. Thus, understanding why blacks and Koreans engaged in violence in Los Angeles in 1992 requires looking past the edges of the television screen, and thus beyond Los Angeles, which limited the scope of our vision to burning buildings. What forms have black-Korean conflicts taken? When and where have they occurred? What have they been fought over? How common have they been?

In fact, confrontations between blacks and Koreans occurred in more than a dozen cities during the 1980s and 1990s. They assumed various forms, often nonviolent.

After conducting a large-scale, systematic survey of local news sources that identifies public confrontations between blacks and Koreans, many of which were missed by the national news media and by scholars, I was able

Table 1.1. Cities Covered by Newspaper Survey
(Listed by State)

Mesa, AZ	Louisville, KY
Phoenix, AZ	New Orleans, LA
Scottsdale AZ	Baltimore, MD
Tempe, AZ	Boston, MA
Berkeley, CA	Detroit, MI
Inglewood, CA	Minneapolis, MN
Long Beach, CA	St. Louis, MO
Los Angeles, CA	New York, NY
Oakland, CA	Cincinnati, OH
Pasadena, CA	Cleveland, OH
Pomona, CA	Columbus, OH
San Francisco, CA	Philadelphia, PA
Hartford, CT	Pittsburgh, PA
Washington, DC	Arlington, TX
Hialeah, FL	Dallas, TX
Miami, FL	Fort Worth, TX
Orlando, FL	Houston, TX
Atlanta, GA	Arlington, VA
Chicago, IL	Seattle, WA
Indianapolis, IN	

to identify the forms taken by black-Korean conflicts, when and where they took place and—equally important for a proper understanding of the phenomenon—when and where they did *not* take place. These data make it possible to answer empirical questions about black-Korean conflicts without relying exclusively on well-known cases.

Methodologically, this survey is unprecedented. Most social scientific analyses of events across a wide expanse of time and space draw on a single source for data, most commonly the index of the *New York Times*. My data on black-Korean conflicts, however, come from a direct search of the full text of scores of newspapers that provide local reporting coverage of thirty-nine cities (all of which have populations of at least 100,000). A list of cities represented in the search appears in Table 1.1. (For a detailed account of the data collection, see the Appendix.)

DISTINGUISHING BETWEEN PROTEST AND VIOLENCE

In order to document variation in the form of conflict as well as the frequency and location of its occurrence, I distinguished between two types of reported events, both of which involved blacks and Koreans in active, public confrontations: (1) incidents of protest and (2) incidents of violence.

Protest consists of nonviolent forms of collective action such as demonstrations, pickets, and marches. However, one particular type predominated: publicly staged boycotts led by African Americans against Korean-owned establishments in predominantly black neighborhoods. For the purposes of this book, I define a boycott as a campaign that mobilizes participants to protest at the scene of a targeted establishment. Thus, campaigns that merely issue a call to boycott, without actively mobilizing protesters, fall outside this definition and were not counted. Other types of protest took place as well, though much less frequently. For example, Koreans sometimes organized public demonstrations in response to black-led boycotts.

Violence consists of reports of interpersonal violence (such as shootings, assaults, and other physical disputes) or reports of property damage (such as looting or arson) in which the perpetrator (or perpetrators) and target (or targets) were positively identified, one of them as black and the other as Korean.[1]

THE BOYCOTTS

Forty black-led boycotts of Korean stores took place during the 1980s and the first half of the 1990s in thirteen of the thirty-nine cities covered by the survey. Among these were boycotts that targeted a beauty shop in Indianapolis, an entire block of stores in Chicago, a flea market in Miami, a shopping center in Dallas, and a mini-mart in Philadelphia. Table 1.2 contains a complete list of cities that experienced boycotts.[2]

A few of the boycotted stores were franchises of chain operations, such as C-Town in New York City or Stop 'N Go in Philadelphia, but most were small businesses of the "mom and pop" variety—individually owned and

Table 1.2. Cities with Reports of Boycotts

Atlanta, GA	Los Angeles, CA
Berkeley, CA	Miami, FL
Chicago, IL	New York, NY
Dallas, TX	Orlando, FL
Fort Worth, TX	Philadelphia, PA
Indianapolis, IN	Washington, DC
Inglewood, CA	

family operated. Very few shops bore Korean names; instead they had names like "Village Inn Cafe," "John's Liquor," or "Jacob's Food Mart."

In just under half the boycotts (seventeen), protest was sparked by a report of violence—usually an altercation between a Korean merchant and a black customer. In a typical case, customer MarQuette Jones and storeowner Taek Won Kim scuffled over a bottle of orange juice in Berkeley, California, and Kim reportedly sprayed mace at Jones. Four times the provocation was a shooting—all of which resulted in deaths, and in all four cases the victim was black. In one such incident, a Fort Worth, Texas, storekeeper named Jason Noh chased after and shot Darrell Bivins, a man he suspected of shoplifting. Four of the protests followed verbal disputes or alleged racial slurs by merchants. In Orlando, for instance, picketing began after a customer named Carol Ricksand and a store employee, Joshua Lee, argued over the sale of lottery tickets.

In at least eight of the boycotts, protesters said they began their marches outside Korean stores in response to problems with the way the store did business: prices were too high (when the protesters were customers), prices were too low (when black business owners led demonstrations), service was rude, or the store was selling alcohol in a neighborhood oversaturated with liquor stores. The sale of liquor became an issue in protests in just two cities, Los Angeles and Philadelphia. In those cases, protesters argued that the overconcentration of liquor outlets in inner city neighborhoods contributed to high crime rates.

In six more boycotts, demonstrators identified other triggers for their actions. In an instance in Washington, D.C., neighborhood activists targeted a grocery store that had recently been bought by Korean Americans in a foreclosure sale. In Dallas, a black shopkeeper had been evicted by the Korean American owner of a shopping center. In Indianapolis, a black organization targeted a beauty supply shop that it said had refused to make donations to community causes.[3]

However, a common thread ran through nearly all the boycotts: protesters made demands that went beyond initial provocations, explicitly linking their actions to the impact of stores on the surrounding community. Boycott leaders almost always claimed that they were defending the economic self-sufficiency of black neighborhoods or the dignity of black residents, twin themes in ideologies of black nationalism. In one such instance, Elombe Brath, an activist in the boycott of the Red Apple grocery in New York City, contrasted black neighborhoods with the ethnic enclaves of other groups, where businesses tend to be owned by residents: "Nobody else would tolerate the kind of situation we have in our community. We reserve the right to be as logical as anybody else" (Baillou 1990b). In this

way, the incidents that triggered protests—even when touted as important
in themselves—served even more importantly to highlight activists' broader
concerns.

More than two-thirds of the boycotts involved members of new or existing organizations. So rather than reflecting the spontaneous or discon-
nected gathering of random neighborhood residents, most of the boycotts
were the product of conscious organization and mobilization. During the
boycotts, new organizations were built and existing ones were strength-
ened.

The organizations that led demonstrations at Korean stores varied in
purpose and orientation. However, most of the organizations leading boycotts had black nationalist orientations. Examples include the Black Panther Militia in Indianapolis; Black Women for Economic Parity in Chicago;
the Brotherhood Crusade in Los Angeles; the Black Unemployed Youth
Movement, the December 12 Movement, the Flatbush Coalition for Economic Empowerment, and the African Nationalist Pioneer Movement in
New York City; and the Malcolm X Memorial Park Coalition in Philadelphia.

Other protest groups focused on neighborhood concerns, such as the
Southeast Neighborhood Interest Coalition in Fort Worth; the Organiza-
tion of Mutual Neighborhood Interest and the South Central Concerned
Citizens Committee in Los Angeles; and the Concerned Citizens of Harlem,
the Brownsville Consumer Action Coalition, and the Lefrak City Tenants
Association in New York City. In Miami, protesters (some of whom were
merchants themselves) formed an organization called People Resolved and
Organized to Ensure Courteous Trade (PROTECT).

A few boycotts involved the support or leadership of black clergy—one
in New York, one in Chicago, and one in Los Angeles. Three more were
organized by college students: one by the African American Theme House
at the University of California at Berkeley, one by the Black People's Union
at George Washington University, and one by students at Howard University.

In only a couple of instances, groups that took part in demonstrations
were trade or labor organizations: a group named African-American Business Concerns in Atlanta and a chapter of the United Food and Commercial Workers union in Los Angeles. In only one case did a traditional civil
rights organization—a chapter of the National Association for the Advancement of Colored People (NAACP) in Los Angeles—become involved
in a boycott.

Another boycott, in Chicago, involved gang members. Reflecting how
black-Korean conflicts often mirrored the political contexts of the cities in

which they took place, this boycott was actually led by a gang-affiliated organization—called 21st Century VOTE—whose purpose was to field candidates for public office. Chicago's reputation for its infamous political machines of old persists with the legacy of strong local party organizations. Chicago's traditional style of politics no doubt continues to influence new entrants to the game. Indeed, as George Papajohn (1993) explains, the leaders of 21st Century VOTE likened "their efforts to those of white ethnic gangs of decades ago that got involved in politics."

The demonstrations at Korean-owned stores usually fluctuated in size over the course of their development. Information on the number of protesters was available for half of the boycotts. Of these, thirteen peaked at fewer than 50 protesters, three peaked at between 50 and 100 protesters, and four peaked at more than 100 protesters.

In at least eleven of the boycotts—and probably more—local organizations representing Korean American communities and merchants responded to black protesters' demonstrations. In some cases, these organizations attempted to negotiate resolutions to the boycotts on behalf of storeowners. In a few instances, they rallied Korean communities to lend financial and moral support to storeowners during boycotts.

African American community organizations also intervened to resolve boycotts (in twelve cases). In doing so, they occasionally registered public opposition to the boycotts. Other times, black civic and merchant organizations took neutral stances. In these cases, leaders of the intervening organizations attempted to use their status in communities to create public spaces where the conflicting parties could talk and bridge their differences.

Public officials—from all levels of government—intervened in about half the boycotts (eighteen). Mediators from the U.S. Justice Department responded to conflicts in a number of cities, including Chicago, Los Angeles, and New York. In some cases, state legislators and human rights commissioners intervened. Most of the public officials who sought to influence the course of boycotts came from city and county governments, including mayors, commissioners, city council members, police officials, and district attorneys. In a small number of cases, courts became involved in conflicts.

Mayors (and their staff) were the officials who most frequently intervened (ten cases), followed by city council members (six), and officials from police departments (five). Like community organizations, public officials worked to end boycotts at times by opposing them and at times by attempting to create neutral public spaces where conflicting parties could talk.

Information on the duration of boycotts was available for about thirty of the forty boycotts (for a number of these, the lengths had to be estimated). The shortest boycotts were over in a day or two; but the Red Apple boycott in New York City endured for more than a year. Fifteen of the boycotts lasted longer than two weeks, and the average duration was about fifty days.

In the twenty cases for which information was available on why boycotts ended, resolution came most often (twelve times) through negotiated agreement. Usually this meant that Korean merchants agreed to hire black employees, contribute to black neighborhoods, or make changes in store policies. Of the various concessions granted by storeowners (and sometimes by merchant organizations) in these agreements, the most common was the promise to hire African American employees (ten cases).

The next most common reason why protests at Korean stores ended was an unnegotiated store closing due to financial and other pressures imposed by boycotters. In the five cases in which this happened, the stores went out of business or their owners sold them and moved to new locations. In the boycott of John's Liquor Store in South Central Los Angeles (and possibly others for which information was incomplete), negotiations between conflicting parties resulted in the closing of the Korean store. (See chapter 5 for more on the John's Liquor Store case.)

INCIDENTS OF VIOLENCE

Local newspapers reported sixty-six incidents of violence between African and Korean Americans in sixteen of the thirty-nine cities in the survey, many of which were also the locations of boycotts (see Table 1.3).[4]

Of these, eleven were against property (including the 1992 riots and several smaller riots) and fifty-five were against persons. The violence against property included one minor instance of looting and four fire bombings by blacks against Korean stores in Los Angeles and Chicago. (Police in Washington, D.C., initially attributed several more instances of arson to black-

Table 1.3. Cities with Reports of Violence

Atlanta, GA	Long Beach, CA
Baltimore, MD	Los Angeles, CA
Berkeley, CA	New York, NY
Boston, MA	Orlando, FL
Chicago, IL	Philadelphia, PA
Dallas, TX	San Francisco, CA
Fort Worth, TX	Tacoma, WA
Inglewood, CA	Washington, D.C.

Korean tensions, but later decided they were more likely perpetrated by Korean gangs.)

Six instances of rioting in black neighborhoods resulted in property damage to Korean stores, two in 1991 and four in 1992, including the Los Angeles riots. The 1991 lootings took place in New York (during the Crown Heights riots that mainly targeted Hasidic Jews) and Chicago (following the Chicago Bulls victory in the National Basketball Association championships). Of the three riots in 1992 in which Korean stores incurred damage (aside from Los Angeles), one took place in Atlanta (simultaneously with Los Angeles), and two took place within the next two months in Dallas and Chicago. All these events were small in comparison to what happened in Los Angeles.

Twenty-four physical assaults were reported, including a case of mistaken identity (when a Vietnamese man was attacked by black youths in Brooklyn who thought he was Korean). Two assaults resulted in deaths (both Korean), twelve in injuries, and the rest in minor or no injuries. Blacks were the alleged or confirmed perpetrators in ten cases and Koreans in fourteen.

Finally, thirty-two shootings were reported between African and Korean Americans. In twenty-six instances, blacks were the shooters and Koreans the targets; in the remaining six, Koreans shot blacks. Twenty-five shootings resulted in deaths (four blacks and twenty-one Koreans), six in injuries, and one in no damage.

Formal charges were filed in twenty-three cases of reported violence; at least six of these cases resulted in convictions (four black and two Korean). Police identified only three of the sixty-six incidents as bias crimes, all physical assaults by African Americans against Korean Americans.

COLLECTING DATA FROM NEWSPAPERS

Although newspapers provide an unrivalled and detailed source of information on political and social events, relying on them for an accurate understanding of complex phenomena presents certain problems. How and to what extent do newspapers distort the reporting of conflict? How might the professional, racial, or other biases of journalists and editors distort the picture of black-Korean conflict that emerges from the data presented in this chapter?

Studies of racial conflict in the United States during the 1960s and 1970s drew heavily on newspaper reports, but virtually none of them sufficiently addressed the matter of data validity (Danzger 1975). Often, researchers relied on a single newspaper for nationwide data or on multiple sources that drew from a single common source. More recent studies have also relied on single sources for newspaper data. Doug McAdam (1982) uses the story index of the *New York Times* to measure protest activity during the civil rights movement; Susan Olzak (1992) codes events found in the text of stories from the *New York Times* to measure racial and ethnic collective action during the late nineteenth and early twentieth centuries.

Reliance on a single newspaper for measures of national phenomena may be unavoidable due to technological limitations, lack of indexes, or other problems of accessibility. However, regional, editorial, and other biases are inevitable. For a major newspaper to report on an event that takes place in another city, that event must first reach the attention of its editors— something that may not happen without the presence of some kind of national concern—and then be deemed important enough to warrant coverage. The process by which this happens is by no means completely arbitrary. The fact that an event fails to be recognized by the news media on a national scale may not mean that the phenomenon is unimportant, just that it has not been awarded a high level of salience. In such cases, a multiple-source method is critical. Researchers routinely make convincing cases for the replicability of event data by formalizing and documenting the data collection process. But too often they do not devote enough attention to the validity of its measurement (Franzosi 1987).

Advances in information technology now allow researchers to draw on a large sample of newspapers with relative ease using electronic databases that contain the full text of news stories from multiple publications. Electronic newspaper databases provided the sources of conflict data for this book. The process eliminated many of the biases inevitable in single-source methods. As evidence of the insufficiency of a single source, a search of the *New York Times* alone would have missed roughly 90 percent of the events from cities other than New York that were found in the multiple-newspaper search.

Nevertheless, potential problems with data validity remain even when using multiple-source data on black-Korean conflicts. First, it is possible that the newspapers covered by electronic databases are not a random sample of the whole universe of U.S. newspapers. Whether or not a database contains a given publication depends on various factors, including whether its publisher has made it available.[5] The influence of particular publishers cannot be completely avoided, even when using a large number of publications, as newspapers have increasingly been consolidated under the ownership of a small number of national or regional chains. Moreover, the databases rarely index neighborhood weeklies, which might be reporting conflict events that never get picked up by the larger metropolitan dailies. However, on average, small weeklies probably have less news-gathering resources and thus do not report these events any more than the dailies. In field work in New York City and Los Angeles, upon which later chapters are based, I found only a couple of boycotts not reported by major newspapers.

The second validity problem has to do with changes in reporting over time. The occurrence of certain events—such as the Los Angeles riots or some of the more widely publicized boycotts—may make newspapers more likely to report smaller incidents of black-Korean conflict that they would not have considered reporting otherwise. Bigger events may make smaller ones more newsworthy. Sharp increases in levels of reported conflict following such well-publicized events would indicate that this is taking place.

However, the majority of incidents took place before the Los Angeles riots of 1992, during which the most well known conflict between blacks and Koreans occurred. Reports of violence between blacks and Koreans peaked in 1991, then dropped afterwards. So it does not appear that the riots increased the media's reporting of violence. However, reports of violence did increase after the 1990 Red Apple boycott in New York City.

The frequency of black-led boycotts of Korean stores was low during the first half of the 1980s, with no more than one boycott reported per year, but then rose during the second half of the 1980s and into the 1990s: between two and seven boycotts are reported each year. Since this increase took place prior to both of the nationally televised events, it does not appear that the data on boycotting was severely biased upwards by media attention.

A deeper problem with using newspapers as the source of event data is introduced by biases other than geography or timing. The picture of black-Korean conflicts that most Americans have is likely distorted by the fact that the news media does not merely report events but frames them as well. Newspapers or television news can exaggerate the importance of individual disputes, play up the role of racial differences (Ong, Park, and Tong 1994, 275–77), or interpret events differently depending on the readership or viewing audience (Umemoto 1994). The result is that media reports may inaccurately portray individual disputes as group conflicts.

Given its reliance on news reports, the data collection for this book may be criticized on the same grounds. All the events counted for analysis cannot be assumed to have racial motives, or even to be instances of intergroup conflict. However, including only those events obviously motivated by hostility toward the other group (such as those officially classified by police as "hate crimes") would be undesirable for several reasons. First, such motivations are not always clearly reported and in any case are difficult to establish reliably. Second, the uncovering of larger patterns in these events across time and space might itself be used to address the question of the existence of group conflict. Third, individual incidents of violence not motivated by intergroup hostilities may prompt collective mobilization that does pit the groups against each other.

Certainly, sifting indiscriminately risks catching *too much* in the process and overestimating what might in reality be a smaller phenomenon. However, my arguments do not end with descriptions of the frequency with which such incidents occur; rather, they serve as a beginning point. Black–Korean conflicts are to a large extent constructed locally. Indeed, if the national-level data collection emphasizes too heavily the similarities among black–Korean conflicts, the case studies of New York and Los Angeles in chapters 4 and 5 focus more heavily on their differences.

Moreover, if media effects shaped the process of reporting on conflicts between African Americans and Korean Americans by increasing the number of reports of conflict, the effects would not be limited to a single city.[6] Conflict would be exaggerated across cities, and media effects (at least as they have been described) would not distort large comparisons among cities.[7] At least for measures of protest activity, newspapers actually make excellent sources of data. Protesters require media exposure for their very success in achieving goals and mobilizing supporters and seek to ensure that they receive coverage (Lipsky 1968, 1151). As Peter Eisinger observes, "Newspaper coverage, however dubious the scholar might be about its objectivity or comprehensiveness, is vital in itself to the projection of protest" (1973, 16).

In any case, it is clear that conflicts between African Americans and Korean Americans happened more often, and in more locations, than is commonly recognized. That said, however, it is hardly the case that these conflicts were common occurrences in the daily lives of African and Korean Americans. In many cases, they have existed together without conflict. Episodes of collective violence were especially rare. Contrary to the assertion that blacks and Koreans have been constrained to a violent relationship, when they have engaged in conflict, they have often found avenues other than violence.

Indeed, intergroup conflicts nearly always involve factions of different groups rather than entire ethnic communities. "Collective action is usually the metier of small bands of partisans, and there is no guarantee that activists accurately mirror the thinking of the community of the whole," as

Jonathan Rieder puts it (1985, 171). This was certainly the case with black-Korean conflicts. Indeed, there were often multiple factions on both sides, all with their own motives and goals. Ultimately, comprehending black-Korean conflicts requires understanding the webs of relationships among these factions.

Chapter 2

Explaining Black-Korean Conflicts

The distinction between peaceful and violent conflict is typically conceived in normative terms and often explained in terms of the personal values or strategic choices of individual leaders. In fact, however, leaders often lose control of the decision to prevent protest from turning violent: labor strikes become violent clashes, peaceful social movements degenerate into civil warfare, and competition over turf or jobs gives way to rioting. Although leaders may play a role, such instances suggest that other factors act to constrain intergroup conflict, nudging it down one road or the other. What larger forces, beyond the control of individuals, might be at work?

With the national data on black-Korean conflicts, we can begin to make sense of this larger issue by addressing several basic questions. Why does conflict break out when and where it does? What role do intergroup tensions play in generating different forms of conflict? Can violence be explained by the same dynamics as peaceful protest?

Most existing explanations of black-Korean conflict—as well as most other types of intergroup conflict—fall into two broad categories: those that see conflict as rooted in ideas—values, customs, and ideologies that lead groups to clash—and those that see conflict as rooted in interests—the material stakes of participants, usually economic in nature, that lead groups to compete. Neither distinguishes between protest and violence. Consequently, understanding black-Korean conflicts, and resolving the larger dilemma of protest and violence, requires a third, supplemental approach: one that sees conflict as shaped by political institutions.[1]

This chapter critically assesses theories of racial and ethnic conflict belonging to these three categories, proposes ways for measuring their observable implications using quantitative indicators, and then uses the national data on black-Korean conflicts to test their empirical validity. The results demonstrate that the timing and location of Korean store boycotts have more to do with political processes than with the sociological phenomena typically presumed to generate tensions. Overt, nonviolent conflicts take place more often in cities where traditional, machine-style political organizations have strong roots and where African Americans have greater political representation. These factors lend structure to political life, making greater resources available for the kind of grassroots organization necessary to sustain protest. Violent incidents, although they appear to be weakly related to boycotts, do not follow the same dynamic.

IDEAS

Theories that pinpoint ideas as the cause of conflict vary in certain respects, but all share a basic assumption: they view group aggression as driven by participants' abstract or idealized notions of social or political relationships, manifested as either values or ideologies. One values-oriented explanation sees the different cultural norms of black Americans and Korean immigrants as quite innocently provoking ill will and misunderstanding. Another more explicitly blames the racial and ethnic prejudices of participants. Of the several theories that attribute conflicts to social or political ideologies, one argues that Korean Americans and African Americans clash because the former subscribe to an "immigrant ideology" which gives them an optimistic view of American society, whereas the latter do not. Another ideological explanation proposes that conflicts are rooted in black nationalism, which leads African Americans to reject the presence of Korean merchants in their neighborhoods in order to achieve community control over social and economic resources. A third ideological explanation views black-Korean conflicts as the product of a racial ideology promulgated by white society, which pits racial minority groups against one another via a discourse of racial hierarchy.

Culture

Close observers of black-Korean conflicts often point to cultural differences as the cause of tensions. Indeed, conflicts often appear to have been triggered by misunderstandings—gestures or words mistaken for disrespectful or offensive behavior—between Korean merchants and black customers.[2] In this view, members of each group bring certain "cultural baggage" to encounters with members of the other. For instance, Koreans have pointed out that their culture discourages shopkeepers, especially women, from smiling, touching, or looking into the eyes of customers (Lee 1991; Sa 1995). Because members of each group are unfamiliar with the customs and values of the other, and because linguistic barriers prevent explanations, they misinterpret one another's actions. For many African Americans, respectful treatment in commercial establishments carries special meaning, as it has long been linked to the struggle for black advancement and civil rights (Fiske 1994, 481). Researchers have noted the apparent significance of cultural differences in creating a backdrop of tension, and attempts at conflict resolution often have focused on changing such perceptions (Freer 1994, 190–92; H. C. Lee 1993).

Ironically, whereas some community leaders point to cultural differences, others, probably with better reason, claim that black-Korean interactions are more often friendly than tense. In fact, in interviews, some Korean merchants have said they prefer black and Latino customers to white customers because they tend to be more friendly and complain less than whites (Park 1991, 181). Whether black-Korean relations are more friendly or more tense in general than other customer-merchant relations is a murky question, with no clear answer.

Without resolving that question, however, the cultural distance between a host group and an immigrant group might be said to vary with the extent to which the immigrant group has assimilated to the host culture. Because barriers to communication are central to this perspective, the linguistic abilities of Korean Americans can serve as a measure of cultural distance between the two groups. Immigrants acquire the language of their host country, and through it the customs as well, in varying degrees. As a result, Korean communities in some cities may be more linguistically insulated than those in other cities, and thus more culturally distant from African American residents.

Indeed, considerable variation exists across cities and across time in the extent to which Korean Americans collectively have acquired English language skills. At one end of the spectrum, 24 percent of Koreans living in the Minneapolis metropolitan area in 1990 were reported as not speaking English "very well" by the U.S. Census Bureau. By contrast, 81 percent of Koreans living in the Los Angeles-Long Beach area in 1980 did not speak English "very well." Across the thirty-nine cities for which conflict data was collected, the average rate is 53 percent. (Baltimore's rate falls closest to the mean) (U.S. Bureau of the Census, 1980a, Special Report 1E, Sec. 1, Table 43; U.S. Bureau of the Census, 1990, Table 49).

Prejudice

Attributing conflicts to cultural differences, however, may represent a convenient way of smoothing over tensions, avoiding criticism for racial bigotry, or redirecting attention away from more important issues (Park 1992, 41). Explanations that attribute conflict to racial prejudice attribute the blame for conflict more explicitly. Black boycotters of Korean grocery stores have hurled accusations of racism at the merchants who run them, and critics of boycotts have responded with the same claims about boycotters.

The targeting of an immigrant group by native-born Americans can be placed in the context of the wave of nativism that swept the United States in the 1980s and 1990s (Cheng 1996). A 1992 survey of New Yorkers living in neighborhoods containing Korean stores found significant (if not overwhelming) support for negative stereotypes of Koreans: 23 percent of the ninety-seven black respondents agreed with the statement that "Koreans are in general rude and nasty people" (compared to 8 percent of white respondents), 45 percent believed "Koreans are overly concerned with making money" (compared to 26 percent of whites), and 34 percent agreed that "Koreans do not try to learn English and American customs" (compared to 24 percent of whites) (Min 1996, 124).

Similarly, Korean immigrants are not immune to the traditional racial prejudices against blacks that are ingrained in American society (Abelmann and Lie 1995, 150; Cho 1993, 199). In the 1992 survey, more than 60 percent of the ninety-three Korean respondents living in black neighborhoods in New York City agreed that blacks are generally "less intelligent," "less honest," and "more criminally oriented" than whites. Asked if blacks were "lazier" than whites, 45 percent agreed (Min 1996, 121).

Survey data on the racial prejudices of blacks and Koreans do not exist for other cities. However, despite abundant examples of the proximity of racial prejudice to conflict, critics have pointed out that prejudice may be more of a symptom than a cause of conflict (Blalock 1967; Cheng and Espiritu 1989, 526). Moreover, certain contexts may breed stereotyping. Korean Americans' perceptions of other ethnic and racial groups often depends on the nature of their workplace encounters. The attitudes of professionals and workers "contrast markedly with those of small businessmen," with the latter most likely to transfer their own perceptions of discrimination by whites onto blacks (Park 1991, 181). This suggests either that cultural differences matter *only* in conjunction with situational factors or that class, not culture, is the culprit.

Thus, a major difficulty with explaining conflict via prejudice is causal priority—establishing which comes first. Beliefs may be an endpoint rather than a beginning—that is, the product of conflict, not its cause.

Explanations of black-Korean conflicts based on values, generally speaking, are flawed by a fundamental imprecision. For instance, neither theories of cultural difference nor theories of racial prejudice explain why blacks and Koreans in particular engage in conflict. Why have similar conflicts between other culturally distinct groups been absent, or at least less visible? Why has the same atmosphere of tension or number of overt conflicts not occurred between black customers and Chinese or South Asian merchants, for instance? (Tensions have been reported between Arab shop owners and black customers, but with much less frequency and in only a handful of places.) Or what about conflicts between Koreans and Latinos? By one estimate, Korean merchants in Los Angeles have more Latino than black customers—17 percent versus 10 percent (Ong, Park, and Tong 1994, 271).

Immigrant Ideology

In another idea-based explanation, black-Korean conflicts arise from a clash of social ideologies. As immigrants who arrive in the United States seeking social and economic advancement, Koreans are said to possess strong beliefs in the notion of the American dream, which contrasts with the much more pessimistic beliefs held by blacks. Consequently, Koreans and other immigrant groups share an immigrant ideology, a commonality lacking between Koreans and native-born Americans, such as blacks. "This frame of reference allows Mexicans to regard Koreans as legitimate competitors—or even models—and not enemies," write Lucie Chen and Yen Le Espiritu. "On the other hand, blacks can claim the prerogative of nativism and thus regard Korean and other immigrants as uninvited guests at a meager meal"(Cheng and Espiritu 1989, 531).[3]

In a similar vein, Edward Chang hypothesizes that "Korean immigrants must believe in the American *dream*. . . . If they do not, they probably have no purpose for living a hard life in America. Black Americans, in contrast, have been so profoundly impacted by racism that their views are not as optimistic" (Chang 1991, 175–76).

Chang further argues that Koreans pursue an "individual" approach to economic survival, whereas blacks pursue a "group approach" by seeking economic security through political activism.

The immigrant ideology argument implies that encounters between two different immigrant groups will always be peaceful. However, nearly equal proportions of native-born African Americans and African-Caribbean immigrants supported the 1990 boycott of a Korean store in New York City (Min 1996, 117–18). Also, Central American immigrants who lived in or near Koreatown were heavily involved in looting Korean stores during the 1992 Los Angeles riots (Rutten 1992).[4]

Moreover, Koreans' approach to business is hardly as "individual" as traditional entrepreneurial stereotypes suggest: Korean entrepreneurs rely heavily on family, friends, and other members of their ethnic community for the labor, capital, and social resources they need (Abelmann and Lie 1995, 130–37). Korean merchants frequently act collectively to gain advantages from suppliers, landlords, and government (Min 1996, 169–92). Still, the notion that the two groups have followed different routes to advancement is affirmed by an important distinction: Korean Americans have certainly been less active in politics than African Americans.[5] However, the notion that the two groups compete in separate spheres suggests that they could have avoided contentious encounters.

More importantly, however, the immigrant ideology explanation provides no systematic evidence for the assumption that each group subscribes to a different world view. Take, for example, the assessment by a policy analyst for the Washington-based Progressive Policy Institute: "The American Dream is alive and well for the nearly 30,000 Koreans who arrive on our shores each year. . . . In cities such as New York, Los Angeles and Washington, such success is plainly visible in the scores of brightly lit, well-stocked and open-at-all hours convenience stores which dot every street corner" (quoted in Hamilton 1992). Beliefs cannot be inferred from behavior so easily. In fact, many Korean storeowners in this country (especially earlier arrivals) did not set up groceries or dry cleaners because they believed doing so was the path to the American Dream; rather, they did so because their initial "dreams" of success as professionals, trained in Korea, failed to materialize after they encountered obstacles—such as financial, licensing, and language difficulties—here in the United States (Abelmann and Lie 1995, 127–28).

Black Nationalism

If the immigrant ideology explanation focuses on the ideas of Koreans, another ideological explanation focuses on the perspectives of African Americans. This variant proposes that black nationalism—which advocates total black control over communities and over economic resources and rejects racial integration—has been a primary cause of conflict between Koreans and blacks. In this view, because black nationalism existed long before the arrival of Korean merchants in black neighborhoods, it must therefore be a more "basic" and primary cause than any particular grievances between blacks and Koreans (Light, Har-Chvi, and Kan 1994, 76–77). In contrast to the immigrant ideology explanation, this one concludes that "Latinos have not displayed the same hostility toward Korean merchants in their neighborhoods because they lack a similar nationalist ideology" (ibid., 79).[6] Moreover, black nationalism explains not only boycotts of Korean grocery stores but violence and criminal activity directed at Koreans as well. As Ivan Light, Hadas Har-Chvi, and Kenneth Kan assert:

> In a way, the black nationalist ideology that later justified the burning and looting of Korean stores [in the 1992 Los Angeles riots] also justified individual and team robberies of the same stores. After all, thieves

were only repatriating property that ought to have been theirs in the first place. (ibid., 75)

These scholars see evidence for this in the fact that Korean stores in South Central Los Angeles suffered more fire damage during the riots than Korean stores in Koreatown, which has a larger Hispanic population, and other areas of the city. They reason that black rioters "evidently had a stronger component of hatred of and revenge against Korean merchants than did rioters elsewhere in Los Angeles where acquisitiveness generally prevailed" (ibid., 80).

Some evidence exists for an ideological foundation to anti-Korean hostility by blacks. The 1992 survey of New Yorkers living in neighborhoods containing Korean stores found that perceptions of economic exploitation by Korean merchants were common, if not overwhelming, among blacks. Among the ninety-seven black respondents, more than a third agreed that "Korean merchants become rich by exploiting black people" and that they represent "an economic invasion of the black community," and about half agreed that Korean businesses reduce opportunity for black entrepreneurs and "drain black economic resources by taking money out of the black community" (Min 1996, 111). However, the survey's designer, Pyong Gap Min, argues that black *rejection* of Korean merchants is not widespread. Only 14 percent of black respondents agreed with the statement that "blacks should not buy from Korean stores" (Min 1996, 97–98). National survey evidence, on the other hand, indicates a fairly widespread attraction among blacks to the views that underlie economic nationalism. In 1984, a majority of respondents in the National Black Election Study supported "shopping in Black-owned stores whenever possible" (Tate 1993, 155).

Explanations based on ideology at times suffer from the difficulty not only of proving them but also of disproving them. Sometimes they are phrased so broadly that scholars using different arguments are able to make them responsible for almost any outcome, or contradictory outcomes. In one version, Light and his colleagues argue that black nationalism explains boycotts, riots, *and* inner-city crime. Political scientist Adolph Reed, on the other hand, characterizes black nationalism as a fundamentally conservative ideology that affirms traditional middle-class values and encourages passivity (Reed 1991, 87–88). In Light's version, black nationalism explains almost any kind of conflict; in Reed's, it is more likely to produce none.

Another problem is that the entirely different integrationist ideology of the civil rights movement produced some of the same outcomes—commerical boycotts—claimed for black nationalism in the case of black-Korean conflicts. If the desire for integration also produces boycotts, then how can we say for sure that black nationalism is responsible? Complicating matters further, a variety of strands of black nationalism exist—cultural, political and economic nationalism, for instance. Each strand may have different behavioral consequences.

However, the way black nationalism manifests itself in different cities might be important. In-Jin Yoon suggests that the organizational form of black nationalism is a critical factor in propelling black-Korean conflicts. Specifically, Yoon argues that local organizations tend to be more militant than national organizations (such as the NAACP and the Urban League), so that in cities where local groups are more influential, "black boycotts of Korean businesses are more numerous, longer-lasting, and more violent than elsewhere" (Yoon 1997, 206–7.) In my own data (see chapter 1), I found no real distinction between local and national organizations: in some cases, local community organizations that boycotted Korean stores were more radical; however, in many others they were quite moderate in their demands and ended their boycotts peacefully. Yoon's conclusion may be the result of his focus on only the longest and most contentious boycotts in several cities. Still, Yoon is correct in pointing out that black nationalism varies in its organizational and ideological manifestations, and, as I will argue, these variations play a key role in explaining black-Korean conflicts.

For the purposes of testing the validity of either the immigrant ideology or the black nationalism explanations across space and time, measures of ideology would have to come from surveys that sample sufficient numbers of black and Korean residents of many cities. Although national-level surveys of African Americans include questions about black nationalism, no surveys exist that do this for a large number of cities. Even if survey data like this were available, they would have to predate conflicts in order to establish that ideological causes were at work rather than mere hostile feelings created by conflicts.

Racial Discourse

Racial discourse theories explain black-Korean conflicts as the inevitable product of dominant, racist ideologies. John Abelmann and Nancy Lie, for example, assert that American racial ideology paints Korean Americans as a hardworking, "model minority" and African Americans as a dangerous, undeserving underclass, thereby framing the two groups as social opposites and pitting them against one another (1995, 162–65). A similar perspective, put forth by Claire Jean Kim, argues that the "racial order," defined as "a shared cognitive map classifying different groups with concrete distributional consequences," set the stage for the Red Apple boycott in New

York City (and presumably other black-Korean conflicts as well). In this view, the racial order continuously regenerates itself, "racializing" Koreans as Asian Americans, "valorizing" them relative to blacks, and "ostracizing" them from politics (2000, 17).

Traditional American racial ideologies have certainly influenced both the news media's portrayal and the public's conception of black-Korean conflicts. And even though racist portrayals of African and Korean Americans rely on utterly false premises, they endure and continue to inform Americans' preconceptions about the two groups (Abelmann and Lie 1995, 165–75). Critics of the news media charge that it exacerbated tensions by "spotlighting" conflicts and by framing Koreans as "unfathomable aliens" (particularly during the Los Angeles riots, when television broadcasts showed merchants shooting from rooftops) (Kim 1993, 221–22).

Scholars who have advocated such explanations make powerful arguments about the usefulness of interminority conflicts in maintaining a status quo of white racial dominance. Moreover, long traditions of white racism and negligent social and economic policies certainly helped to ensure that blacks and Koreans would be forced to coexist under conditions of scarcity and intolerance.

However, broad theories of racial power appear to be insufficient for explaining why, when, where, and how black-Korean conflicts actually *occur*. As Abelmann and Lie acknowledge in their critique of the very concept of black-Korean conflict, "challenging its explanatory power or noting its ideological construction does not fully explain particular instances of African American-Korean American tension" (Abelmann and Lie 1995, 148). Conflicts have taken place in some cities, but not in others. They have become media spectacles in some places, but not in others. They have taken different forms in various places and at different times. Media outlets have covered conflicts differently in varying contexts. Theories based on broad notions of American racial hierarchies—even if they contain much truth, as I believe they do—cannot explain such anomalies.

Indeed, theories that posit black-Korean conflict as the product of a self-generating racial discourse do not suit themselves to empirical testing, since they imply (and often argue explicitly) that dominant narratives predetermine the outcomes of conflict (Kim 2000; Robinson 1993). Moreover, they implicitly deny the importance of local variation and resist quantification, making them difficult to include in an analysis of competing theories. The fact that variation exists, however, suggests that much more is at work than the single variable of racial ideology. This is not to deny that race plays a profound role in structuring the way Americans think and act. Rather, we must look to other explanations as well which can account for variation in the timing, location, and form of conflict.

Local variation in racial power could, however, be measured as the degree to which white politicians were entrenched in city government. Such a measure hardly captures the broad sweep of racial power theories, but political representation usually plays a role. For instance, Claire Jean Kim explains the phenomenon of black-Korean conflict in New York City as part of a reaction by radical black nationalist organizers to the unyielding dominance of entrenched white politicians, specifically the long-lived, racially conservative mayoralty of Ed Koch (2000, 24–27).[7] If theories of racial power have any merit, then conflicts between African Americans and Korean Americans may tend to happen in places with low levels of black political representation.

INTERESTS

Theories that focus on economic interests view conflict as driven by the concrete material stakes of participants and by the structure of capitalism. Competition theory explains intergroup conflict as the product of social proximity: groups are more likely to engage in overt conflict when they come to occupy similar positions on the socioeconomic ladder and are forced to compete for scarce resources. Middleman minority theory, on the other hand, posits social distinctiveness as the cause: conflict breaks out when groups on the lower rungs target intermediary groups, who serve as buffers for the interests of those on the upper rungs. In the case of black-Korean conflicts, both emphasize the high concentration of Korean immigrants in small business ownership. The discussion that follows does not attempt to account for the phenomenon of Korean ethnic entrepreneurship; several excellent studies provide an extensive documentation and explanation of the phenomenon (Light and Bonacich 1991; Min 1996; Yoon 1997).

Competition Theory

Competition theory attributes black-Korean conflicts to group competition over scarce resources. For instance, in this view, conflicts between blacks and Koreans derive at least partly from similarities in the economic positions of blacks and Koreans, who each have insufficient economic opportunities (Freer 1994, 176). Sociologist Susan Olzak, articulating a more general theory of conflict between racial and ethnic groups, similarly argues that "conflict ensues under conditions of *niche overlap*. That is, conflict arises when groups come to compete for the same jobs, housing, or territory. Under conditions of niche overlap, competition among groups rises, which in turn encourages attempts to exclude the competitors" (Olzak 1992, 114). This is not to say that the fundamental blame for conflict lies with the competing groups, only that competition between them is the proximate cause.[8] As Edward Chang writes, economic restructuring and increased scarcity of resources in American cities may have "intensified the conflict between the various groups of 'have-nots'" (1991, 175).

A problem with competition theory, however, lies in specifying the objects of the competition. Jobs—the most common focus of competition theory—have generally not been a major object of contention between blacks and Koreans. Although protesters do commonly demand that Korean stores hire black workers who live in the neighborhood, their targets are the Korean merchants who own the stores, not their employees. Moreover, the small grocery and convenience stores targeted in conflicts tend to be family-run and have few employees (Abelmann and Lie 1995, 131). Housing has not become an object of contention either, as Koreans tend to live outside the predominantly black communities where they own stores (Abelmann and Lie 1995, 105–6). Neighborhood territory and resources, however, might serve as the objects of contention in the form of control over business ownership (Cheng and Espiritu 1989, 529–60). In fact, the object most commonly identified by black protesters at Korean stores—and thus the possible "niche overlap"—is small business ownership. Disparities in the rate of business ownership may serve as signs of larger inequalities in economic opportunity and are said to spark hostility among blacks toward Koreans (Cheng and Espiritu 1989).

As a result, a testable hypothesis that arises from competition theory concerns the relative number of businesses owned by members of each group: the level of conflict should be higher in cities where black business ownership is smaller relative to Korean business ownership. Using data from the *Survey of Minority-Owned Business Enterprises* (U.S. Bureau of the Census 1987), I constructed an index of competition by taking the ratio of black-owned firms to Korean-owned firms.[9] In Seattle and Los Angeles-Long Beach, the metropolitan areas with the lowest ratios in the thirty-nine cities, there are 1.4 black-owned firms for every Korean-owned firm. By contrast, in the Miami-Hialeah metropolitan area, the ratio is 46.5 black-owned firms for every Korean-owned firm. Houston and Orlando fall closest to the mean, which is about eleven black firms per Korean firm.[10] To provide support for competition theory, this variable should bear an inverse relationship with intergroup conflict.

Middleman Minority Theory

Middleman minority theory posits that immigrant groups that concentrate in particular commercial occupations and exhibit a high degree of ethnic solidarity attract hostility from native-born groups, both above and below them on the socioeconomic ladder (Bonacich 1973). Conflict with low-status groups occurs not because the middleman group is competing to occupy the same niche as other groups, but because it occupies a highly vulnerable intermediary position in the social and economic hierarchy between consumers and producers. "The middleman group serves as a scapegoat for the injustices of the system that they did not create," asserts sociologist Edna Bonacich (1994, 405–6). Similarly, Paul Ong, Kye Young Park, and Yasmin Tong argue that Korean merchants are merely "actors in a play scripted by larger forces" but are targeted by blacks because they are "nonetheless the immediate agents conducting business. High prices, poor-quality merchandise, no-return policies, and the like [are] seen as small but persistent incidents of exploitation" (1994, 276). Some theorists subsume middleman minority theory under competition explanations (Olzak 1992), but the fact that the middleman minority does not directly compete with host groups distinguishes it from competition explanations.

Korean Americans certainly meet the requirements of a middleman group: in a number of large cities, they have higher rates of self-employment and business ownership (in retail and other typically middleman sectors) than other immigrant groups (Min 1996, 50–52). They also exhibit high degrees of ethnic solidarity—although solidarity may be as much or more the *result* of intergroup conflicts as the cause (Min 1996, 219). In order to test the suitability of middleman minority theory as an explanation for black-Korean conflicts, we can determine the extent to which conflict is related to the "middleman-ness" of Korean Americans in different cities: if the theory is right, then the more that Koreans fit the definition of a middleman minority (by being overconcentrated in the traditional commercial occupations of middleman groups), the greater the conflict.

Two empirically measurable factors can be identified that could work to make Korean merchants, as a middleman minority group, vulnerable to targeting by black residents or activists: (1) the extent to which Korean merchants fill the traditionally defined niche of the middleman; and (2) the presence of economic strain on black residents that would generate class tensions. A major factor in determining middleman status is "self-employment within the immigrant group at a rate much in excess of the general rate," as Light and Bonacich (1991, 18) have pointed out.[11] In the United States, Korean Americans fit the criterion of self-employment at a higher rate than the general population, but the difference varies geographically. The indicator of Korean middleman minority status I use is thus the ratio of the Korean self-employment rate to the self-employment rate for the whole population, using metro area data from the U.S. Census (1990, Tables 36 and 50; 1980a, Special Report 1E, Sec. 1, Table 45A; 1980b, Table 120).[12]

Korean Americans range from a middleman minority status of .7 in Minneapolis (actually indicating that Koreans are not a middleman group, since the value is less than one) to 6.2 in Baltimore (indicating Korean self-employment is more than six times the city's rate for all groups), with a mean of 2.9 (close to the rate in the Los Angeles-Long Beach metro area in 1980). The only places in the sample besides Minneapolis where Koreans were not a middleman minority, as measured in this way, were Columbus, Missouri, and Boston. Economic strain is represented by the black unemployment rate (U.S. Bureau of the Census, 1980a, Special Report 1E; 1980b; 1990, Table 134). Black unemployment ranges from 1.7 in Scottsdale, Arizona, to 22.2 in Detroit. Black unemployment in New York City in 1990 fell closest to the mean for all thirty-nine cities, a rate of 13.0. A positive correlation of both middleman minority status and black unemployment with the level of conflict in a city would lend support to middleman minority theory.

POLITICAL INSTITUTIONS

There is no question that ideas and interests play some part in generating intergroup tensions. However, ideas and interests only account for the presence of latent tensions and cannot explain why groups act (or fail to act) on those tensions or why their active expressions assume one form or another. A third approach is necessary, which emphasizes the role of political institutions in structuring behavior. In this view, tensions are inspired to some extent by ideas or interests, but overt conflicts are activated and given form by opportunities and constraints that originate in the political system. More specifically, this view stresses the organizational resources and political motives of participants, which are influenced by the nature of local political institutions.

A venerable tradition in political science holds that political institutions shape collective action. Political institutions—the established norms, rules, and structures of politics—create incentives and constraints that shape the way groups behave. When E. E. Schattschneider declared famously that "organization is the mobilization of bias," he meant essentially that political institutions structure conflict by giving expression to certain issues and ignoring others (Schattschneider 1957). In a classic statement of this perspective, Robert Lineberry and Edmund Fowler (1967) argued that urban political institutions filter conflicts, making some governmental designs more responsive to group interests than others. Often, such perspectives explained political institutions as reflections of dominant social groups. In recent years, however, a "new institutionalism" has gained currency which emphasizes the autonomy, stability, and continuity of institutions in structuring behavior: institutions matter because they persist over time, are not easily changed, and do not merely reflect the interests of dominant groups. The institutional perspective has also shed light on the historical development of public policies. Theda Skocpol observes that "the changing institutional configurations of national polities advantage some strategies and ideological outlooks and hamper others"; thus, the practice of politics may produce certain policies, but "policies also remake politics" (1992, 22, 58).

The lesson is this: ideas and interests influence politics, and even impact the very design of political institutions at their formation. Once in place, however, institutions have a life and a force that is all their own, independent of ideas and interests. By structuring the choices in conflicts, they even help to define the ideas and interests of those taking part.

For the most part, scholars of American politics who have used institutional arguments have limited their focus to explaining phenomena that lie within the realm of formal politics, such as voter turnout, the formation of interest groups, and the development of public policy. Far less attention has focused on applying the logic of political institutions to collective action that takes place outside the formal realm—contentious activities that do not adhere to formal or agreed-upon rules, such as protest.

I argue that the impact of political institutions in patterning behavior extends beyond the boundaries of formal politics. This notion has gained greater acceptance in the study of comparative politics, which continuously presents scholars with reminders of the variety of institutional designs among nations (Horowitz 1985; Jenkins 1995). In the United States, however, "movement organizations have frequently been detached by scholars from the mass phenomena that are thought to produce them and from the institutional politics that surrounds them," as Sidney Tarrow (1994, 2) points out. There is no better way to enhance our understanding of the impact of political institutions on social conflicts within a nation than by studying the variation in institutional arrangements and in conflicts that exists among cities.

Explanations of black-Korean conflict—and other racial and ethnic conflicts as well—have neglected to consider the impact of political institutions, or more broadly the role of politics as a powerful and independent factor in shaping the expression of tensions. Most existing explanations rely on social and economic factors. On those rare occasions when politics enters scholarly accounts of black-Korean conflict, it appears as an epiphenomenon; it simply mirrors other factors such as demographics (Umemoto 1994), race (Kim 2000), or economics (Freer 1994). When political institutions figure into the equation, they tend to be seen as part of a homogeneous, unitary "state," which works solely to further economic development

(Freer 1994) or social control (Ong, Park, and Tong 1994). The political process thus tends to seen as more a symptom than a cause (Ong, Park, and Tong 1994, 282–89). Missing is a consideration of political institutions as a set of arrangements that pattern the behavior of groups, independent of social and economic factors, acting as "more than simple mirrors of social forces" (March and Olsen 1984, 739). A political institutions approach goes beyond explanations rooted in social or economic phenomena.

The connection between political institutions and intergroup conflict lies in the mediating effect of community organizations and activists. The actions and motives of community organizers are key to understanding cases of intergroup conflict and to placing it in the context of politics. Most accounts of black-Korean conflicts have overlooked the political incentives that exist for community activists to advocate and engage their groups in conflict. There have been a few exceptions to this tendency. Heon Cheol Lee (1993) analyzes black-Korean conflict as the product of protests and counterprotests. In-Jin Yoon argues that black-Korean conflict is "an essentially political phenomenon, not merely an economic competition or a cultural clash" (1997, 206). These perspectives help shift attention away from the generalized phenomena of attitudes and antagonisms toward the recognition of intergroup conflicts as problems of leadership, politics, and collective action.

Drawing a connection between political institutions and intergroup conflict requires three steps: first, setting forth a framework for distinguishing among different types of ethnic antagonism; second, establishing the role of activists in generating conflict and identifying their relationship to politics; and third, accounting for the capacities of different political-institutional contexts in facilitating community organizing.

A New Framework for Understanding Ethnic Antagonism

Most explanations of black-Korean conflict—and many theories of race relations in general—do not adequately distinguish between different levels of ethnic *antagonism*. Edna Bonacich, for instance, identifies three types, and implies that the same dynamics explain each: "The term 'antagonism' is intended to encompass all levels of intergroup conflict, including ideologies and beliefs (such as racism and prejudice), behaviors (such as discrimination, lynchings, riots), and institutions (such as laws perpetuating segregation)" (1972, 549). Social scientists lack an appropriate means for differentiating among the causes of such phenomena. The resulting lack of clarity impedes the explanatory power of theoretical models. As a corrective, I propose a framework consisting of two levels of ethnic antagonism, each drawing an important distinction.

The first level of antagonism distinguishes between *tensions,* which represent a latent hostility, and *conflict*, which consists of active, observable engagement. Saul Alinsky, the radical organizer and founder of the Industrial Areas Foundation, makes this distinction in his timeless manual for activists, *Rules for Radicals:*

> The organizer is immediately confronted with conflict. The organizer dedicated to changing the life of a particular community must first rub raw the resentments of the people of the community; fan the latent hostilities of many of the people to the point of overt expression. ([1971] 1989, 116)

Although he was not addressing the topic of ethnic conflict per se, Alinsky's observation suggests two points that are relevant: first, that "latent hostilities," or tensions, exist prior to and separate from collective action; and second, that community activists—an often overlooked set of political actors—themselves play a pivotal role in the generation of conflict from tensions. Tensions consist of attitudes, in this case resentment by the members of one group toward those of another group. The presence of tensions may be necessary for conflict to take place, but it is not sufficient. Instead, conflict only occurs when tensions are actively mobilized. Activists are central to that process.

The second level of ethnic antagonism makes the distinction between two types of conflict: protest and violence. Tensions, once they become conflict, can be expressed in either form; however, the conditions that facilitate protest may be different from the ones that generate violence. Apart from the types of behavior that define them, protest and violence may be distinguished from each other in several ways. The most common distinction has a moral dimension.

Protest and violence may also reflect different strategic choices by group leaders. As Peter Eisinger has pointed out, protest represents a rational calculation of costs and benefits. By engaging in protest, relatively powerless groups leverage the implicit threat of violence that most members of society attribute to disorderly behavior, but without suffering the cost of severe repression that more often follows outright violence. In other words, protest allows groups to challenge the status quo while maintaining for themselves a measure of legitimacy, something that is sacrificed by those engaging in violence (Eisinger 1973, 13–14).

Furthermore, for activists protest may have additional, instrumental advantages over violence. The act of organizing demonstrations or marches allows activists to forge direct links with supporters, establishing themselves as visible leaders and strategists for the group and setting up a hierarchical organization that can be maintained over time. The public nature of protest allows activists the chance to draw new supporters, build their organizations, and make themselves known to others as contenders in the larger political arena. Collective violence, on the other hand, makes the pursuit of political power a much more difficult prospect for activists. The illegitimacy of violent action limits the possibilities for repeated public mobilization and reduces the number of potential supporters. In short, protest presents better opportunities for nonelectoral political entrepreneurs. Larger, more stable organizations can be built by leading demonstrations than by instigating riots.

Like theories of ethnic conflict more generally, most explanations of Korean-African American conflict collapse these two sets of distinctions into one. Instead of considering the possibility that different factors contribute to tensions than to conflict, or to protest than to violence, they only really suggest causes for latent tensions and merely assume that the same causes produce various forms of overt conflict. In one exception, sociologist Heon Cheol Lee makes a similar distinction between individual merchant-customer disputes and organized, collective action: "Most misunderstandings of black-Korean conflict and erroneous solutions stem from confusing these two distinct, though related, levels of conflicts" (1993, 226). By doing so, most explanations can only provide explanations for why, in the words of Ong, Park, and Tong, Koreans and blacks are exposed to "a set of interactions potentially filled with conflicts" (1994, 273)—but not why those conflicts actually occur. A complete explanation must provide a mechanism that translates tensions into conflict, and then causes them to be expressed in the form of protest or violence. That mechanism lies in the motives and capacities of community activists.

The Political Process Model of Protest

In a crucial contribution to understanding the politics of protest, Michael Lipsky (1968) emphasized the strategic goals of protest organizers. Rather than portraying activists solely as ideological purists driven by adherence to their stated goals, Lipsky saw them as profoundly constrained by (and aware of) the realities of politics: specifically, the need to build and maintain organizations comprised of their supporters while simultaneously appealing to other groups in the political system for exposure and resources (1968, 1144).

Powerful evidence for Lipsky's claim comes from Saul Alinsky, who sheds light on a basic aim of the activist in another passage in *Rules for Radicals*:

> Every move revolves around one central point: how many recruits will this bring into the organization. . . . The only issue is, how will this increase the strength of the organization. If by losing in a certain action

he can get more members than by winning, then victory lies in losing and he will lose. (1989, 113)

For Alinsky, the point of bringing neighborhood residents together into organizations was to strike at their apathy, build bases of power, and produce confident, capable, and effective individuals. He rejected the use of race as a means of stirring conflict (1989, 119, 122). Why, then, would this be relevant to explaining intergroup conflict? When activists use ethnic conflict as a tool for organizing a community, intergroup relations suffer. But activists need not agree with Alinsky's stance on race in order to share his strategic concerns or his awareness of the fruits of organizing. Conflicts may have ideological goals or they may seek to eliminate opponents, but they also serve as a way to mobilize followers and build organizations. Seen through this lens, the escalation of ethnic conflict reflects not only the degree of hostility toward a rival group but also the larger political and organizational climate.

A useful way to think about the relationship of activists to this larger climate is the notion that protesters respond to openings in the overarching "structure of political opportunities," even though their challenges to the status quo take place outside the arena of formal politics. Herbert Kitschelt, in a comparison of nations, writes that "political opportunity structures are comprised of specific configurations of resources, institutional arrangements and historical precedents for social mobilization, which facilitate the development of protest movements in some instances and constrain them in others" (1995, 57). The same can be said for comparisons across cities. Collective action by community groups, according to Peter Eisinger, "is not simply a function of the resources they command but of the openings, weak spots, barriers, and resources of the political system itself" (1973, 12). In this way, the political environments of cities shape the lives of groups within them.

Of particular importance is the way that politics influences the resources available to groups for engaging in conflict. Doug McAdam identifies the crucial role of *organizational* resources; the intensity and endurance of collective action "depends, in part, on the level of organizational resources" (1982, 56). In McAdam's view, such resources emerge from internal and external social processes. However, formal political institutions may play their own part, shaping the course taken by racial and ethnic conflicts by influencing patterns of community organization.

Scholars who have developed political process models of protest have focused on insurgent challenges by relatively powerless groups against governing institutions. However, this understanding of protest can also be applied to groups engaged in conflict with one another that do not exhibit a clearly hierarchical relationship, such as African and Korean Americans.

By influencing the level of political competition and organizational resources available to a local community, the arrangement of political institutions can facilitate or limit the ability of activists to organize tensions in their community. As political scientist John Mollenkopf points out: "A relative density of institutions which create collectively-oriented ties will enhance community mobilization" (1974, 381). Thus, certain local, institutional contexts may foster greater degrees of ethnic and racial mobilization than others. Political and community organization, in turn, may produce more nonviolent collective action such as protest.

Political Settings and the Capacity for Organization

When racial tensions overwhelm the level of organizational resources of a community, violence—rather than peaceful, organized protest—can result. In this vein, Donald Horowitz argues that American race riots of the 1960s and 1970s occurred more commonly in the North than in the South because, at the time, the North lacked the organizational infrastructure of the civil rights movement, and thus "the movement could not be transplanted readily" (1983, 196). In his study of black insurgency, McAdam confirms this, pointing out that movement leaders failed to establish strong organizational networks in the North (1982, 190–91).

Northern protesters adopted much of the southern movement's symbolism. However, as Horowitz asserts:

> [whereas] the movement in the South was carefully planned and organised (especially in preparing demonstrators to respond peacefully to police abuses), and was therefore non-violent, the disorders in the North were neither carefully planned nor organised. What small element of protest demonstration there was to one or two of them in the first instance quickly dissolved into violence. (Horowitz 1983, 197)

However, as the level of political resources and organization among northern blacks grew—quickened by enhanced political consciousness, the demise of white-controlled urban machines and the passage of the 1965 Voting Rights Act—rioting began to fade. As Horowitz argues, black rioting subsided in the 1970s after

> urban political institutions were finally performing for the black community the functions they had historically performed for white immigrant groups, integrating them into a previously alien political system by means of patronage, the exchange of tangible benefits for votes, or simply the more reliable delivery of basic municipal services. (1983, 204)

This era marked the beginning of widespread independent mobilization and acquisition of concrete political gains by blacks, at least in northern and midwestern cities where pluralistic machine systems had worked for other ethnic groups in the past (Joyce 1997).[13] This led to further changes in the political context, as Horowitz explains:

> With the growth of organisation in the North, presumably strategies of protest were more developed and more smoothly executed. Furthermore, with the background of violence in the Northern cities, protest strategies, which depend on the threat (but not the use) of violence, would probably be more effective. . . . As black representation and organisation increased, it would be reasonable to expect an increase in protest and a decline in violence. (1983, 204)

This line of reasoning suggests that urban political institutions have their impact on the development of intergroup conflict chiefly through two factors: levels of political organization and levels of political representation.

Traditional Party Organization

If community activists are central to the process of translating latent tensions into overt, nonviolent conflict, then what features of urban political institutions tend to facilitate community organizing, that is, the work of activists? Cities differ in the nature of their political processes and in their capacities for organization. In particular, political systems with traditional political institutions—those with histories of machine-style politics—should be more likely than those dominated by reform-style institutions to produce nonviolent, protest-oriented ethnic conflict.

Clarence Stone (1989) observes that different configurations of political institutions promote different types of politics. How a city is governed depends largely "on how the populace is organized to participate in a community's civic life." Machine politics, for instance, promotes political activity that resembles its "organizational network oriented toward patronage and related considerations." On the other hand, reform politics "heighten[s] the role of organizations connected to business" and discourages activity by "working-class organizations and nonprofit groups unsupported by business." By influencing the levels of different kinds of political expression in a city, then, the pattern of local politics also influences the quantity and kind of groups that mobilize.

When formal and informal political processes are considered together, traditional cities tend to be less centralized in their power structures than reform-style cities. True, traditional-style cities were once highly centralized due to the informal power of political machines (Banfield 1961). Reform-style cities were designed to be fragmented institutionally precisely in order to prevent machines from controlling them (Schockman 1996, 59). However, centralized machines are all but gone.

What remains in traditional cities are *patterns* of machine politics, which continue to influence political behavior (Wolfinger 1972). Thus, cities with traditional-style politics retain high levels of organization but lack centralized control. Reform-style cities, however, have been highly susceptible to informal control by tight circles of business elites and public officials, a phenomenon Stephen Elkin calls the "entrepreneurial political economy" (1987, 61; see also Stone 1989). The decision-making processes of reform cities have been found to exhibit more centralized, informal power structures (Clark 1971, 303–4, 312). Higher levels of organizational activity in a community without centralized leadership—the conditions present in former machine cities—can lead to greater degrees of competition between organizations and thus spur more mobilization.

Furthermore, in machine cities, political parties themselves are highly elaborate and formalized institutions (unlike the more fluid, informal, and business-dominated partnerships of reform cities). In a system where "every formal organization gives rise to an informal one," this leads to a proliferation of political activity (Stone 1989). This activity is increased at the grassroots level by the orientation of machine politics toward material stakes. The more the patronage, services, or other stakes available from government, the more that citizens will organize to compete for them. Mobilization to gain political rewards or protect one's stakes provokes others to do the same, and the formation of groups begets the formation of more groups. Organizational networks are built up over time which ultimately allow neighborhood activists and other community and political entrepreneurs to mobilize supporters more easily for conflicts—whether those conflicts are with government or with each other. In reform cities, by contrast, political life lacks the structure provided by such ubiquitous organizational networks.

To measure the organizational climate of cities, I use the state-level index of the strength of local traditional party organizations (TPOs) developed by David Mayhew (1986). The TPO score ranges from 1 to 5, with 5 representing the existence of strong parties.[14] A positive relationship of this score with protest and a negative association with violence would support my argument.

Black Political Representation

The presence of traditional party organization indicates a high level of structure in political life at a citywide level that patterns organizational activity. However, a second factor crucial to explaining the impact of the political process on black-Korean conflicts is the political representation of African Americans. The formal officeholding of a particular ethnic or racial group provides a measure of that group's relative strength in political resources and also signals an opening in the political opportunity structure of a city.

Black representation in politics thus reflects a shift in the system-level balance of power, signaling to black activists that the political system might be more responsive to their demands. As mentioned, in boycotts of Korean stores, black protesters nearly always highlighted the larger community implications of their demands. Under more favorable political conditions, activists might see greater chances that third-party actors would support their efforts, and they might therefore be more likely to mobilize neighborhood residents to protest. Without such conditions, tensions might remain without channels for organized protest and develop into violence. An analysis by Peter Eisinger of protests from a single year in the late 1960s lends support to this notion: he finds that racial violence follows a different dynamic from protest, with only the latter tied to an opening of political opportunities (Eisinger 1973).

The degree of black political resources can be measured by the percent of black representation on city councils.[15] Higher levels of representation are associated with higher levels of political efficacy, sophistication, and resources, which in turn facilitate collective mobilization for protest activities, and activists who lead boycotts might figure this feature of the opportunity structure into their cost-benefit calculations. Black political representation on city councils for the thirty-nine cities ranges from zero to 85 percent, with an average of 27 percent. A positive relationship with protest would support the explanation.

An important aspect of the institutional explanation for black-Korean conflict is that protest and violence have different causes. When the political life of a city lacks structure, generating fewer organizational resources in communities, tensions are more likely to transform into violence. Thus, unlike theories of conflict based on ideas or interests, the institutional explanation hypothesizes that violent conflict follows a different dynamic from protest: intergroup violence should *not* be related to political and organizational factors. Or if it is, intergroup violence should be greater where political life is less structured.[16]

TESTING THE THEORIES

Which explanations actually account better for the distribution and expression of black-Korean conflicts across space and time: ideas, interests, or institutions? Using the conflict data described in chapter 1 and the quantitative indicators identified in this chapter, multiple theories can be tested

Table 2.1. Quantitative Measures of the Theories of Black-Korean Conflict

---

Political Institutions
   Traditional party organization (scale of 1–5)
   Black city council representation (percent)

Ideas/values
   Proportion of Koreans who don't speak English well (percent)

Interests (middleman minority theory, competition theory)
   Percent of Koreans self-employed to percent of city
      population self-employed (ratio)
   Black unemployment (percent)
   Black-owned firms to Korean-owned firms (ratio)

Demographic factors
   City population (natural log)
   Black population (percent)
   Korean population (percent)
   Violent crime rate (per 100,000 population)
   Occurrence or not of boycott/violence in previous year

---

simultaneously for their ability to explain empirical reality. Since the data available are at times limited in richness and depth, the findings from these tests should be taken as suggestive rather than conclusive—the results of rough tests of complex social phenomena.

Nonetheless, the breadth of statistical analysis is its greatest strength: without it, empirical testing of multiple competing theories using a large number of cases is next to impossible. Certainly, nowhere else has this approach been applied to explaining black-Korean conflicts. Moreover, this breadth makes the perfect companion to the depth offered by comparative case studies, which, for reasons that will become clear later, comprise the remainder of the book.

Of the theories reviewed in this chapter, four have observable implications that can be measured with available data: cultural differences, competition, middleman minority, and political institutions. The measures associated with each set of theories are listed in Table 2.1.

As Table 2.1 shows, the political institutions argument is represented by two variables: the strength of traditional party organizations in a city and the percentage of city council members who are black. Interest-oriented explanations are represented by three variables: (1) representing middleman minority theory, the percentage of Koreans who are self-employed relative to the percentage of the general population that is self-employed and the level of black unemployment; (2) representing competition theory, the ratio of black-owned business firms to Korean-owned firms; and (3) the black unemployment rate. For idea/value-oriented explanations, only cultural difference is formally represented as a variable, using a measure of Korean Americans' English language skills. However, a negative relationship between black city council representation and the incidence of conflict would support the racial discourse explanation.

Because the thirty-nine cities vary not only along these dimensions but also in other ways that might be said to matter to the occurrence of conflict, a variety of demographic attributes are included in the analysis as well. These include the city population size,[17] the percent of the population that is black, and the percent that is Korean. Additionally, the rate of violent crimes (the number per 100,000 population) is included in order to control for the possibility that some cities may be more conflictual than others.[18] In such places, a social environment laced with higher levels of apprehension might generate overt intergroup conflict independently of other factors. Finally, variables are included to represent the possible contagion effect of previous conflict—that conflict the previous year increases (or decreases) the likelihood of conflict the next year—for both protest and violence.

The following discussion reports the results of two separate statistical models: one that estimates the impact of the variables in Table 2.1 on the probability that boycotts will happen, and one that does the same for incidents of violence. Both models use what statisticians call pooled time-series data: each data point is a "city-year," representing one year in one of the thirty-nine cities. The number of years for which there is a data point is different for each city: some cities have six years (1990 to 1995) and some have as many as eleven (from 1985 to 1995), depending on the number of years of newspaper coverage that was available for each city in the newspaper survey.[19]

Tables 2.2 and 2.3 show the probabilities that each explanatory variable

Table 2.2. Chance of a Boycott Happening in One City in One Year When Increasing Explanatory Factors from Their Minimum to Maximum Value (Percent)

Explanatory factor	Minimum	Maximum
Traditional party organization (1–5)	3.4	13.6
Black city council representation (0%–85%)	1.8	49.9
Black unemployment (2%–22%)	27.4	2.6
Violent crime rate (215–4,352 per 100,000 population)	2.0	32.8

Note: Only statistically significant factors are shown. City population is also significant, but not included in the table.

Table 2.3. Chance of a Report of Violence in One City in One Year
When Increasing Explanatory Factors from Their Minimum to
Maximum Value (Percent)

Explanatory factor	Minimum	Maximum
Proportion of Koreans who don't speak English well (24%–81%)	16.6	1.7
Black-owned firms to Korean-owned firms (ratio: 1.4–46.5)	19.6	2.6
Black unemployment (2%–22%)	23.9	2.5
Violent crime rate (215–4,352 per 100,000 population)	1.7	26.2

Note: Only statistically significant factors are shown. City population is also significant, but not included in the table.

has on the chance of an incident happening in any given year in any given city. Only the variables that achieve statistical significance (meaning that the numerical value of their correlation with incidents of boycotts or violence can reasonably be expected to differ from zero) are included. Tables 2.2 and 2.3 both indicate the independent impact of each explanatory variable on the probability of conflict when the variable is increased from its minimum value to its maximum value, with all other variables held constant at their mean values.[20]

The Occurrence of Boycotts

As Table 2.2 shows, boycotts are more likely when four criteria are met: traditional party organizations have greater presence, the level of black representation on city councils is high, the level of black unemployment is low, and the violent crime rate is high. The analysis suggests that political institutions indeed impact conflict by making nonviolent expressions more likely.

Cities lacking traditional party organization—reform-style cities such as Los Angeles or Miami—are unlikely to experience black-led boycotts of Korean stores, all other things equal. Thus, with all the other factors in the analysis—economic, cultural, and demographic variables—held constant at their average values, such cities only have a 3.4 percent chance of a boycott happening in any given year. By contrast, cities with high levels of traditional party organization, such as New York or Chicago, have a 13.6 percent chance of experiencing a boycott, making them four times as likely as those without high levels of party organization to experience nonviolent conflicts between blacks and Koreans.[21]

Black city council representation has a similarly powerful impact on the likelihood of boycotting. Increasing the level of black representation from its minimum value of 0 percent to its maximum value of 85 percent leads to a correspondingly large change in the chance that a boycott will happen, from 1.8 percent to 49.9 percent. Much of that increase takes place only for levels of black council representation above 50 percent, which only six of the thirty-nine cities experienced. Thus, the real-world impact might also be expressed in another way. For all thirty-nine cities, the average proportion of African Americans serving on city councils is 27 percent, roughly the figure for Houston, Philadelphia, and Cincinnati in the early 1990s. Raising the level of black political representation from one standard deviation below the mean (7 percent, the proportion in Minneapolis) to one standard deviation above the mean (47 percent, roughly the proportion in Detroit, St. Louis, and Inglewood, California) increases the probability of boycotting fivefold, from a 2.2 percent chance to an 11 percent chance in any given year.

Surprisingly, none of the explanations based on ideas or interests, which would account for the causes of latent tensions between groups, receives support. Of the three variables representing economic interest-based theories, only black unemployment achieves statistical significance in the analysis. Middleman minority theory suggests that the higher the economic pressures on black city residents, the more likely they would displace anger onto middleman merchants. However, the analysis shows that higher levels of unemployment are associated with lower probabilities of boycotting. Increasing black unemployment from its minimum value for the thirty-nine cities, 2 percent, to its maximum value, 22 percent, correlates with a drop in the probability of boycotting from 27.4 percent to 2.6 percent.

Similarly, racial discourse theory suggests that black political representation should be negatively related to boycotting, the argument being that the exclusion of blacks from politics instigates greater protest activity against status quo arrangements, including the presence of Korean businesses in black neighborhoods. However, the results demonstrate that black representation has a positive effect on the likelihood of boycotts.[22]

Interestingly, the only other statistically significant variable is the violent crime rate, which increases the probability of boycotting from 2 percent to 32.8 percent when raised from its lowest level of 215 crimes per 100,000 population to its highest level of 4,352. As was the case with black city council representation, the bulk of the impact happens at the upper end of the distribution, when the violent crime rate is higher than 2,700 crimes per 100,000 population. Only five cities fall into that unlucky category. An increase in the crime rate from one standard deviation below its mean (940) to one standard deviation above (2660) is associated with an increase in the probability of boycotting of about seven percentage points. The violent crime rate is most likely related to the probability of boycotting because higher crime rates generate more fear, and thus higher levels of general social tension generally, not because boycotts have anything to do with crime or violence directly. (I will return to this relationship below.)

The Occurrence of Violence

Violence clearly follows a different dynamic from protest in the case of black-Korean conflicts. As Table 2.3 shows, neither of the political-institutional variables bears statistically significant relationships with reports of violence between blacks and Koreans. Given the expectations of the institutional model, this is somewhat surprising.

This lack of support for political factors is not the only difference from the boycott model. In another important contrast, variables for all of explanations based on ideas and interests yield significant relationships. However, this does not translate into *support* for all of these theories. Instead, these factors at times appear to work in the opposite directions expected of them.

For instance, the percentage of Korean Americans who do not speak English well is related to the probability of violence, but not in the direction suggested by explanations of conflict focused on cultural differences. Rather than supporting the notion that reports of violence are more likely where the linguistic gap is larger, this finding indicates—rather counterintuitively—that violence is more likely where the linguistic gap is smaller. Increasing the proportion of Koreans without good English skills from the variable's minimum value of 24 percent to its maximum value of 81 percent results in a decline in the probability of reported violence, from 16.6 percent to 1.7 percent. Similarly, higher levels of unemployment, which economic interest explanations posit should be related to higher levels of conflict, are actually associated with a lower likelihood of violence. Raising black unemployment from 2 percent to 22 percent, its lowest and highest values in the thirty-nine cities, corresponds to a drop in the probability of reported violence, from 23.9 percent to 2.5 percent.

The only explanatory variable that yields a statistically significant relationship with violence that works as expected is the ratio of black-owned to Korean-owned firms, representing competition theory. As competition theory predicts, the smaller the ratio (and thus the closer Koreans and blacks are to each other in their levels of business ownership), the greater the chance of conflict. As Table 2.3 shows, increasing that ratio across its entire range, from 1.4 to 46, leads to a decrease in the likelihood of reported violence of 19.6 percent to 2.6 percent. Los Angeles and Seattle have the minimum value; Miami has the maximum. Orlando and Houston have ratios closest to the mean, or about twelve black-owned firms for every Korean-owned firm. Additionally, the general violent crime rate in a city is positively related to reports of violence involving blacks and Koreans.

A Relationship between Protest and Violence?

Across the entire sample of years and cities, the two forms of conflict seem to be related to each other. The simple correlation of boycotting and reports of violence in city-years is .25, meaning they appear in the same cities in the same years a quarter of the time. Moreover, both forms of conflict are related to the general level of violent crime in a city, suggesting that the degree of contentiousness of life in a city may be part of what drives conflicts. But can it be said that protest is related to reports of intergroup violence? Does the previous occurrence of one generate more of the other, as a matter of course?

It appears not. When this idea is tested in the boycotts model, by including a variable indicating previous violence, it fails to yield a statistically significant effect. The same holds true when testing for the effect on violence of previous boycotting.[23]

GAPS IN THE PUZZLE

The political institutions of cities influence when and where blacks boycott Korean stores. The more highly structured the political life in a city—as indicated by the degree of traditional party organization—the more likely it is that blacks will boycott Korean-owned businesses. And the greater the political resources of African Americans, as indicated by their representation on city councils, the greater the likelihood of boycotts.[24] Party organizations play an important role in structuring political life, and black elected officials represent the presence of political resources in black communities and an opening in the political opportunity structure.

Gaps remain in the puzzle of black-Korean conflict, however. Specifically, three questions remain unanswered by the statistical analysis. First, why are objective conditions thought to be responsible for tensions only related to violence and not to boycotts? Black-Korean conflicts do not appear to be the provoked by the conditions thought to generate mass-level, intergroup tensions. This finding seems to contradict the fact that boycott leaders, although separated widely by time and place, stated aims that bore striking resemblance to one another, appearing to reflect such conditions. Thus, the question remains: What role, if any, do tensions play in producing nonviolent conflict?

Second, why is the political-organizational setting not related to violence? A political-institutional argument may be taken to suggest that the more structured the political life of a city, the less violence. If politics plays a hand in producing protest, and does so by channeling tensions into nonviolent actions, then why does it not appear to lessen violence as well? For the sake of drawing practical lessons, this may be the most important question of all. What role, if any, does the political process play in preventing violent intergroup conflict?

Third, why does there appear to be no relationship between protest and violence? Regression analysis found no evidence that protest leads to violence, or vice versa, from one year to the next. Still, the two forms are correlated. Moreover, contrary to the results of my statistical analysis, common sense suggests that tensions produced by one might feed the other. Observers of boycotts have argued that boycotts tend to generate their own antagonisms that then lead to violence (DeLeon 1996; H. C. Lee 1993). As noted in the previous chapter, boycotts often have followed reports of violence. This matter, too, seems unresolved. What is the relationship, if any, between the two forms of conflict?

There are two possible explanations for why the analysis leaves these three gaps in the puzzle. First, imprecise measurement of the variables representing some of the theories may hinder the analysis, preventing it from capturing true relationships. Perhaps we just need better data. (For a discussion of this possibility, see the Appendix.) Second, intermediary steps in the puzzle may be missing from the analysis, requiring researchers to dig deeper into actual cases of conflict and trace processes on the ground. This second possibility not only makes sense but points to the next step in solving the puzzle.

Most likely, the statistical analysis excludes important steps in the process of conflict generation. If factors like competition, middleman minority status, and cultural differences matter, they produce latent tensions—in the form of attitudes—between blacks and Koreans. Political and organizational resources then help to determine the form of collective action and severity of conflict that ensues from these tensions. However, since inter-city measures of tensions, such as the attitudes of blacks toward Koreans and vice versa, were not available for a large sample of cities, they could not be included in this analysis.

What effect would including a measure of tensions have on the analysis? Tensions are hypothesized as being the direct product of sociological factors. These would not only contribute to the generation of overt forms of conflict, but might also in turn be affected by them, introducing the possibility of feedback effects. Currently the closest the analysis gets to this is accounting for the possibility of contagion effects from previous conflicts, which do not achieve statistical significance. As noted, neither boycotts nor incidents of violence are more likely when similar events preceded them the year before. Substituting the opposite event for the contagion variable (testing to see if violence makes boycotts more likely or if violence makes boycotts more likely) also fails to produce a relationship.

Another element missing is the lack of an indicator for ideological explanations for conflict. The solution to the problem of missing measures for both tensions and ideology would lie in opinion surveys. However, to avoid uncertainty about the direction of causality, even these would have to predate conflicts, or at least represent multiple points in time. Such data are unavailable for more than a couple of cities.[25] The role of ideology may be discernable through the examination of case studies in which the development of conflict is traced over time and in greater depth than statistical analysis. Doug McAdam has argued that the generation of protest must be preceded by a subjective evaluation of objective conditions, a "mood" that directs or frames the need for action (McAdam 1982). In the case of black boycotts of Korean stores, black nationalism may provide this kind of subjective evaluation, and it may do so in a more complex manner than has been supposed.

Finally, the statistical analysis suggests that political institutions do not dampen the prospects for intergroup violence. However, cities with traditional party organizations and greater black political representation are more likely to have established traditions and networks of community organizing, which channel tensions directed at Korean Americans into boycotts. When cities lack traditional organization and black representation, it would seem that black activists would have a more difficult time channeling tensions, allowing violence to result. The reason this argument does not appear to be borne out by the analysis may lie in yet another missing element in the puzzle.

These two features of the political process may act in conjunction with other factors, making violence less likely only when such factors are present. Intermediary political factors, which have yet to be discovered, can only be identified using a closer and deeper level of analysis. Even more important, political institutions may make a difference only for large-scale violence. Individual reports of violence may simply not be related to intergroup tensions, as some explanations of black-Korean conflict have suggested. Including reports of such incidents was necessary to evaluate claims about the explanatory power of theories of conflict. However, an indiscriminate method of collecting data on violence may obstruct our view of a more specialized role for politics.

Evidence for this last possibility already exists. An analysis of data on race riots during the second half of the twentieth century found that rioting was more likely to take place in cities with reform-style political institutions than in cities with more traditional political institutions (Olzak and Shanahan 1996, 946–48, 950–51).[26] Little has been made of this finding. However, it suggests that different contexts of local politics may provide not only different sources of grievance for racial violence (the most commonly hypothesized link), but they may also provide different capacities for channeling hostilities into protest rather than into violent conflict.

Chapter 3

Comparing New York City and Los Angeles

From the national-level analysis, we know two things about the relationship of politics, protest, and violence in black-Korean conflicts: political institutions have influenced when and where boycotts have taken place, and protest has followed a different path from violence. Statistical analysis excels at identifying broad patterns such as these, but its dependence on the quantification of complex phenomena sets limits. As useful and even indispensable as it is, statistical analysis remains a blunt instrument. When faced with the challenge of picking an intricate lock, one needs a finer tool.

In particular, the national-level analysis left the answers to three important questions unclear: (1) What role do intergroup tensions play in generating boycotts? (2) Do political institutions dampen collective violence? and (3) What exactly is the relationship between protest and violence? Theory and data analysis have given us the broad outlines of a solution; the next step is to delve into the thicket of actual conflicts, with a closer examination of how they emerge and develop on the ground. In order to answer these questions and to more fully illuminate the relationship between politics and social conflict, I shift the focus back to the two cities that framed the initial puzzle.

Why Los Angeles and New York City? First, as readers will recall, the major conflicts in these two cities offered contrasting images of black-Korean conflict: one was extremely violent, the other decidedly not. However, these climactic events could not have happened anywhere; they were tied to specific local contexts. The 1990 Red Apple boycott in New York and the 1992 riots in Los Angeles reflected broader tendencies in each city. Second, the two cities have a great deal in common socially and economically, but they differ markedly in their political institutions. Thus, comparing the two cities provides the opportunity to discover precisely *how* politics shapes conflict. The task of this chapter is to lay the groundwork for that comparison.

DIFFERENT PATTERNS OF CONFLICT

The nature of conflict between blacks and Koreans was different in New York City and Los Angeles. Table 3.1 presents the comparison. Over the course of a decade and a half, New York City experienced twice as many black-led boycotts of Korean stores as Los Angeles: fourteen versus seven. Additionally, boycotts in New York City lasted, on average, four times as long as those in Los Angeles: 120 days compared to 30. Boycotts, therefore, not only happened more often in New York, but once they had begun, were more protracted. This fact suggests a fourth question to add to the first three: Why are boycotts more intractable in some places than in others?[1]

Although reports of violence involving blacks and Koreans were more numerous in New York City, Los Angeles had many more reports of severe violence. The latter experienced more shootings: fourteen in Los Angeles and only one in New York.[2] Reports of physical assaults account for most of the violent incidents in New York, and many of these were merely scuffles that resulted in minor injuries.[3] Moreover, in a number of cases in New York, claims about the severity of attacks were contested. Shootings, on the other hand, were always verified by police.

Most important, Los Angeles experienced the participation of both blacks and Koreans in the civil unrest of 1992. During the entire course of the rioting, forty-six Korean Americans were reported injured and more than 2,000 Korean-owned businesses were looted, burned, or both (Ong and Hee 1993b, 7–14; Min, 1996, 90).[4] By contrast, only one Korean business is known to have suffered similar damage in New York City, during the Crown Heights rioting in New York in 1991 (which targeted Hasidic Jews, not Koreans) (F. Lee 1993). Of course, Crown Heights demonstrated that violent intergroup conflict is certainly possible in New York City, even if the chief combatants were not African Americans and Korean Americans. Compared to Los Angeles, however, the scale of rioting in Crown Heights

Table 3.1. Black-Korean Conflict in New York
and Los Angeles, 1980–1995

	New York	Los Angeles
Boycotts	14	7
Average duration of boycotts	120 days	30 days
Riots	No	Yes
Arson	1	5
Shootings	1	15
Assaults	12	5

was miniscule. In the Crown Heights riot, about 200 individuals (mostly police officers) suffered injuries, and six businesses experienced significant losses (Girgenti 1993, 130–31). The unrest took place within an area of one square mile, led to fewer than 130 arrests, and produced no deaths (ibid., 112, 224). The rioting in Los Angeles, by contrast, covered nearly sixty square miles, led to more than 16,000 arrests, and produced fifty-two deaths (Morrison and Lowry 1994, 19; Sears 1994, 238).

THE TWO CITIES COMPARED

New York City and Los Angeles appear to have a great deal in common. As Table 3.2 shows, Korean Americans exhibited roughly the same aggregate level of English fluency in 1990 in each city: 67 percent were unable to speak English well in New York, compared to 63 percent in Los Angeles. Koreans were thus about equally "culturally distant" from blacks in both cities. Korean Americans were also self-employed relative to the general population roughly to the same degree, indicating similar degrees of middleman minority status: in both cities, they were 3.3 times as likely as other city residents to be self-employed. African Americans had similar unemployment rates on both coasts, 12.9 percent in New York and 13.5 percent in Los Angeles. The two places also experienced similar levels of violent crime: 2,383 incidents per 100,000 people in New York, and 2,404 in Los Angeles.

Of course, the two cities were not identical. In Los Angeles, there were only 1.4 black-owned businesses for every Korean business—one of the smallest ratios in the country—compared to a ratio of 4.6 in New York City. The proportion of blacks in the population in Los Angeles in 1990 was about half that in New York, 14 percent versus 29 percent. Los Angeles had a proportionately larger Korean population, 2 percent compared to 1 percent in New York. Finally, Los Angeles was about half the size of New York (with 1990 populations of 3,485,400 and 7,322,560, respectively).

With regard to politics, as Table 3.2 shows, New York City and Los Angeles had similar levels of black representation on the city council in 1990: 13 percent in Los Angeles, and a slightly higher rate of 17 percent in New York. Moreover, each city was governed at that point in time by an African American mayor: David Dinkins governed in New York, while Tom Bradley was mayor of Los Angeles. (Dinkins, however, had just been elected the city's first black mayor, whereas Bradley had been in office since 1973.)

On the other hand, Los Angeles and New York City lay at opposite ends of the spectrum of traditional party organization (scores of 1 and 5 respectively). This contrast indicates the wide divergence between political

Table 3.2. New York and Los Angeles Compared, 1990

Quantitative measure	New York	Los Angeles
Political institutions		
Traditional party organization (1–5)	5	1
Black city council representation	17%	13%
Ideas/values		
Proportion of Koreans who don't speak		
English well	67%	63%
Interests		
Self-employment of Koreans relative to		
city population (ratio)	3.3	3.3
Black unemployment	12.9%	13.5%
Ratio of black-owned firms to Korean-		
owned firms	4.6	1.4
Demographic factors		
City population (millions)	7.3	3.5
Black population	29%	14%
Korean population	1%	2%
Violent crime rate (per 100,000		
population)	2,383	2,404

institutions in the two cities, a chasm that extends to a number of the components in their political structures. Traditional party organization both contributes to and is molded by the array of formal, governing institutions in a city. As I have argued, these institutions have consequences not only for conventional politics but also for forms of social conflict that take place outside their boundaries.

POLITICAL INSTITUTIONS IN NEW YORK CITY

Political life in New York City is highly structured. It is not too great an exaggeration to say that every interest is organized, although every group does not get its way or have an equal impact on policy. City government here, as elsewhere, is powerfully constrained by economic forces and by the interests of dominant political coalitions. But many interests *attempt* to make their voices heard and compete for attention in politics, frequently and repeatedly. This tendency has not escaped the notice of scholars studying New York. In other cities, particularly those dominated by reform-style institutions, the scope of organized interests is relatively narrow, allowing business interests to dominate. However, as John Mollenkopf writes, "In

New York, business interests, while large and powerful, appear to be less cohesive and less well organized, . . . while the power of city government is greater, public sector producer interests stronger, and its political constituencies better organized" (1992, 40).

Why are interests so active and well organized in New York City? First, traditional party organizations maintain an enduring influence. The first political machines emerged in the late nineteenth century and structured political life with extensive ward organizations (Bridges 1984). Over the course of the twentieth century, the machines met with recurring challenges by reformers, which whittled away at their dominance, but the patterns of organization they had established persisted. Inescapably, reformers adopted the methods of the machines, and New York became one of many American cities with "machine politics" but without a cohesive, all-powerful "political machine" (Wolfinger 1972). In fact, the Democratic Party is highly fragmented internally, due largely to the independence of separate party organizations in each of the city's five boroughs, but also to continual conflicts between its "regular" and "reform" wings (Mollenkopf 1992, 77; Wolfinger 1972, 376).

A second feature of New York City politics that generates an active political life is the enormous size of the material stakes made available by city government. The bureaucracy employs hundreds of thousands of public servants, easily more than any other big city in the nation—both in absolute terms and in proportion to population. Roughly five percent of New York's population works for the city, giving the individuals in that group a direct stake in the political system (Sonenshein 1993, 232). Politicians are keenly aware of this fact and have used the bureaucracy to shore up electoral support and to advance the interests of racial and ethnic groups. Public employee unions have thoroughly organized the city workforce, ensuring political activity among city workers (Mollenkopf 1992, 73).

As many city jobs as there are, however, much more than public employment is at stake in New York City politics. Unlike other big cities, New York pays for and controls education and social services (Fuchs 1992). This means that organizing, protesting, and demanding funding for schools and government programs takes place much more at the municipal level than might otherwise be the case.

A third important feature of the political system is the visible presence of government institutions in the city's neighborhoods, which links city government to the grassroots and constantly exposes residents to political activity. An excellent illustration of the profound impact that New York City government has on neighborhood life is the city's system of fifty-nine community boards, established in 1969 during the mayoral administration of John Lindsay. The move both reflected and deepened city government's traditional attachments to neighborhoods. Community board members are appointed by elected officials and ostensibly advise municipal agencies on policy implementation.

More important, however, the boards provide New Yorkers with incentives to mobilize politically, often right in their own back yards. As Douglas Yates describes:

> Most boards play the role of a community forum in which local needs
> and grievances are articulated. . . . [They] become lightning rods for
> community opposition to government initiatives [and] operate as semi-
> institutionalized critics of government. Having developed this habit
> of criticism, community boards tend to adopt and amplify whatever
> antigovernment feeling is running in the neighborhood. . . . In general,
> the activity pattern of the boards is one of protracted debate and griev-
> ance-articulation punctuated by an occasional burst of protest. (1973,
> 39–40)

In effect, this component of the city's institutional design actually draws residents into politics at the neighborhood level, stirring potential controversies and providing forums for mobilizing and organizing around them.

The community boards demonstrate only one aspect of the neighborhood decentralization of New York City government. Another is the system of thirty-one elected community school boards, instituted in 1969 to reform the educational system. Moreover, an extensive network of nonprofit organizations, funded by city hall, perform a variety of governmental functions (Mollenkopf 1992, 71). The resulting decentralization of city functions "strengthens the neighborhood's capacity for sustained protest by expanding its organizational base," as Yates (1973, 154) points out.[5]

The fourth feature that makes for a vigorous political life in New York City is the centralized power structure at the upper tiers of government. In spite of the way governmental functions are decentralized at the neighborhood level, formal authority over decision-making within city government is highly concentrated in the office of the mayor. New York City has a "strong mayor" political structure, meaning that the chief executive wields greater say over major governmental policies than the relatively weak city council. Moreover, the commissioners of dozens of city agencies answer directly to the mayor, serving at his whim. The fact that the mayor sits alone atop the massive machinery of New York's municipal bureaucracy establishes clear lines of authority, making it easy for New Yorkers to assign credit or blame—and giving them a highly visible target against which to mobilize when they feel their interests are threatened.

The mayor's formal authority does not translate into power over realms outside the halls of city government, however. Although his appointive and budgetary powers are great, the mayor spends much time fending off challenges from other actors in New York politics. Some of these challenges come from other levels of government, such as the New York state legislature, or from quasi-independent bodies like regional transportation authorities.[6] However, even actors from within New York City can destabilize the mayor's authority, particularly when they hold the right cards, like economic assets or blocs of votes. Ultimately, the mayor faces the same informal constraints as any other mayor in any other city in the United States. The mayor of New York, however, is more visible than most, raising expectations that are often out of proportion with the capacities of the office.

The fifth and final institutional feature important to New York City's organizational life is the large number of opportunities for individuals to hold elected and appointed public offices. More offices means more entry points for city residents into politics, whether they are running for office themselves, working on campaigns, or contacting representatives. Elected officials in the city include the mayor, public advocate, comptroller, five borough presidents, five district attorneys, fifty-one city council members (thirty-five members before the reform of the council in 1991), the members of the thirty-one community school boards, and numerous state judges. In addition, the city sends sixty representatives to the state assembly in Albany.

All of these features promote a relatively high level of political organization and activism at the grassroots in New York City. But in the absence of the Democratic machine's once-centralized control of political life, the organization of interests lacks a cohesive guiding force. Instead, the city's politics exhibits what Douglas Yates calls "street-fighting pluralism," which he defines as "a pattern of unstructured, multilateral conflict in which many different combatants fight continuously with one another in a very great number of permutations and combinations" (1977, 34).[7] This pattern spills over the boundaries of conventional politics. Andy Logan describes how New York's "hyper-organization" is evident outside the halls of government, and not just in a figurative sense: "Every few days—and sometimes several times a day—fist-shaking, placard-waving crowds converge on City Hall to protest budget cuts, say, or ethnic bias on the part of city agencies, or the inhumane treatment of carriage horses" (1992, 91). For many New Yorkers, politics is no distant affair; instead, it exhibits an "in-your-face" quality. Politics provokes community organization. Structure in political life compels community activists to mobilize their neighborhoods, establishing dense networks of community organizations that become active even on issues that lie outside the arena of formal politics.

POLITICAL INSTITUTIONS IN LOS ANGELES

A very different system is at work in Los Angeles, where politics lacks structure, fewer interests are organized—especially at the grassroots—and those which are well organized tend to be business-oriented. In a political context with little structure, relatively few voices are mobilized to make themselves heard. Why is this so, and what are the consequences?

Los Angeles is the opposite of New York on all five dimensions of governmental structure: it lacks the enduring influence of traditional party organizations, city government makes available few material stakes to draw residents into politics, it has virtually no presence in the city's neighborhoods, the upper tier of government is fragmented, and there are few entry points into politics.

First, Los Angeles has always had weak party organizations. At the turn of the century, Protestant migrants rose to dominance in politics and "sought to build a new type of metropolis, freed from the ethnic, heterogeneous influences of eastern and midwestern cities," and thus "consciously designed to differ" from cities like New York and Chicago, as Raphael Sonenshein (1993, 26) asserts. As part of a wave that swept the West and Southwest, where strong political machines had never existed, the reformers adopted nonpartisan, at-large elections and other measures in order to centralize power, promote economic growth, and prevent influence by immigrants and minorities. These moves ensured that parties would never ensconce themselves in city politics. With politics "removed"—as the reformers saw it—business interests and localities were ensured continued dominance over the political scene (Bridges 1992; Judd and Swanstrom 1994, 89).

Second, local government in Los Angeles makes available relatively few material stakes to connect people directly to politics. Historically, without the patronage system of machine politics, there has been less of an incentive for politicians to provide jobs and services. The municipal bureaucracy in Los Angeles is dwarfed by New York City's, not just in absolute terms because the city's population is smaller, but also proportionally: city employees only make up about one percent of the population in Los Angeles, compared to five percent in New York (Sonenshein 1993, 232). The number of city jobs in Los Angeles (about 40,000) is about the same as in Chicago, a city closer in size to Los Angeles than is New York, but civil service rules place far stricter limits on political control over hiring decisions in Los Angeles (ibid., 232; Joyce 1997). Consequently, few individuals have direct or even indirect stakes in the fortunes of city government. Moreover, the city relies on other levels of government (county, state, and federal) for many of its functions, especially social services such as welfare and education. Mayors earlier in the century, like Sam Yorty, did not see city government as a provider of social services; Tom Bradley, who did, sought increased funds primarily from the federal government (Davis 1987, 74; Saltzstein, Sonenshein, and Ostrow 1986, 62). With few material stakes available from the city, there is far less reason for groups making demands on government to organize and protest for them at the local level.

Third, city government functions are highly insulated from political pressures at the neighborhood level (Skerry 1993, 75), where it has traditionally had almost no presence. Indeed, this was the intention of Progressive Era reformers, who designed the system in order to prevent the corruption of neighborhood-based machines and to remove politics from mundane matters of service delivery. As noted above, some functions are not even provided by the city but by other levels of government entirely.

In the 1960s, Los Angeles toyed with the idea of implementing a system of neighborhood councils, but unlike in New York, the idea failed to take hold and died. Reflecting its lack of institutionalized connections to the grassroots, Los Angeles city government thus lacked a real equivalent to New York's system of community boards to act as lighting rods for activism. Generally speaking, there are few formal outlets for input into decision-making processes, giving residents little reason and few opportunities to organize politically at the neighborhood level.

Fourth, formal authority is spread widely at the upper tiers of government, among the mayor, city council, and city agencies, blurring lines of authority and thereby discouraging interest-group organizing. In contrast to New York's strong mayoral control over city agencies, services tend to be provided by highly independent agencies in top-down fashion. The Los Angeles Police Department is a classic example. For nearly half a century, prior to reforms in the early 1990s, the LAPD was "virtually autonomous and free from political control," thanks largely to the efforts of Chief William Parker (after whom the city's downtown police headquarters is named) (Cannon 1997, 74). For years, the department resisted community policing reforms, which might have decentralized its authority. Mayor Tom Bradley did not encourage such reforms either, possibly because a police department with community roots presented a political challenge to the mayor (Cannon 1997, 89–91).

Fifth, Los Angeles offers few entry points into politics. The school board, "one of the lowest rungs on the electoral ladder," is an independent authority that governs a territory larger than the city itself and consists of only seven members, each of whom represents a district with an average of more than 600,000 residents (Skerry 1993, 76–77). Likewise, the City Council has only fifteen members. Only a handful of other elected positions are available for which residents can run or work on campaigns: the mayor, controller, and city attorney at the city level; and five supervisors, a number of judges, the district attorney, sheriff, and assessor at the county level. The city sends only five representatives to the state assembly (and the County of Los Angeles, which includes the city of Los Angeles as well as other municipalities, sends twenty-five) (Los Angeles County Clerk 1999). This amounts to fewer than a third the number of elected officials representing New York City.

Consequently, in contrast to New York City, political institutions in Los Angeles do not promote grassroots political organizing. Even the efforts of the United Neighborhoods Organization, which is highly skilled at such organizing and operates in cities across the country, have been "stymied by the obstacles and disincentives to neighborhood politics" (Skerry 1993, 203). Instead, as an "entrepreneurial city," Los Angeles is more receptive to effective political organization by business interests than by other groups, and major policy decisions tend to be dominated by a "regime" of elites and downtown business interests that practice a consensus-over-conflict political style (Elkin 1987; Stone 1989). As a matter of course, the mayor and the council refrain from open conflict in Los Angeles more than in other cities (Rohrlich 1997; Saltzstein, Sonenshein, and Ostrow 1986, 70). Thus, although formal power in city government is fragmented among actors at the upper tiers, political power in informal terms is highly centralized. The city may have a "weak mayor" in formal terms, but successive mayors have been able to amass power informally, as both Tom Bradley and Richard Riordan showed during their respective peaks in power (Saltzstein, Sonenshein, and Ostrow 1986, 64; Starr 1999a; Starr 1999b). Indeed, the fragmentation of formal government institutions means that mayors develop informal means of governing.

Historian Kevin Starr aptly describes the impact of reform politics on the political participation of Los Angeles residents:

> In contrast to the boroughs of New York and the wards of Chicago, Los Angeles was organized voter by voter, with no intervening structures like political parties or labor unions standing between the voters and the city as a whole. When voters were aroused, which is to say, when they were concentrating, it became a plebiscitary democracy, with each atomized voter entering momentarily into the political system on a one-to-one basis, then forgetting about it. In nonpolitically

intense times, which is to say most of the time, Los Angeles as government, as politics, tends to disappear from voters' consciousness like a movie no longer being watched. (Starr 1999b)

To put it more bluntly, if politics in New York City is "in your face," politics in Los Angeles is "out of sight, out of mind." Politics does not loom large in the daily life of most Angelenos, and consequently neither does neighborhood organizing.

LOOKING DEEPER

The next two chapters examine Korean-African American conflicts in New York City and Los Angeles. They trace the development of conflicts over time, from the early 1980s to the mid-1990s, in order to illuminate the impact of the city's political environment on intergroup relations. In order to reconstruct events in the two cities, I drew on scores of newspaper stories, a variety of public documents found in city government archives, and personal interviews with twenty-one individuals involved in conflicts. Previously published academic studies supplemented these primary sources.

With all three types of primary sources, my aim was to discern the nature of interactions among players in and around black-Korean conflicts. In order to compensate for the tendency of major news media to perpetuate dominant interpretations of issues involving race and class, I drew on a variety of newspapers: conservative-leaning tabloids like the *New York Post;* liberal-leaning establishment broadsheets like the *Los Angeles Times* and the *New York Times;* upstart competitors like *New York Newsday* (which led a short-lived existence but provided some of the best coverage); newspapers with primarily black or Korean readerships like the *Korea Times,* the *Amsterdam News,* and the *Los Angeles Sentinel;* and alternative weeklies like the *Village Voice* and *LA Weekly.* (Older editions and English versions of Korean-language newspapers were often difficult to find; however, to some extent, I was lucky to be able to draw on the work of other scholars who had used these sources to document black-Korean conflicts.) Drawing on a range of publications, I hope, allowed me to steer clear of reflecting the biases of any single one.

The twenty-one interview subjects were individuals whom I chose in order to reflect a balance of different vantage points on conflicts: protesters, Korean merchants, public officials, etc. They were conducted in-person for an average of one and a half hours. The interviews not only yielded new perspectives and provided new information on conflicts, but also allowed me to confirm contrasts in the patterns of conflict in the two cities. Because many of my interview subjects were in unique positions to know about the history of intergroup relations in their respective cities, I used the information they gave me to check and supplement press and other reports. Indeed, it was the job of some of the individuals I spoke with—such as the staff of local human rights commissions and of the Justice Department's Community Relations Service—to monitor occurrences of conflict. I found that there had been only a couple of boycotts that had gone unreported by newspapers. The public documents I drew on included transcripts from public hearings and reports by city and state government agencies.

The stories these two chapters tell complicate the lessons learned so far. They demonstrate that politics matters to conflict, but in ways that are more subtle and varied than a particular model would predict. By demonstrating how black-Korean conflicts developed differently in the two very different political contexts of New York City and Los Angeles, chapters 4 and 5 help to answer the three questions left unresolved by the broader analysis. They do so by opening windows to human agency, revealing how individuals reacted to their surroundings, impacted their environments, and interpreted their own actions. They make it possible, by tracing actual processes of conflict with precision and depth, to identify mechanisms of causation more concretely. Close examination of cases of conflict in New York City and Los Angeles allows us to draw the connection between politics and conflict more sharply.

The case studies also tackle the new, fourth question, presented at the beginning of this chapter, concerning why boycotts are more intractable in some places than others. In chapter 1, the nationwide survey of black-Korean conflicts revealed that third party actors—groups or individuals other than those immediately involved in disputes—frequently intervened. Indeed, as Michael Lipsky (1968) has observed, protesters must activate third parties to respond to their actions if they want success. Moreover, Doug McAdam argues that protest is "profoundly affected" by the responses of "other organized groups" (1982, 56). A political-institutional approach suggests reasons why third parties become involved and how they may tend to shorten or extend conflicts. Third party actors may see protests as opportunities for mobilizing their own constituencies and building organizations though countermobilization, extending the life of conflict. The degree to which this happens depends on the degree to which the political and community setting encourages such mobilization and organization. On the other hand, local political systems have varying capacities for resolving intergroup conflicts. In addition to shaping the emergence of conflict, political institutions shape the availability and responses of third parties, especially elected officials.

Chapter 4

New York City: Heat without Fire

"A LONG, HOT SUMMER"

It was May 1990, and *New York Newsday* warned of "a long, hot summer" ahead (Duggan 1990). The Big Apple's summer heat was felt halfway across the country, and readers of the *Chicago Tribune* learned that it had nothing to do with the weather: "N.Y. Racial Violence Shatters New Mayor's Gorgeous Mosaic," the paper's headline proclaimed (Curry 1990). The previous November, voters in New York had made history by electing their first African American mayor, David Dinkins, on a promise of racial harmony. This event set the context: racial tremors in New York were bound to attract attention across the nation. The *Tribune* used Dinkins's own "gorgeous mosaic" metaphor to declare his campaign promise dead.

The headline reflected a common impression, but it went too far. Actual "racial violence" in New York that summer was minimal for a city of seven million with racial tensions running as high as they were. As the *Tribune* pointed out, white City College professor Michael Levin had publicly called blacks "less intelligent." His black colleague Leonard Jeffries had called whites "ice people." Pulitzer Prize-winning newspaper columnist Jimmy Breslin had been suspended for calling a Korean colleague "slant-eyed" and a "yellow cur." In a trial that provoked rivalries of race and turf, two white youths faced murder charges in the death of sixteen-year-old Yusuf Hawkins the previous summer. And the boycott of a small Korean market by black activists in Brooklyn grew into a citywide political crisis.

Angry voices and raucous demonstrations filled the streets and halls of New York City in the summer of 1990. But if anything shattered the gorgeous mosaic, it was not *violence* so much as *protest*. Like other contentious intergroup conflicts in New York City, black-Korean conflicts were expressed as protest more often than as outright violence. The city's highly structured, competitive, hyper-organized political context shaped the development of relations between blacks and Koreans, as latent tensions transformed into overt conflicts.

Political institutions influenced conflicts indirectly—by providing a particular context that shaped the expression of tensions—and directly—by encouraging attempts at intervention by public officials and other third parties. From the beginning of tensions in the early 1980s through a climactic event—the Red Apple boycott in 1990—and beyond, the ever-present flurry of political and community organizing in New York's neighborhoods lent black-Korean conflicts the distinct characteristic of active protest without violence. Hardly a year passed without demonstrations outside a Korean-owned store somewhere in the city.

Politics played more than a background role in shaping conflict. Throughout the period under study, but particularly in the case of the Red Apple boycott, political actors and other third parties who intervened directly in conflicts helped to shape their development. Examining the ways these players interacted makes for more than an interesting story; it also suggests avenues for theory-building and helps to provide preliminary answers to the four questions that remain in the larger puzzle of politics, protest, and violence in black-Korean conflict.

THE EARLY 1980S: BEGINNINGS OF CONFLICT

Tensions between African Americans and Korean Americans emerged in the early 1980s in different parts of the city. The conflicts that took place in these years acquired enduring features that would characterize similar conflicts more than a decade later. Most notably, from the beginning black New Yorkers were divided—between voices of resentment and voices of moderation—over how to respond to the growing presence of Korean merchants in their neighborhoods.

Among black community leaders, the division fell along ideological lines, with radical organizers on one side and moderates on the other. The former group consisted of black nationalist activists, whereas the latter included members of the traditional civil rights community and heads of black business organizations. The split also coincided somewhat with lines of geography and class, although not always neatly. The divisions mirrored and to some extent grew out of an older fracture between two competing centers of black political power: the Harlem-based members of the old Democratic machine who advocated traditional politics and the Brooklyn-based insurgents who emphasized community power and other more militant directions (Mollenkopf 1992, 89–90).

Tensions in Harlem

The initial outcries against Korean merchants in black neighborhoods came not from radicals, however, but from the owners of small businesses with whom they competed. In 1981, New York's largest black readership newspaper, the *Amsterdam News,* reported on the presence of an "anti-Korean-hysteria" among black merchants in Harlem. "The situation is tense among both sides of the business community, and is seen in some circles as by far the most explosive issue to come out of the Black community since the Harlem riots of 1943," the paper reported. Notably, the three-part series took pains to portray Korean storeowners sympathetically, charging that black businessmen who felt threatened by Korean entrepreneurs had succumbed to envy and ignorance. "Such ignorance can only retard forward progress for Harlem and its people," the paper declared (Noel 1981b, 16). For those who perceived the threat, however, the increasing visibility of Korean merchants spoke for itself: Korean Americans owned about one-quarter of the 160 storefronts along the bustling section of 125th Street between Fifth and St. Nicholas Avenues, the heart of Harlem's shopping district (Douglas 1985; Noel 1981b).[1]

By contrast, the leaders of several Harlem business organizations downplayed the emerging tensions and instead pointed to opportunities for cooperation. Founders of the 125th Street Business Association viewed their mission as helping merchants of different ethnic and racial backgrounds work on common problems, such as inadequate police protection. Similarly, officials of the Uptown Chamber of Commerce declared that they were "trying to get away from a race issue to an economic issue." The view of the chamber's vice-president was that Korean merchants who actively took part in Harlem life were welcome to do business there: "Our major concern is dealing with people who are contributing to the development of the community. Currently there are many Blacks who have stores on 125th Street who live outside of the community and take money out of the community and who don't contribute to the community" (Noel 1981a, 39). Some of Harlem's business leadership even saw their Korean counterparts as "vital to Harlem's economy" (Noel 1981b, 3).

At least some moderate business leaders, however, believed that tensions were inevitable, and felt that they could do little to prevent those with resentments toward Koreans from attempting to force them out of the neighborhood. Malvin Locus, president of the 125th Street Business Association, put it this way: "If they want to drive them out, there's absolutely nothing I can do to stop them. I am only one person and our organization is only one organization. There are many other organizations. The voice of the community will rule" (ibid., 3). In fact, moderates soon lost control of the issues that gave shape to black-Korean relations.

Early on, the closest that tensions came to overt expression in Harlem was the posting of flyers denouncing a Korean store in 1981—likely the actions of resentful black merchants. No demonstrators protested at the store

(Kim 1995, 74; Min 1996). However, the following year, a radical organization known as the Afrikan Nationalist Pioneer Movement took up the call and launched a "Buy Black" campaign aimed at closing every Korean-owned store in Harlem by encouraging residents to refuse them their patronage. Again, no actual demonstrations took place at stores. Almost immediately, however, the campaign provoked reactions in the black press. Although it had supporters, several leading Harlem businessmen criticized the campaign and took the opportunity to advocate harmony with Korean Americans (Browne 1982b).

The varied reactions of community leaders to Korean merchants found mirror images among Harlem residents. In a letter to the editors of the *Amsterdam News*, one resident, Sheila Boyd, appealed to activists to focus their energies on larger targets: "If you want to boycott, maybe you should try boycotting Macy's, Alexander's, and all the other big department stores that are owned by whites, and who have been your enemy long before the Korean arrived in Harlem. I mean, why boycott something so small and petty?" (Boyd 1982).

The nature of their work makes community organizers uniquely sensitive to the irony of this plea: effective protest movements require good targets, but the best targets were largely missing from black neighborhoods. Department stores and other large establishments had all but abandoned black neighborhoods, one of the very reasons an economic niche existed for Korean entrepreneurs to fill with small businesses. The twin forces of racial segregation and neighborhood decline limited the options available to organizers who wished to strike at community apathy. Left with only small targets, community organizers would have to find other ways to stir the passions of residents. Radical activists in New York's black neighborhoods saw the growing tensions with Korean merchants, which had begun as pockets of resentment among black merchants but soon spread to customers, as opportunities to mobilize communities, advance their own organizational needs, and achieve their political goals.

Korean shopkeepers in Harlem did not sit passively as ethnic tensions brewed in the neighborhood. As the threat of their competition sparked resentment by black business owners, Korean merchants' own fears prompted them to organize separate merchant associations, such as the 125th Street Harlem Korean Merchants Association. In fact, much early organizing in New York's Korean American community was motivated by the strategic need to defend against threats from other groups—not just the hostile attitudes of some resentful black merchants, but active discrimination by white landlords and suppliers as well (Kim 1981, 259; Min 1996, 169–79).

As the organizational activity among Korean merchants grew, the consequences for intergroup relations were twofold—and somewhat contradictory. First, it enabled Korean and black trade associations to attempt cautious truces, in which Korean merchants often agreed to join or contribute to black organizations (Douglas 1985; Noel 1981a, 39). Second, the new level of organization among Koreans made their small, family-run grocery stores part of a network of similar establishments. They therefore appeared to be larger targets than they actually were, which made them all the more viable as objects of black community activism.

It is worth emphasizing that Korean immigrants encountered hostility from white New Yorkers as well as black. Since the late 1970s, Korean merchants had faced discrimination from white wholesalers who supplied their stores (Min 1996, 170). Moreover, in 1982, the *Daily News* reported the statement of a white state senator implying that Korean Americans universally followed Rev. Sun Myung Moon, the controversial and much-reviled head of the Unification Church. After publication of these comments, the Korean Produce Association reported a steep decline in sales at member stores (Browne 1982a). Later, in the 1990s, a white City Council member accused Asians of "invading" Queens, a borough with many Korean residents (Cheng 1996).

Koreans in New York City also experienced harassment from police. Later, discriminatory treatment led to the formation of an organization called Koreans Against Anti-Asian Violence, which rallied more than 300 people outside a precinct house to protest an incident of brutality against a Korean man from Queens (Iverem 1987). Early on, police protection and treatment could have been issues around which blacks and Koreans coalesced. Instead of forging coalitions around concrete concerns like these, however, efforts at peacemaking between the two groups came to focus on prayer meetings and goodwill trips to Korea.

Boycotts in Brooklyn and Queens

At about the same time as tensions and the efforts to address them were reported in Harlem, the first active engagement of black protesters with Korean merchants took place in the outer boroughs of New York. In 1981 and 1982, two black-led boycotts targeted Korean stores in Brooklyn and Queens. These early boycotts took on further characteristics that would continue to mark confrontations between the two groups and attracted some of the same activists that would return to future scenes outside Korean stores. Starting with these, Table 4.1 lists all the boycotts that broke out in New York City between 1980 and 1995, along with the neighborhoods where they took place, the dates they began, the number of days they lasted, and their peak sizes in numbers of active protesters.

The city's first overt clash between members of the two groups, a boycott of two stores in the neighborhood of Jamaica, Queens, was triggered

Table 4.1. Black-Led Boycotts of Korean Stores in New York City,
1980–1995

Store (Neighborhood)	Date[a]	Duration[b]	Peak Size[c]
Produce stores (Jamaica)	June 1981	35	NA[d]
Red Apple (Flatbush)	Feb. 1982	27	Under 50
Ike's (Harlem)[e]	Oct. 1984	97	Under 50
Fish store (Jamaica)	1986	NA	NA
Tropic (Bedford Stuyvesant)[e]	Aug. 1988	125	NA
Koko's (Harlem)[e]	Sept. 1988	420	50–100
Red Apple and Church Fruits (Flatbush)[e]	Jan. 1990	505	400
Blue Ribbon (Bay Ridge)[e]	Jan. 1990	NA	50
R & N (Brownsville)[e]	Aug. 1990	12	Under 50
C-Town (Elmhurst)[e]	Feb. 1991	4	40
Lee's Fancy Fruit (Flatbush)[e]	April 1991	3	Under 50
Church Ave. stores (Flatbush)	April 1992	NA	NA
125th St. stores (Harlem)	Sept. 1994	2	Under 50
Hat store (Greenwich Village)	1995	90	NA

[a]Indicates month in which boycott began.
[b]Number of days.
[c]Number of protesters.
[d]Information not available.
[e]Boycott followed a report of violence.
Note: Some dates, durations, and peak sizes are approximate.

by a fight between an employee and a customer in one of the stores and lasted about five weeks. The complaint that angered residents to boycott in Jamaica would be echoed in future clashes: a store employee claimed a customer had shoplifted, and the customer claimed to be the innocent victim of an attack by the employee (Min 1996, 74).

Activist Robert "Sonny" Carson led protesters in demanding that the employee be fired, that this and other Korean stores in Jamaica lower their prices, and that they hire more black employees (Min 1996, 74). Carson, who helped lead later boycotts as well, had a history of organizing protests in black communities. During the late 1960s, he had chaired the Brooklyn chapter of the Congress on Racial Equality (CORE) and had been one of the radical activists fighting for community control of schools in the Ocean Hill-Brownsville section of Brooklyn (Murphy 1990; Sleeper 1990, 100).[2]

From the Korean American community, several organizations responded to the Jamaica boycott. Leaders of the Korean Association of New York and the Korean Produce Association of New York, organizations that had emerged in the mid-1970s, met with boycott leaders in an attempt to end the protest, and Korean merchants in the immediate vicinity formed a new organization during the boycott called the Jamaica Korean Merchants Association. The conflict ended after a "Korean-black friendship meeting" gathered almost a hundred people together with community leaders and elected officials—an event that apparently stole the boycotters' thunder (Min 1996, 74).

The second boycott, in February 1982, targeted three shops in the Flatbush neighborhood of Brooklyn. Fifteen members of a group called the Black Unemployed Youth Movement led residents in demonstrations outside these stores over the course of several weeks. The organization began its boycott after the shop owners reportedly backed out of an agreement to hire neighborhood residents. At first, the protest leaders attempted unsuccessfully to bargain with a Brooklyn Korean merchants association. Afterwards, however, the storeowners themselves agreed to hire four black youths part-time to end the boycott.

Although the overt expression of tensions in these cases differed from what was going on in Harlem, the sentiments were similar. "Our thrust is not that many of these merchants are Korean," said the boycott's organizer, Omowale Clay, head of the Black Workers Organizing Committee. "We just want to know what they are doing for the community" (Jones 1982). Like Carson, Clay would figure into future black-Korean conflicts. In fact, both would reappear at precisely the same location in Flatbush, near the corner of Eighteenth Street and Church Avenue, eight years later. In 1990, two of the stores at that location were targeted in the city's most severe black-Korean conflict, the Red Apple boycott. Observers would see Clay wielding a bullhorn on the picket lines, chanting to marchers.

The fact that boycotters targeted the same stores twice probably had more to do with their location than with their owners. At least one of the stores, and probably the other as well, changed hands before 1990.[3] More important, Church Avenue runs through the heart of East Flatbush, a busy shopping district with a nearby subway stop, and the boycott leadership no doubt recognized the strategic value of the location in mobilizing supporters. This was also the hub of the city's biggest West Indian community, a fact that offered radical organizers an opportunity to pursue an ongoing mission: unifying New York's increasingly ethnically diverse black population behind a common political front.[4]

THE MIDDLE TO LATE 1980s: THE ESCALATION OF CONFLICT

During the rest of the 1980s, three major boycotts took place: two in Harlem and one in Brooklyn. With these cases, public officials began to intervene in black-Korean conflicts, and police appeared at the scene of protests. Ironically, however, conflicts only became more intractable: each lasted three months or more.[5]

A Boycott in Harlem

Harlem saw its first boycott of a Korean store in October 1984, when Ike's Grocery Store and other nearby shops on West 125th Street became the targets of a group calling itself the Concerned Citizens of Harlem.[6] Protests by the group began after a fight broke out between the store-owner's wife and a customer, Mark Jinks. In the altercation at Ike's, police arrested Jinks for assault and disorderly conduct after he reportedly attacked the officers as well, but protesters claimed that Jinks had been assaulted first by store workers. Rev. Juanita Hogan, a boycott leader who told reporters that Jinks had been the victim rather than the aggressor, had this to say: "I am just demanding a little respect for my brothers and sisters. I have watched a senior citizen—an elderly lady—mistreated by the merchants and I am tired of looking at it" (Matthews 1984). Other protesters walking the picket line claimed they had either witnessed or been subject to assaults in the past, at Ike's and a neighboring store owned by the same family, the Shins.

After about three months, the Shins sold the two stores to another Korean American merchant (Douglas 1985). Apparently, however, this did not end the boycott. Protests dwindled only after sparking an investigation by the Federal Bureau of Investigation and attracting public criticism from community leaders in Harlem (Min 1996, 75).

City officials also intervened in the boycott. City Clerk (and future Mayor) David Dinkins and City Council member Frederick Samuel joined Lloyd Williams, president of the Uptown Chamber of Commerce and one of Harlem's moderate voices on black-Korean tensions, in talks with three Korean organizations: the Harlem Korean Merchants Association, the Korean Produce Association (led at the time by Sung Soo Kim, a business activist who would later set up his own alternative service for merchants, the Korean Small Business Service Center, and continue to intervene in black-Korean disputes), and the Korean Association of New York. The plans that had been worked out in the early 1980s for Harlem's black and Korean trade groups to merge their memberships still had yet to be realized. But new negotiations over the Ike's boycott brought an agreement for Korean merchants to hire more black youths, support local civic activities, and receive "sensitivity training" (Douglas 1985).

A flyer distributed by demonstrators showed how they linked their protest at Ike's with larger issues. The demonstrations were sparked by a single report of violence, but the flyer's banner read, "Boycott all Korean merchants in this block"—indicating that the boycotters targeted stores by their owners' ethnicity, or at least by the fact that they were not black, rather than by particular incidents of abuse. Indeed, the text of the flyer moved straight from the issue of Korean business ownership to the issue of disrespect toward black customers to the issue of physical violence, and back to business ownership, exemplifying the rhetoric used by boycotters of Korean shops at other times and places, in New York City and elsewhere. By focusing on the issue of community control, activists linked relatively minor disputes at neighborhood groceries to the larger cause of black nationalism. In New York City, contradictions in this logic would emerge later and face wide scrutiny, as boycotters tried to justify their actions to the public and ultimately widened existing splits among African Americans.

In the late 1980s, the stakes for interracial harmony mounted. Rev. Jesse Jackson, having built national support among African Americans in his 1984 bid for the presidency, expanded his appeals to other groups in his 1988 presidential campaign and made a stop in New York City. Jackson's "rainbow" candidacy that year made the resolution of racial conflict a nationwide project and provided the context that might have soothed tensions surrounding Korean stores in New York. In April 1988, some 300 Korean Americans cheered Jackson at a fundraiser sponsored by a group calling itself Korean Americans for Better Racial Relations. They roared when he called for the reunification of South and North Korea. Striking a chord closer to home, Jackson called for "better relations between Blacks and Asians" (Anekwe 1988). Electorally, at least, Jackson's campaign spurred efforts that contributed to the success of multiracial organizing in David Dinkins's mayoral victory the following year. However, the Rainbow Coalition that Jackson built centered more on his candidacy than it focused on the goal of constructing long-term grassroots cooperation among ethnic groups, thus limiting the potential for concrete and lasting impacts on interminority relations.

Partisans of black-Korean conflicts in New York did not heed Jackson's call for harmony. George Tait, leader of the Harlem-based Afrikan Nationalist Pioneer Movement, continued the group's ongoing general call to black residents to stop shopping at Korean-owned stores in Harlem. Tait's organization, however, did not typically organize demonstrations. He made this clear in a column he wrote for the *Amsterdam News:* "All we have to do is not patronize them [Korean-owned stores]. We don't have to picket, protest or march" (Jamison and Browne 1988). In saying this, Tait effectively distanced his "Buy Black Campaign" from the various boycotts that targeted particular Korean stores with public protests. The former aimed to rid black neighborhoods of "all non-Black businesses," whereas the latter focused only on stores where there had been "incidents of atrocity and abuse." As election day approached, however, Tait reflected that his own campaign found it difficult to evoke emotional responses (Tait 1988). Boycotters who organized actual demonstrations, on the other hand, knew precisely how to provoke supporters into action: by linking reports of Korean merchants' abuses, via the backdrop of intergroup tensions, to goals of community control and black power.

Two boycotts staged in the late 1980s were organized by a newly formed group of activists who became particularly adept at this strategy: the December 12 Movement, a group notorious for its antiestablishment posture. In order to understand these conflicts, one first needs to know something about the organization and how it fit into politics and activism in New York City.

The December 12 Movement

Sonny Carson's name, well-known to New Yorkers of all racial and ethnic backgrounds, became synonymous with controversial racial conflicts during the 1980s. However, Carson's aggressive public persona contributed to the misperception that he was in exclusive control of a number of contentious protests, particularly those involving the December 12 Movement. Consequently, accounts of the group's protests at Korean stores often portrayed him as the lone driving force behind boycotts, a charismatic leader without genuine grassroots or organizational support (See, for instance, Sleeper 1990, 300). However, the December 12 Movement was not merely Carson's vehicle, and his personality alone did not account for the frequency and intensity of black-Korean conflicts in New York City.

Three points about Carson and the December 12 Movement are relevant to the development of black-Korean conflicts in New York. First, Carson was one of a coterie of radical black power activists who together exercised control of the organization—and thus its campaigns against Korean stores. Second, the group's relationship with other black activists was complex: sometimes cooperative, but often bitter and divisive, heightening intragroup conflicts that intensified the quest for leadership in New York's black communities. Third, the December 12 Movement behaved like a revolutionary, "underground" organization, but at the same time maintained links to the formal political system. It both influenced and was influenced by conventional politics.

The leadership first came together in 1987 to protest the beatings of black and Latino inmates by jail guards in upstate New York—the group's name commemorates the date of that gathering (Lucas 1995). Much of their subsequent activism has targeted the criminal justice system. In style and substance, the December 12 Movement strongly resembles the Black Panther Party, the revolutionary black power organization whose notoriety peaked in the 1970s. Like the Panthers, the group's leaders subscribed to a radical, internationalist version of black nationalism, and most were veterans of earlier black power protests. Their antiestablishment posture was reflected in the way they were regarded by the criminal justice system: several of the December 12 Movement leaders were defendants in the infamous "New York 8" racketeering case in 1985, and some have criminal records. For a number of years, law enforcement officials labeled them "urban terrorists" and tracked their activities (Hornung 1990, 27; Noel 1992, 25).

Sonny Carson has been the December 12 Movement's most visible figure, claiming the mantle of leadership in interviews with the press. The group's other leaders have had lower public profiles; however, they were no less important to the organization. Some led other organizations, whose memberships were brought together under the umbrella of the December 12 Movement. Each contributed different functions to the organization, belying the common impression of Carson as its sole leader. Behind the scenes, for instance, activist Coltrane Chimurenga played the role of chief strategist. Chimurenga exemplified the intellectual as well as street credentials of the December 12 Movement: he was a student organizer at San Francisco State University in the 1960s and then earned a masters degree at Harvard University's School of Education. Attorney Roger Wareham coordinated legal strategies for the group in its ongoing battles with police. Activist Viola Plummer spread the organization's Marxist ideology and rallied support among black women. Omowale Clay and Arthur Majeed Barnes typically coordinated marchers at the group's demonstrations. Lawrence Lucas, a Catholic priest with a checkered past in the Church,[7] crucially played dual roles for the organization. On the one hand, he acted as the organization's public voice, writing newspaper columns both to communicate its agenda and to castigate rival activists and public officials. On the other, Lucas maintained channels of communication with public officials (Hornung 1990; Lucas 1995).

The group's founding marked its split with other prominent nonelectoral black leaders, especially local activist Rev. Al Sharpton and Nation of Islam leader Louis Farrakhan. During the 1987 jail protest, they fought over control of plans for a massive march on the Brooklyn Bridge. After that, the December 12 Movement leadership regarded Sharpton and Farrakhan as bitter rivals and as traitors to black America (Hornung 1990, 27; Noel 1992, 26–27). Their approaches distinguish them further. Whereas Farrakhan espouses a conservative brand of black nationalism, based on separation and coexistence with mainstream American society and its governing institutions (Reed 1991), the December 12 Movement advocates eventual overthrow of the state via a revolutionary vanguard (Hornung 1990). Sharpton, on the other hand, accepts the legitimacy of mainstream institutions and often chooses to use, instead of undermine, them. His campaigns during the 1990s for the New York mayoralty and the U.S. Senate can be seen as logical extensions of his approach rather than departures from it. Even before his campaigns for public office, Sharpton built his leadership on relatively mainstream church foundations.[8]

These divisions reflect the fractious nature of New York City politics, which has meant that political movements often follow a path of involution as much as evolution. New York's tradition of decentralized machine politics impressed a pattern of increasing internal complexity on black politics, just as it has on other racial and ethnic communities in the city. Consequently, Sharpton and his allies, the leaders of the December 12 Movement, a number of other community organizers, and a host of elected politicians competed frequently and viciously for leadership among the same constituencies of disaffected black New Yorkers.[9] Multiple sets of organizers and officials continually made simultaneous and overlapping attempts to mobilize the same black neighborhoods for different ends.

Like many of these interconnected activists and organizations, the December 12 Movement became tied to conventional politics, despite its revolutionary agenda. Activities of two of its leaders are worth mentioning. First, Sonny Carson was a paid staff member on David Dinkins's 1989 mayoral campaign. Carson, undoubtedly aided by his leadership in the December 12 Movement, worked on a voter turnout effort, part of an unprecedented and massive community mobilization citywide (Murphy 1990). He resigned from the campaign, presumably to spare Dinkins a major scandal, after the press reported accusations that he was being paid with checks to a phony organization (Levitt 1989). Second, the December 12 Movement possessed ongoing links to officialdom through another of its leaders, Lawrence Lucas. Lucas held dialogues with officials in the New York Police Department (NYPD) and with mediators at the U.S. Justice Department, and he even occupied a seat in Harlem on one of New York City's community boards, the network of neighborhood-based citizen advisory councils whose members are appointed by the city council members and borough presidents (Lucas 1995).

Moreover, the activist origins of at least one of the leaders of the December 12 Movement lie in the character and traditions of New York City politics and community organization. The Ocean Hill–Brownsville school dispute of 1968, during which Carson made a name for himself, was propelled by black militancy, but it also came out of a movement to decentralize political power—an issue that was rooted in the neighborhood orientation of New York City politics. The dispute was also a product of the structure of New York City government. The city's direct control over public schools (which is unusual because cities usually share the responsibility with state governments or leave it entirely to special districts) has created a huge stake for groups to fight over at the local level (Sonenshein 1990, 200). It was out of this context that Carson, a street activist allied with black teachers in Brooklyn, rose to prominence as a powerful community organizer.

The December 12 Movement's first two boycotts of Korean stores, to which I now turn, began within weeks of each other in the fall of 1988. In the boycott of the Tropic Market in Brooklyn, rival black community leaders who cooperated with Korean merchants made a successful end run around the boycotters and reached a public accord, although the store eventually closed down. In the case of Koko's, a store in Harlem, no accord ended the boycott; instead, the shop outlasted protests and remained open.

The Tropic Boycott: Resolution by End Run

On August 27, 1988, Ivy King and her daughter were shopping at the Korean-owned Tropic Market in Bedford-Stuyvesant, Brooklyn. On their way out the door, owner Woo Yang Chung stopped the pair, accused them of shoplifting a package of dried fish, and demanded to search their bags. King and her daughter refused, and a fight broke out. Both sides claimed injuries: the Kings said the owner and several employees punched them and threatened them with a knife; Chung reported that the Kings hit his wife and his employees. Newspaper reports carried no indication that any of the injured required hospitalization (Jamison and Browne 1988; Min 1996, 75).

Following the encounter, the December 12 Movement rallied support in the neighborhood for a boycott by charging that a black grandmother had been severely beaten. The day after the dispute, they approached a number of Korean merchants along the surrounding commercial strip on Fulton Avenue and demanded that they shut down until further notice. Protesters later claimed that police had instructed merchants to keep their shops open (Jamison and Browne 1988, 39; Lee 1988; Min 1996, 76).

The December 12 Movement did not organize the boycott alone; instead, it sought aid from black community organizations based in the neighborhood. This became the group's working practice in boycotts: combining its own leadership, strategic resources, and citywide reputation for radical activism with the local membership base and grassroots legitimacy of neighborhood organizations. In the Tropic case, one such organization called the United African Business Association had been considering a boycott of the market well before the dispute between King and Chung, hoping to shut down all the Korean-owned stores in an area encompassing four police precincts. The manager of a local record store, Joe Long, said: "We saw this coming, but just couldn't get the right people involved. We were looking for people who want to work and do something. We're going to push our politicians to let them know what's going on out here" (Jamison and Browne 1988, 40). The association's business-oriented agenda may not have fit a radical Black Power agenda. But the December 12 Movement, experienced in planning protests, stepped in and provided the leadership.

Several weeks into the boycott, Brian Parks, a representative of a Brooklyn Korean merchants association, approached the protesters outside the Tropic and offered a public apology, financial rewards, or even a change in ownership in order to end the boycott, according to Carson. The same association contacted George Tait, the Harlem "Buy Black" campaign organizer, with similar offers and an appeal for attempts at reconciliation between the two communities (even though Tait was not involved in the Tropic boycott). The offers were rejected. "We don't want no dinners, no dollars and no deals. We are engaged in an economic war," Tait told Parks (Jamison 1988a).

Rebuffed by protesters, Korean merchants contacted other black community leaders, including businessmen and professionals. Negotiations followed—seven rounds in all. The black and Korean negotiators had not been directly involved in the boycott, but each one brought a different claim of legitimacy for representing the neighborhood: Albert Vann, a Democratic politician from Brooklyn, was the district's State Assembly representative; Roscoe Reynolds was executive director of the local YMCA; Sung Soo Kim was president of the Korean American Small Business Service Center; and Rev. Choong-Sik Ahn was pastor of the Korean Church of Brooklyn (Jamison 1988b; Min 1996, 194).

An accord reached by the negotiators in late December garnered enough support in the neighborhood to effectively end the protests outside the Tropic Market. In return for the black negotiators' public appeals for an end to the boycott, Korean merchants represented by Kim's Small Business Service Center agreed to undertake measures that would support the neighborhood economically.[10] Kim, whose organization frequently lobbied city government for municipal policies favorable to its dues-paying membership, exercised wide latitude during the negotiations and agreed to the final terms despite his view that boycotters had chosen the wrong target.

"Theoretically, I am very sympathetic," he said. "But their resentment should be toward American society as a whole. We are the wrong target. To picket all Korean stores is racism" (Lee 1988). Kim refused to give in to several other demands, but the concessions he did make drew criticism from others in the Korean community (Min 1996, 76).

The dynamics among black leaders in Brooklyn were complex. During the mediation, Al Vann, the State Assembly representative, had agreed in principle with many of the December 12 Movement's charges against Korean merchants, and believed that the alleged attack on Ivy King demanded justice. Underlying his perspective on the conflict was the issue of community control: "We have to address under what circumstances do we allow persons who do not live in our community to continue to operate," he said (Jamison 1988c). In fact, initially the assemblyman's team had demanded that the Tropic's owner turn his store over to black owners and leave the neighborhood, a call that Kim rejected (Boyd 1988a). Unlike the boycott leaders, however, Vann eventually advocated a resolution short of closing the Tropic or any other Korean-owned establishments.

This opened a rift between the negotiators and the boycotters over who best represented the black residents of Bedford-Stuyvesant. The dispute reflected the continuing divisions among black community leaders in New York City over how to deal with Korean merchants in black neighborhoods. Vann's argument was that no individual alone could speak for the entire community, but that elected officials could make greater claims to legitimacy than unelected activists. Arguments by December 12 Movement leaders implied the opposite.[11]

Ironically, Vann and Carson had been allies among the insurgent black activists who fought the Ocean Hill-Brownsville school wars in the late 1960s (Sleeper 1990, 57, 219). Their paths had diverged in 1974, when Vann made a successful run for the State Assembly. During the Tropic boycott, members of the December 12 Movement portrayed Vann as selling out his constituents and dismissed his intervention as betrayal. "The agreement is not worth the paper it's written on," Lawrence Lucas told reporters. Carson and Lucas charged that the negotiators failed to consult residents of Bedford-Stuyvesant, a charge that Vann and other members of the mediation team refuted (Lee 1988).

Although the December 12 Movement's demonstrations at the Tropic Market were halted by the accord, the group's presence continued to be felt in Bedford-Stuyvesant in an arrangement it dubbed the "People's Farmers Market," which consisted of fruit and vegetable peddlers it helped set up outside Korean stores on weekends.[12] As the peddlers spread, they caused "enduring problems" for Korean merchants in Brooklyn; together, the boycott's (limited) support among residents and the peddlers' competition forced the Tropic and several other Korean stores in the neighborhood to close (Min 1996, 76).[13]

African and Korean American community leaders were not the only third parties intervening in the affairs surrounding the Tropic boycott. Brooklyn Borough President Howard Golden (a white incumbent who had defeated Vann in a race for the borough presidency just a few years earlier) helped link the Korean American Association of Brooklyn with thirteen black churches, which agreed to distribute food for Thanksgiving dinners donated by the Koreans. Golden's office also aided the Urban League and the Korean American Small Business Service Center in setting up seminars for Korean merchants to help them avoid misunderstandings with customers (*Amsterdam News* 1988).

Golden's intervention went further than that, however. He sent his staff to meet with senior aides to Mayor Ed Koch, who were quietly concerned about the boycott going on in Bedford-Stuyvesant. "It was more internal debate than true collaboration," according to Michael McQuillan, Golden's advisor on race and ethnic affairs. Koch and Golden hardly enjoyed good relations, and differences in opinion among their aides at the meeting led to heated debate. Koch's staff wanted to "give Carson something" to make him end the boycott, but Golden's aides wanted to address "underlying issues" (McQuillan 1995). In the end, the Koch administration told Korean merchants in Brooklyn that all it would do was support them if they chose to file a civil suit against the protesters. Police Commissioner Benjamin Ward, however, warned that "court intervention could galvanize the demonstrators and expand the protest" (Roberts 1990). Ward's prudent advice was heeded in the Tropic boycott. Later, the Red Apple boycott would prove his point; court cases linked to the conflict actually helped to drive up the stakes.

The Koko's Boycott

The second of the December 12 Movement's boycotts began in September 1988, just a few weeks after the incident at the Tropic Market, and it targeted a produce store called Koko's. Unlike the Tropic, Koko's retained greater support among black shoppers and survived its fourteen-month-long boycott (H. C. Lee 1993, 5). The same storefront, under different ownership, had been the target in the 1984 Harlem boycott; like the Red Apple in Brooklyn, it occupied a strategic location in a busy shopping district. The charges and countercharges sounded a familiar refrain: store employees were said to have attacked customers—in this case an elderly black couple—who the employees in turn accused of shoplifting. Protesters who lived in the neighborhood maintained that the attack had merely been the latest in a long pattern of abuses by the store's owners, and the merchants claimed that they had been the victims of assaults. Police made arrests on both sides (Mwalilino 1988).

The owners of Koko's did not want intervention from the larger Korean community, and thus the boycott went largely unnoticed in the Korean press (Min 1996, 75)—even though it was covered for black readers by the *Amsterdam News*. However, Koko's owners accepted the assistance of Sung Soo Kim of the Korean American Small Business Service Center, who had responded to the Tropic Market boycott. A cast of public officials and clergy intervened, including Al Vann, City Council member Enoch Williams, and Rev. Calvin Butts of the Abyssinian Baptist Church in Harlem (Browne 1988). Despite the efforts of mediators, more than a year passed with no end to the boycott in sight.[14]

The end of the boycott was not accompanied by a high-profile agreement among public figures acting as mediators, as in the Tropic boycott. Instead, it was spurred by the changing context of city politics. David Dinkins—then the Manhattan Borough President—was running for mayor that fall, and his campaign was seeking to piece together support among the city's traditionally fragmented communities of liberal white, black, and Latino voters. In particular, Dinkins's challenge was drawing unprecedented support from community organizations in black neighborhoods throughout the city, aided by Jesse Jackson's consciousness-raising presidential campaign the year before. Unlike the ill-fated Rainbow Coalition, however, the Dinkins campaign was making effective use of community organizers' grassroots connections in order to mobilize voters. Among them was Sonny Carson, in his paid role assisting the campaign with voter turnout. When the press began suggesting (somewhat obliquely) that Dinkins's campaign funds were lining Carson's pockets instead of funding a genuine mobilization effort, however, Carson resigned from the campaign (Murphy 1990). Then, suddenly, the Koko's boycott fizzled. No clear resolution had been agreed to by the negotiators. Korean American observers believed that the boycott's conclusion had been timed to spare a scandal for the Dinkins campaign (Kim 1995).

The Tropic and the Koko's boycotts signaled the entrance not only of politicians but of police into black-Korean conflicts in New York City. Officers stood watch and took crowd control measures at both boycotts, their presence triggered not just by the involvement of individuals they had labeled "urban terrorists" but also by the size of the protests and the threat they posed to public order. At the Tropic Market, officers "were on hand . . . when demonstrators forced Chung to close his establishment and escorted him through demonstrators . . . when he opened his store" the next day (Jamison and Browne 1988, 40). At both of the boycott scenes, police limited where protesters could march. Father Lucas, the December 12 Movement organizer who maintained channels of communication with the NYPD and other authorities, met with police officials and persuaded them to "ease off a little" (Lucas 1995). Remarkably, given a bitter rivalry between police and the December 12 Movement, no violence erupted in either case.[15]

THE COURSE OF A CONFLICT: THE 1990 RED APPLE BOYCOTT

The most severe conflict involving African Americans and Korean Americans in New York was the simultaneous boycott of two stores in 1990, the Red Apple and Church Fruits in the Flatbush section of Brooklyn. Since the initial dispute took place at the Red Apple, and the boycott became associated with it in the public mind, I refer to the conflict simply as the Red Apple boycott.[16] This conflict was followed by seven smaller boycotts, most of which lasted under two weeks: four in Brooklyn, one in Queens and two in Manhattan. I trace the Red Apple boycott in greater depth in order to demonstrate the influence of the political context and third party intervention on the course of conflict, and then briefly describe the smaller boycotts and how they were affected by the larger.[17]

The Incident

We know a few things for certain about what happened the evening of January 18, 1990. Jiselaine Felissaint, a Haitian-born resident of Flatbush in her mid-forties, entered the small Korean-owned Red Apple grocery on Church Avenue. At about 6:00 P.M., two police officers arrived at the store to find her sprawled on the floor, unable to stand up. The officers reported that a "confrontation" had taken place, and arrested the store's owner on assault charges (Noonan 1990).

Beyond those meager facts, the rest is unclear. According to Felissaint, three Korean employees accused her of shoplifting and beat her up—grabbing her neck and slapping, punching, and kicking her—as she was innocently leaving the store to shop elsewhere. According to the employees, Felissaint refused to pay for the plantains and limes she had picked out, then became agitated, screamed at the cashier, and sat on the floor. Embarrassed prosecutors discovered later that they had charged the wrong man; the store's owner had not even been present during the dispute, and by the summer they had switched the charges to the manager, Pong Ok Jang. A year later, in January 1991, a six-member jury composed of four whites, one Hispanic, and one black found Jang innocent of all charges (Lubasch 1991).

The charges alone—mere misdemeanors—hardly carried the gravity necessary to propel New York City into the spasms of racial division for which it became known. Although Felissaint claimed her injuries prevented her from returning to her job as a home-care worker for several months, her accusations in no way approached the severity or terror that catapulted other incidents of interracial violence into the public mind and drew officials and activists into a media circus. The incident pales in comparison to cases like the racial slaying of Yusuf Hawkins in 1989 or the police torture of Abner Louima in 1997.

Yet somehow, the scuffle between Felissaint and Jang—otherwise indistinguishable from the hundreds of minor disputes that must happen every year—managed to trigger a citywide political crisis. It drew massive crowds of demonstrators, not only on Church Avenue but outside the state Supreme Court building in another part of Brooklyn and at City Hall in Manhattan. It tested the resolve of a new mayor, the city's first African American in that office, and challenged the legitimacy of the city's public institutions. It ended only after protesters' energies were spent, more than a year later, defying all efforts at resolution. How and why did the conflict reach such proportions? The answer lies in the efforts of black, Korean, and white activists and public officials to mobilize and countermobilize supporters at a critical juncture in city politics. In the story of the Red Apple boycott that follows, these activities are the focus.

Regardless of what actually happened inside the Red Apple that evening, stories made their way through Flatbush about a Korean merchant's attack on a black woman, and within an hour about forty neighborhood residents showed up outside the store for a spontaneous protest (Noonan 1990). Not long afterwards, the store across the street, Church Fruits, attracted a crowd when a fearful Red Apple employee sought temporary refuge there on his way home. Previously, the only connection between the two stores had been their competition for customers.[18] From that point on, however, their fates were joined. The boycott had begun.

The conflict might have ended after only two days. Concerned about the daily crowds protesting at the store, Korean and black community leaders held talks in a meeting set up by City Council member Susan Alter of Brooklyn and hosted by the police in the basement of the Flatbush precinct house. The aim was to resolve the dispute before it grew out of proportion. Two black participants—Joanne Oplustil of the Church Avenue Merchants Block Association (CAMBA) and Guy Victor, executive director of Haitian Americans for Social Justice—asked that the Red Apple be closed to allow passions to cool and a solution to be found; Sung Soo Kim, of the Korean American Small Business Service Center, agreed to deliver the message to the store's owner, Bong Jae Jang. At first, Jang acceded to the request, but after a few hours, he reopened the Red Apple. Characterized as a "misunderstanding," this had the effect of inflaming the passions of protesters instead of the hoped-for cooling (Kim 1995; New York City Mayor's Committee 1990a, 36–37).

Initially, the major media paid little attention to the conflict developing on Church Avenue. As one close observer recalled, protesters "festered in obscurity" for almost three and half months (James 1995). Most news outlets, print and broadcast alike, neglected the boycott until May (Jones 1990). The *Amsterdam News,* the city's major black readership paper, did not report on the conflict until March, and then had no further coverage for two months (Browne 1990b). Only *New York Newsday,* the vigorous and respected (but now-defunct) newspaper, began reporting on the boycott within its first few weeks (English and Yuh 1990).[19] Korean language newspapers also carried little coverage of the Red Apple boycott before May (Min 1996, 249–56). The paucity of media coverage did not mean other actors were neglecting the boycott, however. Out of public view, the scene was buzzing with activity by organizers, officials, and other third parties, all responding to the initial dispute in their own ways.

Who Were the Boycotters?

As the boycott progressed, it became an object of contention in itself. Boycott supporters and boycott opponents fought over whether it was a "neighborhood" conflict or one created by "outsiders"—an issue that cut to the legitimacy of the protest and those leading it. The challenges to this and other boycotts over whether they legitimately represented the will of local communities became central to their development. Such challenges posed dilemmas for Red Apple boycott organizers and for interested mediators alike. At the heart lay the issue of responsibility for the boycott; beyond its leaders, who were the boycotters? Finding the answer requires recognition of the impact of the political context on processes of group mobilization.

A common perception at the time was that the Red Apple boycott "belonged" to Sonny Carson—that he instigated, masterminded, and controlled it.[20] Like the Koko's and Tropic boycotts, however, this one was organized not just by Carson but by the other leaders of the December 12 Movement as well, with Carson as the most public spokesperson, and by activists from other organizations. Moreover, the December 12 Movement did not achieve leadership of the boycott unproblematically. Other activists had arrived on the scene before it, organizing demonstrations and assuming leadership first.

There are really two separate questions at issue. First, who led the boycott? Second, who made up the base of support—the crowds that marched outside the Red Apple? Most accounts of the conflict have neglected the dynamics linking protest leaders to the crowds that supported them, emphasizing either the "outside" activists leading it or the "neighborhood" residents supporting it. Both sets of actors were necessary components in the boycott, but neither set alone could sufficiently account for the scale of mobilization that occurred. A third set of actors—neighborhood activists, whose presence was guaranteed in many corners of the city by New York's sprawling and hyper-organizing political institutions—provided the crucial link between the two.

The initial dispute on January 18 drew more than an angry crowd. Once news had spread of a Korean merchant's alleged assault against a Haitian woman, leaders of existing black community organizations rushed to Church Avenue. Some, such as Guy Victor of Haitian Americans for Social Justice, and Wilson Desir, the president of Alliance des Emigres des Haitians, had close ties to the Haitian community. Others, including Rev. Herbert Daughtry, a longtime community organizer and protest leader, led larger, Brooklyn-wide organizations. The activists came seeking information about the dispute and bearing offers of assistance to Felissaint, but they also saw opportunities in the emerging conflict to advance their organizations and causes.

The set of activists who worked to mobilize and organize neighborhood residents, however, had close ties to the neighborhood itself. Guy Victor and local activists George Dames, Sabine Albert, and Brenda Bell, who led an organization called the Flatbush Coalition for Economic Empowerment, issued the formal call to boycott. They rallied various community organizations and residents informally under their banners, not only to respond to the alleged attack, but also to tie an incident representing the mistreatment of black customers by non-black merchants to the larger issue of disparate economic opportunities for blacks (H. C. Lee 1993, 172). Although the initial gathering outside the store had been spontaneous, the protests that ensued took the form of "a series of deliberate, purposeful, organized collective actions," in the words of Heon Cheol Lee (ibid., 165, 171).

However, before long, control over the mass demonstrations that breathed life into the boycott began to shift. After a few weeks, members of the December 12 Movement arrived on the scene, establishing an umbrella group called the Flatbush Frontline Collective, with the intent of coordinating the increasing number of neighborhood and citywide activists who were becoming involved. Although the various organizations ran the boycott together (Lucas 1995), the December 12 Movement's entrance served to displace other figures, edging out the neighborhood activists from the exclusive leadership they possessed at the outset (James 1995; H. C. Lee 1993, 172–73).[21] To some extent, different organizations performed different functions. The December 12 Movement exercised control over grand strategy, while neighborhood activists were involved more frequently in day-to-day picketing—as evidenced by their more frequent interviews with reporters at the scene. City Human Rights Commissioner Dennis DeLeon, who observed the protests frequently himself and followed it daily through commission staffers assigned to the site, reported that "Sonny Carson and Viola Plummer and some other folks like that . . . came in at the very beginning, but then their involvement on a regular basis thereafter was sporadic. Sonny would show up on weekends and stand on top of a dumpster and do a little speech" (DeLeon 1996).

The intervention by the December 12 Movement met with varied responses from neighborhood activists. Some became "absorbed in the charismatic personalities" of the December 12 Movement (James 1995). Carson, Lucas, Clay, and Plummer had staged impressive protests in the past, and some neighborhood activists likely saw them as useful to the boycott.[22] Others, such as George Dames, however, responded to the move like "a mother with recalcitrant children," expressing mixed feelings about the new leadership (James 1995). Both Albert and Dames remained active in the boycott for months, crucially providing the new leaders with connections to neighborhood organizational networks and ties that established their legitimacy there. Dames, however, eventually bowed out. Still other neighborhood activists who had initially cooperated in the boycott decried the involvement of the December 12 Movement much sooner and even turned to oppose the boycott.

Even as control over the boycott shifted to a new set of leaders, however, the picket lines continued to draw residents of Flatbush. A committee appointed by Mayor Dinkins to report on the boycott affirmed this fact after holding a massive public hearing just blocks from the boycott site in June (New York City Mayor's Committee, 1990a). According to some observers, neighborhood residents were heavily involved in the demonstrations and comprised the majority of protesters who maintained a consistent presence (DeLeon 1996; James 1995). By no means did all the residents of Flatbush support the boycott, however. Many opposed it, and even greater numbers grew weary of it by fall (Gonzalez 1990d). Moreover, neighborhood residents did not comprise all the demonstrators—the boycott attracted a large number of supporters from outside the neighborhood, many of them mobilized by the December 12 Movement.[23]

The size of the protests outside the Red Apple and Church Fruits Markets fluctuated over time. Table 4.2 culls estimates of the numbers of protesters and police officers from a variety of newspaper reports and official sources and charts them against key events in the conflict. On a number of occasions, the boycott amassed hundreds of protesters, whose raucous marches generated a frightening "wall of sound" (DeLeon 1996). At other times, picketers maintained a presence of several dozen or more. Through late summer and the fall of 1990, a core group of two dozen protesters kept picket lines going daily, with larger crowds on weekends (Flynn and Bowles 1990; Gonzalez 1990b). Thereafter, handfuls of protesters continued to picket the store through June of the following year, when the Red Apple changed ownership and the boycott finally ended (Baril 1991).

What Did They Want? Competition, Mobilization, and the Role of Race

Critics of the boycott—such as former Mayor Ed Koch—called it a form of extortion, suggesting that the protesters threatened the store's business in order to get some kind of material reward for themselves (Murphy 1990). Similar accusations have been leveled against boycotts at other times and in other cities, and in some cases, protesters actually did seek material rewards, although usually in the form of contributions to neighborhoods or community organizations. It was quite common for Korean merchants to offer donations on their own.

In this case, however, the evidence does not support that assertion. In public statements, leaders of the boycott against the Red Apple explicitly rejected contributions and other concessions, countering that by offering such things Korean community representatives were attempting to buy them out (Sinclair 1990). When moderate black community leaders appealed for an end to the boycott in exchange for economic assistance for the neighborhood, December 12 Movement leaders charged that such leaders would "sell out their mommas for a few crumbs" (they made this charge in a flyer distributed at pickets).[24] Instead, the goals of the boycott were a criminal conviction for the storeowner and the closure of the shop itself.

The December 12 Movement was motivated by two factors: by its radical, black nationalist ideology and by its pursuit of informal political power in black neighborhoods. Sonny Carson told Stephen James, an attorney who briefly represented the protesters, that it was "a bigger movement," not just about the Red Apple assault, and not just about the Flatbush community. "This wasn't even about black-Korean relations in this country" (James 1995). The boycott represented an opportunity for the December 12 Movement to advance its revolutionary agenda—and to enhance its organizational base vis-à-vis rival activists.

Table 4.2. The Red Apple Boycott: Protesters, Police, and Key Events

Date	Protesters	Police	Key Events
Jan. 18, 1990	40		Initial dispute and spontaneous protest
Jan. 19	25		
Jan. 20	400		Red Apple reopens after brief closing
Jan. 25	200		
Jan. 27	100	200[a]	
Feb. 6	300		
Feb. 10	100[b]		
April 21			Mayor Dinkins forms committee to investigate boycott
May 7			Court orders protesters 50 feet from stores
May 8	50		
May 10			Dinkins delivers televised address to city
May 12	300[c]	80	
May 14	200		
May 19	200	300	
June 23	30		
June 27			Judge orders police to enforce injunction
Aug. 30			Mayor's committee releases report
Sept. 18	100[d]	150	Koreans rally at City Hall; police begin to enforce court order
Sept. 21	15		Dinkins shops at boycotted stores
Sept. 22	50	400	
Sept. 23	20		
Sept. 29	100		
Nov. 7			City Council releases report
Jan. 18, 1991	50		
Jan. 30			Red Apple manager acquitted

Sources: Jan. 18, 19, 20 (Noonan 1990); Jan. 25 (Jordan 1990); Jan. 27 (McQueen 1990); Feb. 6 (Jordan 1990); Feb. 10 (English and Yuh 1990); May 8 (Purdum 1990a); May 12 (Hevesi 1990b; Palmer and Queen 1990); May 14 (Purdum 1990c); May 19 (Harvey 1990; Howe 1990); June 23 (Lodder and Rist 1990); Sept. 18 (English and Henneberger 1990; Hevesi 1990a; Mandulo 1990); Sept. 21 (Purdum 1990d); Sept. 22 (Gonzalez 1990a; Hornung 1990); Sept. 23 (Bornstein and Jordan 1990; Gonzalez 1990b); Sept. 29 (Gonzalez 1990c; Yamada 1990); Jan. 18, 1991 (English 1991).
[a]McQueen (1990) notes that on this day there were "'hundreds' of police, many in riot gear."
[b]This figure is for Saturdays in general around this time.
[c]In Newsday, Palmer and Queen reported 600 protesters, but in the New York Times, Hevesi reported 300, although the Newsday number contradicts a later report by Newsday that the peak number of protesters was 300.
[d]Average number derived from differing reports.

This point is demonstrated by tracing the relationship between the December 12 Movement and local activists during the early stages of the boycott. Leaders of the boycott maintained that it was built on a consensus with neighborhood activists (Lucas 1995). However, the December 12 Movement used appeals to ideological purity and castigated moderates in order to drown out the voices of activists who differed with its goals for the boycott. For instance, before the December 12 Movement's control was cemented, local organizers of the boycott had called on Mayor Dinkins and his administration to intervene directly in the conflict (Browne 1990b). Reflecting this position, in mid-February, neighborhood activist and boycott organizer Brenda Bell told a *Newsday* reporter: "We would like to have the demands met so we can cease the boycotting. . . . We do want open dialogue" (English and Yuh 1990). Thereafter, however, no one on the side of the boycotters was willing to negotiate. In April, Sonny Carson told the *New York Voice* that appeals for dialogue by the Dinkins administration would fall on deaf ears: "They're not gonna talk to me, 'cause I'm not gonna talk to them. . . . We just want these Koreans prosecuted" (Sinclair 1990). When attorney Stephen James, who was brought in by local organizers George Dames and Sabine Albert, attended a meeting at City Hall in May without the December 12 Movement's permission, he was reprimanded by "Carson's people" (Griffin 1994, 15–16; James 1995). Dennis DeLeon, Dinkins's human rights commissioner, recalled that "initially there were many voices [among protesters]. But that became less true as time went on" (DeLeon 1996). Whatever differences existed among the ranks of the protest leadership early on, they were gone by summer.

Closing ranks helped the boycotters rally and solidify a base of support. The politically charged milieu surrounding the conflict made it appear that there were just two sides: for or against. However, given the fragmented environment of community organizing in New York City, boycott leaders could not assume support from black residents—other activists and other causes competed for the attention of the same constituents. The more controversy and criticism the December 12 Movement received, the more it thrived; among potential supporters, such attention served as a measure of defiance, which lent the organization a reputation for commitment and authenticity.

The streets of Brooklyn gave vivid proof that New York's neighborhoods were a market for political entrepreneurs. Not only were the December 12 Movement and its partners leading pickets in Flatbush, but other organizations were leading countermarches nearby, and Rev. Al Sharpton was organizing marches through Bensonhurst to protest the racial slaying of Yusuf Hawkins. On at least one occasion, Carson and Sharpton even led separate protests, for separate causes, at the same location—on the steps of the Brooklyn State Supreme Court building, each to rally supporters in anticipation of different court rulings. The two never appeared together, however, for either case (H. C. Lee 1993, 214–15).[25]

Boycott leaders thus had to escalate the conflict in order to generate support.[26] Like in other communities in New York City, the task of organization-building was complicated by the diversity of national origins among black New Yorkers. In a drive to unify Haitian Americans, Jamaican Americans, African Americans, and other black nationalities under their own banner, the December 12 Movement chose to frame the choice for potential supporters in racial terms. A boycott flyer issued the call: "African People Unite: Defend Against All Racist Attacks." One speaker, referring to the alleged attack on Felissaint, told a boycott rally: "I don't care if she is a Haitian woman. She is black. She can be my mother" (H. C. Lee 1993, 200).

In their speeches to marchers at the scene, boycott leaders focused on specific issues not directly related to the incident that had sparked the conflict, such as black ownership of community businesses, inequalities in political representation, police brutality, the scourge of drugs, and white racism. Recordings of famous speeches by Malcolm X were "blasted" from loudspeakers at rallies (ibid., 153, 202, 206). The organizers thus *used* the boycott, which had begun as a protest against a single incident, to draw attention to larger concerns. A boycott flyer provided a clear statement of this objective:

> As we enter the 6th week of the boycott of Red Apple and Church
> Fruits, the fundamental contradictions of racism and economic ex-
> ploitation become clearer to us. However, the question for Black folks
> to consider is this: "Who is going to control the economic life of the
> Black community?" . . . People understand that this struggle we are
> presently engaged in is a continuation of our historical struggle for
> self-determination.

Using the boycott to make these connections made sense to organizers because larger targets were more distant, and thus more difficult to target—supporters could be mobilized more easily with local concerns. Korean-owned stores, along with police precincts and community boards, represented some of the few institutions dominated by non-blacks that were immediately visible to residents of the neighborhood.

Even as they mobilized supporters on the basis of race, however, boycott leaders frequently went to pains to explain to critics that the boycott was not targeted against Koreans as a group, but at two merchants who had assaulted black customers and who happened to be Korean. It was the media and public officials, they charged, who made the conflict racial (Lucas 1990a, 1995). When asked to explain racist remarks in flyers and speeches, boycott leaders simply pointed out that they could not control who showed up to demonstrate. The boycotters' record is a mixed bag. On the one hand, past boycotts led by the December 12 Movement had called on supporters to shut down all Korean stores in a neighborhood and frequently had made public statements with racial overtones. Moreover, some leaders of the boycott—such as Carson and local activist Brenda Bell—did explicitly denounce Korean Americans as a group (Carson 1990; English and Yuh 1990).[27] On the other hand, some leaders, such as Lawrence Lucas, refrained from such remarks. Moreover, as its leaders did not hesitate to point out, the boycott did not target other Korean-owned stores near the Red Apple and Church Fruits—despite the apparent contradiction of this strategy to the December 12 Movement's stated goal of community control.

Whether or not organizers of the boycott held prejudices against Koreans, they certainly made use of preexisting tensions between blacks and Koreans in order to rally mass support for the boycott. They were probably not motivated strictly by racism against Koreans. However, at the same time, they cared little about pursuing efforts to transform the prejudices of their supporters into more socially productive beliefs. (Of course, Koreans and whites who mobilized against the boycott were often guilty of the same indifference.) Instead, the chief strategic concern of the boycotters, like most parties to the conflict, was to keep their organization afloat in the city's combative arena of community politics.

Opposition from Other Black Community Organizations

Divisions among black community leaders and organizations became visible during the boycott and affected the course of its development. Eventually, much of the mobilization around the boycott centered on the question of which black organizations best represented the neighborhood. For the December 12 Movement, the goal was to unify black communities.[28] For leaders of some West Indian community organizations in Brooklyn, however, the boycott was an intrusion by African Americans whose bases of power lay elsewhere, outside the neighborhood. The diversity of responses to the boycott mirrored the fragmented nature of black politics in New York, and the multiple attempts at countermobilization expanded the magnitude of the conflict.

Certain community organizations in Flatbush, such as the Church Avenue Merchants Block Association and Umma, a volunteer neighborhood patrol organization, objected to the boycott's leadership and strategy. Like the moderate black business leaders in Harlem in earlier conflicts, CAMBA's leadership found fault with the lack of Korean American participation in local affairs, but disagreed with boycotters' confrontational tactics. Both organizations supported residents who formed groups to cross the pickets and shop in the boycotted stores on a regular basis (H. C. Lee 1993, 211, 213).

The New York chapter of the Congress of Racial Equality took its opposition to the boycott even further, and in June brought a class-action lawsuit against protesters and city officials to try to end the boycott.[29] CORE had played a key role in the civil rights movement (McAdam 1982, 154–56). However, under the leadership of Roy Innis, a former black power activist turned advocate of the National Rifle Association, New York's CORE chapter had moved to the political right of other civil rights organizations. Innis organized countermarches on Church Avenue to protest the Red Apple boycott (Bowles and English 1990).

Some black clergy opposed the boycott and led prayers and marches jointly with Korean ministers to call for racial harmony. One rally outside the Red Apple, which gathered two hundred supporters (mostly Asian American), received a mix of responses from picketers and passersby (Howe 1990). Similar efforts at cooperation occurred in other cities as well, demonstrating the potential for cooperation as well as conflict between African and Korean Americans.

To what extent did these divisions mirror public opinion in New York City's black communities? Two separate surveys show the extent of division among black New Yorkers over the boycott. A CBS-Newsday poll taken in May 1990 found that 27 percent of black respondents and eight percent of whites supported the boycott. A 1992 survey of New Yorkers living in neighborhoods with Korean stores yielded nearly identical results (Min 1996, 97). This does not necessarily mean the balance of respondents opposed the boycott—some may have had more complex opinions, or no opinion at all. Undoubtedly, however, the Red Apple boycott stirred conflict among blacks as much as between blacks and Koreans.

No Closing the Stores: The Response of Korean Organizations

> "They cannot close. We could be next."
> —Byong Yong Chon, manager of a store two
> blocks from the Red Apple (Goldman 1990a)

In most Korean store boycotts in New York City, Korean Americans did not sit idly by. In the case of the Red Apple, however, Korean merchants responded even more vigorously than they had in the past. The boycotters' emphasis on race as a tool for mobilizing supporters helped transform the boycott into an intergroup conflict. However, that was only half of the equation. In their efforts to defend the boycotted stores, Korean New Yorkers—via community and trade organizations—invoked ethnic solidarity as well.[30]

The intervention of Korean American organizations helped propel black-Korean conflict from neighborhood storefronts to larger arenas, in New York City and elsewhere. Korean merchants individually have had few resources with which to defend themselves against boycotts. But civic and trade organizations made a huge difference, using their large membership bases to bolster merchants' capabilities for survival.[31] Ironically, their success in defending individual Korean-owned stores likely intensified the role of race in incidents that had already been framed as interminority conflicts. Had these organizations not rallied Korean communities to support targeted merchants, boycotts might have been shorter-lived (ending in some cases in the closure of stores) and less frequent, since media attention and strong responses fueled black activists' efforts to mobilize followers.

The boycott against the Red Apple and Church Fruits was initially highly effective. Protesters were able to persuade or prevent shoppers from entering the store. Sales dropped precipitously and stayed close to zero for several months. The heavy reliance of the stores on sales of fresh produce made them particularly vulnerable to the boycott, since such items could not be kept on the shelves for long (H. C. Lee 1993, 166).

Two Korean-owned stores on the next block that had formerly competed with the Red Apple and Church Fruits, however, actually saw increases in business. In contrast with past boycotts, the protest leadership actually encouraged neighborhood residents to shop at the other Korean stores, especially when the press and public officials charged them with racism against Korean Americans and exposed contradictions in their goals (H. C. Lee 1993, 167). In fact, plenty of Korean-owned businesses existed nearby. Along Church Avenue's commercial district, within five blocks of the boycott, more than a third of the sixty-seven small stores were owned by Korean Americans. Only thirteen were owned by African Americans, and (due to their second-story locations or types of business) most of these were not visible from the street. By contrast, out of the area's five produce stores—the most conspicuous businesses due to their sidewalk displays—four were Korean-owned (H. C. Lee 1993, 69–70).

Thanks to competition among Korean organizations seeking to speak for Korean New Yorkers, however, the fate of the boycotted stores was not immediately sealed. In fact, Korean organizations jostled for the right to represent the boycotted merchants in the conflict just as African American organizations had endeavored to represent black customers in the neighborhood.[32] On the first day of protests, the owner of the Red Apple telephoned two organizations for help. One was the Korean American Small Business Service Center, headquartered in Flushing, Queens, the neighborhood considered by many to be New York City's "Koreatown" (Min 1996, 38–39). The other was the Korean Produce Association, located at the Hunts Point Market in the Bronx, where storeowners traveled daily to buy produce from wholesalers. Both organizations claimed hundreds of members across the city and had experience dealing with black-Korean conflicts.[33] Dennis DeLeon, who helped coordinate Mayor Dinkins's mediation attempt, met with leaders from both and observed their competition:

> [The organizations] had varying levels of influence, and they always were competing against each other, [over] who represented the storeowners. Or who would bargain with the city for what the storeowner needed and wanted. I was dealing with [the] two groups all the time, and their ascendancy rose and fell, depending on what was going on, and sometimes there was a third group.[34] (DeLeon 1996)

As Heon Cheol Lee points out, membership in the Small Business Service Center and the Korean Produce Organization overlapped, meaning the two organizations competed for organizational growth; intervention in high-profile disputes like the Red Apple boycott presented opportunities to "enhance their prestige" (H. C. Lee 1993, 181).

The Small Business Service Center's director, Sung Soo Kim, had represented Korean merchants in the Tropic boycott and made haste to respond to the Red Apple boycott as well. During the first week, Kim accompanied the Red Apple's owner to a police precinct house to file a countercomplaint in the case against him and attended meetings with neighborhood activists, police officials, and protesters (Kim 1995). Kim also sent letters to newspapers and television stations in hopes of winning their support and thereby ending the boycott quickly. But appealing to the press might only have exacerbated the conflict by giving the boycotters more attention (Min 1996, 107). Eventually, however, the Korean Produce Association, led by executive director Michael Kang, outmaneuvered Kim and won informal recognition as representative of the boycotted stores. Various third parties attempting mediation of the conflict saw Kang as the merchants' chief representative, including Dinkins administration officials (DeLeon 1996), the Justice Department's Community Relations Service (Glenn 1995; Hernandez 1995), and the Brooklyn Borough President (McQuillan 1995).

Although they competed in this way, Korean organizations were nonetheless virtually unanimous on the proper strategy to pursue against the boycott: all agreed on the necessity of supporting the store financially to keep it open. Few voices, if any, were heard advocating the alternative: ending the conflict swiftly by allowing the store to close or be sold. Most argued that allowing it to close would simply open the door to future boycotts in greater numbers. As a result, the two stores came to be seen as community property—ironically, in a sense, confirming the impression of intergroup conflict that many black demonstrators on the picket lines already held.

The storeowners' perspective was different. Before the boycott, neither the Red Apple nor Church Fruits had been a dues-paying member of any major Korean merchant organization (Sa 1995). Once the boycott was in full swing, both owners wanted to sell their stores to end the ordeal as quickly as possible. But community pressure and support from these organizations forestalled them from pursuing that option (H. C. Lee 1993, 183; Min 1996, 149). In fact, as the Red Apple's owner, Bong Jae Jang, revealed to a reporter, other Korean merchants had decided that his store would serve as a test case against future boycotts (Goldman 1990a).

Unanimity on the aims of countermobilization and competition to pursue them ensured a vigorous response. Initially, the Korean Produce Association and the Korean American Association of New York coordinated fundraising to keep the stores open, with the help of the *Korea Times New York* (Sa 1995). Contributions poured in from other sources as well. An independent group of Korean merchants who wanted to avoid the overhead costs incurred by those organizations sent money to the two stores directly (H. C. Lee 1993, 182). Korean American churches and groups from other cities donated funds too, urged by community leaders and editorials in Korean-language newspapers (Min 1996, 148–49).

During 1990, Korean merchants raised about $150,000 to support the two stores (Min 1996, 149). Before the boycott, the Red Apple had grossed $25,000 in weekly sales and Church Fruits had grossed $40,000 (Baril 1991; H. C. Lee 1993, 165). During the boycott, however, the sales volume at both stores fell to near zero (Farber 1990), so donations to the stores were crucial not only in keeping the stores open during the pickets but in sustaining the conflict as well.

The Korean response to the boycott went beyond fundraising. Korean American groups organized an enormous "peace rally" in September to call for an end to the boycott, and more importantly, to protest what they saw as Mayor Dinkins's inaction. About 7,000 Koreans, equal to 15 percent of the city's Korean population, took part (Min 1996, 151). The rally's remarkable size was the product of mobilization efforts by Korean civic, church, and trade groups, the fruit of years of organizational development in New York City's Korean community. The rally was rife with symbols of ethnic solidarity: the crowd sang traditional Korean songs and heard speakers compare the boycott to the Japanese colonization of Korea (Min 1996, 152). Some speakers, such as Jong Duck Byun, president of the Korean Association of New York, urged racial reconciliation with African Americans and pointed to black soldiers' participation in the Korean War as a model for unity. Richard Izzo, the attorney for the boycotted merchants, told the crowd that the Dinkins administration, in its inability to halt the boycott, had failed them—evoking the most enthusiastic response of the day (English and Henneberger 1990).

Despite its enormous size, the rally was tightly controlled by its organizers. Internal dissent over whether to hold the rally—for fear of further angering black New Yorkers—was largely erased after Red Apple owner Bong Jae Jang reported being beaten by blacks on his way home one day at the end of August (Min 1996, 150). Slogans had to be approved by the organizing committee so they would not offend blacks (H. C. Lee 1993, 97). For the most part, placard carriers adhered to the rule. However, rowdier Korean demonstrators booed when Mayor Dinkins addressed the rally and interrupted his speech with jeers. Undoubtedly worried that the crowd would give voice to the widespread racial prejudices against blacks held by many Koreans, rally organizers worked to calm the crowd (English and Henneberger 1990).

According to New York–based sociologist Pyong Gap Min, one of the rally's organizers, "Korean community leaders attempted last-minute negotiations with the New York City government to terminate the boycott, using the planned rally as leverage" (Min 1996, 151). Although they failed to get a "positive response," it is unclear what kind of response they could have expected. The Dinkins administration had no power to halt the boycott unilaterally (without using force), since its organizers in no way answered to the mayor. The attempt, however, demonstrates the extent to which Koreans responding to the boycott believed, correctly or incorrectly, that the real conflict was between Sonny Carson and David Dinkins (Kim 1995). In any case, the Korean rally did appear to have an effect on the mayor—the next day, he ordered police to comply with a several-month-old court ruling ordering them to keep picketers fifty feet from the store. A few days later, Dinkins shopped at the two stores in person as a show of support, something critics had been demanding for months. To many observers, this simply made the mayor appear indecisive and weak. Understanding Dinkins's response to the boycott, however, requires an examination of the constraints and opportunities facing the mayor—any mayor, in fact, but this one in particular.

The Mayor's Response: Inaction or "Delicate Diplomacy"?

"We have a series of boiling pots. And the mayor is like a cook who has to keep an eye on all of them."
—Former U.S. Representative and mayoral candidate Herman Badillo (Carroll 1993)

The role of Mayor Dinkins in the boycott became a flashpoint for controversy, contributing yet another factor that broadened the scope of the conflict. Public expectations of Dinkins's role in healing racial conflict ran high for two reasons: one related to the defining themes of his campaign the previous fall, and the other related to the formal—as opposed to informal—powers of any mayor of New York City.

First, Dinkins ran on a platform emphasizing racial harmony, a theme that enabled his primary victory over his predecessor, Ed Koch. Voters had rejected Koch's brazenness on matters of race, which many came to believe had fueled rather than quelled divisive racial conflicts during the 1980s. Dinkins's portrayal of the city as a "gorgeous mosaic" of racial and ethnic groups and his quieter, less confrontational style offered a fresh alternative. The Red Apple boycott began only a few weeks after Dinkins's inauguration, and the conflict became a test of the mayor's alternative strategy, what he called "delicate diplomacy" (Jetter and Jordan 1990). The historical distinction of being the city's first African American mayor further heightened public expectations of his role.

Second, New Yorkers expect strength from their mayor. This is not so much because previous mayors with big personalities had left big shoes for Dinkins to fill, but because the chief executive in New York City is given broad formal powers by the city charter. The city's structure of political institutions is frequently characterized as a "strong mayor" system because the mayor wields much more power than the City Council over important policy matters such as the budget and the planning process, and because he exercises direct authority over city agencies.

Despite his formal powers, however, Dinkins received massive criticism for "inaction" in the boycott. Critics from all quarters charged him with failing to end the boycott by refusing to denounce it forcibly in public. The charge came especially strongly from Korean Americans, but by no means only from them. Former Mayor Ed Koch, *New York* magazine columnist Joe Klein, and other public figures urged Dinkins to shop at the stores.

When the mayor failed to do that (until September), journalist Jim Sleeper castigated him for failing to "exercise LaGuardian leadership and bring the full moral weight of his office to bear against Carson" (Sleeper 1990, 300), echoing similar remarks by state Supreme Court Justice Gerald Held, who presided over a case related to the conflict. Dinkins received criticism from figures as far-flung as Mel Miller, speaker of the New York State Assembly.

The Dinkins administration was hardly inactive. It began to intervene in the boycott almost immediately after its start through the work of a Human Rights Commission field worker in Brooklyn, who visited the scene daily, met with protesters, and monitored their shifting demands (Jordan 1990). Two Dinkins aides became the point men on attempts to resolve the conflict: first Deputy Mayor Bill Lynch, and later Human Rights Commissioner Dennis DeLeon. The two decided that the best course of action was to "resolve it" rather than condemn it, as the mayor's critics demanded. The intelligence DeLeon received from his staff in the field was that "strong, genuine feelings of disrespect" had been stirred by Jiselaine Felissaint's accusation, and the problem with condemning the boycott "was that when you put yourself in that posture, your ability to play a negotiator is seriously limited" (DeLeon 1996).

By April, the would-be mediators from City Hall grew frustrated with protesters. Virgo Lee, head of the mayor's Office for Asian American Affairs, identified two sources of frustration:

It took months to define the leadership—that was part of the delay. . . . The other part of the delay was the ongoing mediation process—we thought we were making progress. It took us quite a number of months to realize that the final bottom line demand of the protesters was that the Korean stores must close, . . . an unacceptable demand. (Bunch 1993)

Lee also pointed out the difficulties of resolving a conflict in which both sides refused to budge on the closing of the stores:

It is the position of the mayor's office that these stores should not be closed down. . . . The problem we have been facing is that if the position of the people on the picket lines is that there is nothing to talk about, then we have nowhere to go. . . . The Koreans are willing to sit down and talk, but they are not willing to close down the stores. (Sinclair 1990, 22)

One result of the frustration Dinkins's staff encountered was the mayor's decision to set up a fact-finding committee consisting of black and Korean community leaders (none of whom were involved in the conflict directly). The committee's mission was to investigate the original incident and the roots of the conflict. Like other "blue ribbon" commissions set up to investigate racial crises, this one may have been little more than a symbolic tactic to deflect negative attention and make the administration appear to the public to be engaged in constructive activities (Lipsky and Olson 1977). After all, the staff of the Human Rights Commission and other mayoral aides had been collecting and assessing information from the beginning—just without a public face.

Rather than helping Dinkins, the move worked against the mayor and his mediation attempts by expanding the multiplicity of interventions into the conflict. The mayor's mistake in setting up the committee became apparent almost immediately after he announced its members, as it became embroiled in its own scandal over the appropriateness of the selections. Moreover, talks between Dinkins aides and protesters broke down soon afterwards (Jordan 1990). But the extent of the mistake broadened considerably when the committee released its report in September and the City Council took issue with its conclusions, set up its own committee to investigate it, and later issued its own "report on the report."[35]

At times, Dinkins's strategy did seem confused. Although the main thrust was to negotiate a quiet resolution behind the scenes, his administration also hoped that the courts would settle the dispute. The attitude was, "Let's get it to court really quickly and get it resolved" (DeLeon 1996). Relying on the courts was a mistake, however, since in hotly contested social controversies courts can widen divisions rather than mend them (Franklin and Kosaki 1989)—and in the Red Apple case, the conflict had extended far beyond the initial incident. Moreover, despite the preference for quiet negotiations, Dinkins undertook two major public moves: First, on May 11 Dinkins delivered a rare televised address to the city. In the speech, he urged racial harmony, denounced the racial violence of the Yusuf Hawkins killing and other cases, and, compelled by mounting public pressure, called for the Red Apple conflict to end and offered to mediate the settlement himself. "Boycotts can be an appropriate and effective response," Dinkins declared, "but this one is not and the vast majority of the people in that community know it" (Purdum 1990b).[36] Second, on September 21, Dinkins made a highly publicized shopping trip to the boycotted stores. In his view, this move "broke" the boycott (DeLeon 1996), even though smaller groups of protesters persisted long afterward. In addition to the two major public moves, the Dinkins administration held a series of public hearings at the site, which were attended by neighborhood activists, merchants, and neighborhood residents.

Could Mayor Dinkins have ended the boycott earlier by pronouncing his opposition publicly, applying the "full moral weight of his office" in order to undermine support for it? In the past, no mayor had intervened directly in Korean store boycotts, so no cases exist for comparison. However, Mayor Koch's penchant for ending other racial conflicts by denouncing them met with rare success, and eventually contributed to his own defeat. The best test of the mayor's influence in this conflict thus lies in examining the impact of his public actions on the size of protests.

Given the data in Table 4.2, it appears that Dinkins's televised speech had little effect on diminishing the size of protests—if anything, boycotters were energized by outrage at the mayor's dismissal of their claims. The table traces peaks and valleys in support for the boycott. During the first month, crowds numbered in the hundreds. Then, for the two months prior to the speech, the boycott persisted enough to be effective, but without the same level of energy. In fact, in mid-March, protesters talked about suspending their marches (Jordan 1990). Then, on May 12, the day after Dinkins's address, the demonstration drew 300 marchers, as close as ever to its previous high of 400. On the next two days for which numbers are available, 200 picketers marched. Thus, if anything, the mayor's public condemnation boosted support for the boycott instead of undermining it.

Unfortunately, Dinkins's shopping trip to the boycotted stores four months later, in September, does not provide a satisfying test of the potential impact of "moral leadership": by September, the numbers of protesters at the scene had already dwindled (Flynn and Bowles 1990). Shoppers did begin to return to the stores after the mayor's appearance, however.

Explaining the Mayor's Response:
Past Experience, Current Constraints

As noted, the mayor of New York City possesses great formal powers, a fact ensured by the city government's "strong mayor" political structure. Formal political power in New York City is hierarchical and centralized, meaning that city agencies answer directly to the mayor and commissioners serve at his whim. Informal power, however, is highly dispersed. The mayor enjoys much less control over the "informal" arena of organizing around neighborhood, ethnicity, and other interests. The high level of political organization and the extreme fragmentation of politics in New York City—a single centralized party organization being a thing of the past—means that the mayor must deal with a multitude of competing power centers over which he has little influence. And when it comes to intervening in social conflicts, informal power matters more than formal power. The mayor's arsenal of budgetary and appointive powers made little difference in helping him resolve a conflict that took place outside the boundaries of conventional politics.

Three factors explain the manner in which Mayor Dinkins responded to the Red Apple boycott. First, he was constrained by new contradictions that had emerged in the traditional electoral base of liberal mayors, as black nationalists came to challenge black elected officials for leadership and legitimacy—not only in New York, but in a number of cities (Tate 1993, 160–63). The fragile electoral coalition that put Dinkins in office the previous November—he won by a razor-thin margin of two percent, catapulted over the top by an extraordinary mobilization effort among racial minorities—made him pay especially close attention to black communities, which often had ties to radical activists like the boycott leaders as well as to traditional politicians like himself.[37] In 1993, Dinkins lost the mayoralty to Rudolph Giuliani—again, by a margin of two percent—partly because of low turnout among black voters (Roberts 1993).

A second factor explaining Dinkins's response was the political tradition from which he had arisen, a factor that had more to do with organizational style than with racial identification. Dinkins may have appealed for support and built his coalition as a progressive reformer, but he acquired his schooling in politics from the machine tradition of the Harlem clubhouses. The conflict between these two traditions may explain Dinkins's confusion over whether to pursue a quiet, behind-the-scenes strategy or an open, direct one.

A third factor that shaped the mayor's response was the past experience of elected officials' efforts to mediate black-Korean conflicts in New York City. Dinkins himself had made headway with a negotiation strategy during the 1984 Harlem boycott. No doubt, he had also watched State Assembly Representative Al Vann meet with success more recently, in 1988, in the Tropic boycott—by using a combination of negotiation and more vocal leadership. Vann, an insurgent politician from the newer, rival, and more radical current in black politics in New York, and thus someone with no roots in the machine tradition, had condemned an alleged attack and voiced support for black community control even as he achieved an end to the boycott that did not require closing the store.

Several differences between the two cases explain Vann's success and Dinkins's failure. First, Vann had roots in the same radical tradition as the December 12 Movement, and thus did not face the challenge of black nationalism to traditional black politics. Second, among Korean Americans, support and mobilization for the shops boycotted in the Red Apple conflict was much higher than for the Tropic grocery, making the scope of the 1988 conflict smaller. Third, the accord that effectively ended the Tropic boycott did not have the support of the protesters. Vann affected the course of the conflict without even talking to the boycott leaders. The first two differences were beyond Dinkins's control. What about the third difference?

The mayoral aides who coordinated Dinkins's response tried the "end run" strategy that worked for Vann. Human Rights Commissioner DeLeon spelled out the mayor's strategy:

> We tried to use a divide-and-conquer approach with the demonstrators. . . . We tried to peel off the Haitian community from Sonny Carson, and treat them separately and try and strike some bargain, some settlement based upon a set of other concerns—respect, pride, things like that, opposed to this kind of broad-based, diffuse anger. (DeLeon 1996)

This, in essence, was what had made Vann's strategy effective—splitting the boycotters' base of support. The key difference was that whereas Dinkins desired quiet, behind-the-scenes negotiations with moderate neighborhood activists (who had lost their exclusive control over the boycott after the December 12 Movement stepped in), Vann directly engaged Korean community leaders in negotiations that resulted in a highly publicized agreement that bypassed the boycotters. In fact, the mainstream media gave more attention to Vann's accord than they had to the boycott itself. Vann succeeded because he appeared sensitive to both sides *and* undercut the influence of the boycott leaders.

As a mediator in the Red Apple boycott, however, Dinkins was placed in an impossible position. Vann's constituency was a State Assembly district; Dinkins's was the entire city. Vann had black power credentials, which lent him a measure of legitimacy to fend off challenges from radicals; Dinkins had more moderate roots and had cobbled together a complex, easily fractured coalition (Mollenkopf 1990). Dinkins encountered critics from all quarters. He was castigated for pandering to black New Yorkers and was even held responsible for their actions. As an article by Karen Tumulty (1990) in the *Los Angeles Times* noted at the time: "Many of Dinkins' critics seem[ed] to suggest that as a black, he should automatically hold sway over New York's black community—a view that [did] not recognize the diversity of opinion and outlook among blacks in the city." And he was castigated by Lawrence Lucas (1990a) and others for pandering to white New Yorkers: "Dinkins' inability to tell white folks to go to hell causes him to lean on Black folks to end the boycott, thereby blaming the victim in traditional American fashion." In fact, as Brooklyn School Board member Maurice Gumbs (1990) pointed out, the very qualities that earned Mayor Dinkins so much criticism from so many New Yorkers during the Red Apple boycott—his moderation, quiet style, and restraint—were "the same qualities which they considered virtues" just the year before during the mayoral campaign. Having elected a Dinkins, many New Yorkers nonetheless yearned for a Koch: "Today the demand is for a mayor who will shriek: Boil them in oil! Take 'em out and shoot 'em!"

Other Interventions: Multiple, Uncoordinated Responses by Public Officials

Once a solidly white neighborhood, Flatbush had been transformed in recent decades by flight to the suburbs, racial succession, and immigration, into a polyglot of black ethnicities. Political representation, however, lagged behind the demographic transformation of the neighborhood; formal politics was still dominated by whites, even at the borough level. Thanks to the traditional, neighborhood orientation of New York City's political structure, several white-dominated political institutions had actual physical manifestations in the neighborhood: the police, for instance, and the local Community Board. In Flatbush in particular, white residents were overrepresented among the Community Board's appointed members. Because the Boards are situated locally and hold frequent hearings on issues of direct concern to neighborhood residents, they act as lightning rods for neighborhood activism throughout New York City. Flatbush was no different, and the Red Apple boycotters used the conflict to highlight this fact.[38]

Flatbush's Community Board became involved in the boycott within the first month. Alvin Berk, the board's appointed chair, wrote to Mayor Dinkins and demanded his intervention to help end the boycott. Berk reported that protesters had leveled death threats against some of the moderate Haitian activists trying to resolve the conflict and had established "an illegal, green market" near the boycotted stores. Given that the boycott was still in its early stages, Berk's letter was prescient in forecasting the potential scale of the conflict: "They test your administration's resolve," Berk warned the mayor. If the conflict were not cut short soon, he wrote, "You will be remembered as the mayor who presided over the beginning of the end" (English 1990b). A few weeks later, black members of the Board voiced disagreement with Berk's message and tone (English 1990a).[39]

The racial divisions on the Community Board reflected the growing tendency of the conflict to expand and absorb new actors, as public officials, one-by-one, threw their hats in the ring. As the arena grew, it became characterized by multiple, uncoordinated—and often competing—responses by public officials. Rather than referring to their efforts as conflict "resolution" or "management," terms that imply success, a more appropriate term would be conflict "intervention."

Brooklyn Borough President Howard Golden intervened in the conflict with his own attempt to end it, independently of Mayor Dinkins. Golden was the first public official to initiate public negotiations, which were held at Brooklyn Borough Hall in early February. Organizers of the initial protests at the Red Apple, such as George Dames, Ernie Foster, and Guy Victor (who were not members of the December 12 Movement), came to the meeting but walked out before it ended. The remaining participants—including Community Board officers, representatives from neighborhood organizations and Korean merchant associations, clergy, and mayoral aides—issued a joint agreement without the boycotters (McQuillan 1995). In this way, Golden's attempt (more than Dinkins's) resembled Al Vann's negotiations over the Tropic boycott. The participants called for a moratorium on the boycott in exchange for several proposals, including an investigation into the initial incident, cultural education programs, and increased hiring of black workers by Korean merchants (English and Yuh 1990). However, Golden's attempt at an "end run" around the boycotters received little press attention, a necessary ingredient for success, and the boycott only grew as it drew more third parties and public officials to intervene.[40] Moreover, Golden lacked Vann's level of legitimacy among more radically inclined black Brooklynites. During the boycott, aides to Golden and Dinkins interacted frequently, but not productively. Instead, in the view of the Golden camp at least, the Dinkins administration "spurned many willing alliances" (McQuillan 1995).[41]

City Council members intervened as well. The meeting which council member Susan Alter helped to arrange in the Flatbush precinct house just two days into the boycott brought together community leaders, protesters, and police (Kim 1995). Few other councilors became involved until much later in the conflict. Their most significant entrance into the foray did not come until the fall, when the boycott was waning. In September, upon release of a fact-finding report by the committee Dinkins set up to investigate the boycott, a council committee held hearings that questioned not only Dinkins's handling of the boycott but the ethics of the report itself. State Assembly Speaker Mel Miller, a white resident of Flatbush, testified at the hearings and called the report a "disservice to all people in New York," because it had not condemned the boycott outright. Council member Noach Dear of Brooklyn called the report "a sham" (Terry 1990b). Two months later, the council committee issued a formal response, entitled "An Analysis of the Report of the Mayor's Committee Investigating the Protest Against Two Korean-Owned Groceries on Church Avenue in Brooklyn" (New York City Council Committee on General Welfare 1990).

Brooklyn District Attorney Charles Hynes intervened in the conflict by deciding to file assault charges against the Red Apple storeowner. The decision to pursue the case was not inevitable, but instead was bound up with the politics of the boycott. A deputy to Hynes reportedly offered to drop the assault charges against a demonstrator if Felissaint dropped her assault charges in exchange (Browne 1990c). Such an attempt might have worked in a different conflict, but it was likely doomed in the Red Apple case; Felissaint and her attorney, Colin Moore, pursued their case separately from the boycott, with little or no coordination with demonstrators. Hynes, an elected official, was one of a number of public officials who led marches in Flatbush against the boycott (Goldman 1990b). He became further embroiled after receiving sharp criticism in the Dinkins administration's fact-finding report, which charged him with acting too slowly and prolonging the conflict (New York City Mayor's Committee 1990b).

State officials responded to the boycott as well, though less extensively. Assembly Speaker Miller, as already noted, spoke out against the boycott and against Mayor Dinkins's handling of it. The state Division of Human Rights attempted to offer a solution to the conflict by announcing funding for a business ownership training program in Flatbush (Anekwe 1990, 40).

The conflict over the Red Apple even prompted a reaction from the federal government, when a Korean American contributor to the Republican Party successfully urged the administration of President George Bush to intervene. Y. S. Yoo, a business owner from New Jersey, attended a ceremony in the White House Rose Garden and caught the ear of Bush's attorney general, urging him to send a team to investigate what he called an "illegal" boycott (Yoo 1995). As a result, the Justice Department twice ordered Patricia Glenn, the chief mediator in the New York office of its Community Relations Service, to report on the boycott personally to a presidential aide. "There was a lot of pressure from the White House for us to resolve this," Glenn recalls (Glenn 1995). Federal mediators visited the scene periodically and held a number of meetings at their offices in downtown Manhattan.[42] Their meetings included blacks and Koreans, and they managed to hold the only intergroup mediations that included a member of the December 12 Movement, Lawrence Lucas.[43]

The mediators in the Community Relations Service attempted to coordinate their efforts with local officials, meeting with police commanders and Borough President Golden's staff. They encountered resistance from the Dinkins administration, however, possibly because Dinkins's staff perceived them as Republican operatives from the Bush White House trying to embarrass a new Democratic mayor (Glenn 1995; Hernandez 1995).

The courts were drawn into the conflict by seven separate cases: two criminal investigations and five civil suits.[44] But agents of the courts were not merely passive actors; instead, they actively intervened. Most notably, in response to a civil suit, Brooklyn Supreme Court Justice Gerald Held issued two rulings demanding that police prevent or restrain picketing in front of the stores, and even issued what amounted to a public statement calling on Mayor Dinkins to "personally intervene" in order to end the boycott. In one ruling, Justice Held wrote that the court regrets the failure of the mayor of the City of New York to personally intervene and use the prestige of his office and his high standing in the community to convince the parties to bring a suitable end to the dispute. (Jetter and Jordan 1990)

Justice Held had tried in vain to mediate the dispute himself. For his part, Mayor Dinkins, reflecting a desire to shift attention to the courts, had called on demonstrators to wait for a court verdict in the ongoing assault trial.

Indeed, courts are commonly seen as effective instruments of conflict resolution. However, the involvement of courts in the Red Apple boycott served to lengthen and intensify the conflict. The state Supreme Court injunction against the protesters facilitated the task of mobilizing support for the boycott. "It was a big help from my point of view," said Lawrence Lucas. "That simply energized the people more" (Lucas 1995). The ongoing assault cases also helped—every new court date that was announced equipped boycott leaders with new justifications for rallying followers (Lucas 1995; Hernandez 1995). Court hearings were often packed with both supporters and opponents of the boycott, adding to the other public events organized by the mayor, the city council, and the borough president.

If the multiple, uncoordinated responses from public officials achieved anything, they expanded the scope of the conflict and energized the boycotters. According to Dennis DeLeon, the efforts of other officials "were just sideshows. . . . Some of these things just served to keep [the boycott] going. The demonstrators would see these things happening, and knew that none of them were involved. And there were no efforts to deal directly with them [the boycotters], and they would get pissed off, and there would be more fervor than before" (DeLeon 1996). Certainly, Dinkins might have coordinated better with other officials, but he lacked the instruments or leverage to force anyone but his own commissioners to fall into line. Some public officials did in fact invite boycott leaders to mediation attempts, which the latter often rebuffed. However, the disarray generated by New York City's fragmented politics set the stage for separate, competing responses that only served to expand the conflict.

Consequently, the boycott against two small Korean-owned stores grew into a protest against white-dominated political institutions. The role played by courts in the conflict was particularly important. Major newspaper and broadcast coverage of the boycott did not even begin until Justice Held issued the first court order against protesters, which provided news outlets with their first major story on the conflict.

The Police Presence: Containing and Cooperating

On a Saturday in September 1990, one day after Mayor Dinkins shopped at the boycotted stores and several days after homemade explosives were found on a nearby rooftop,[45] a boycott leader described the scene on Church Avenue as "an armed camp, a massive show of force, intimidation designed to show the neighborhood that the police control the street (Hornung 1990, 35).

On that day, the NYPD had dispatched 400 officers to Flatbush. As Table 4.2 shows, this represented a peak in the police presence at the boycott. But there had been a significant police presence throughout the boycott, beginning as early as January and February (Jordan, Jetter, Murphy, English, and Liff 1990; McQueen 1990). And once the police began enforcing the court order to keep picketers fifty feet from the stores, uniformed officers often outnumbered protesters.

The NYPD had intervened in the conflict at its outset. The meeting in January at which community representatives made an attempt to end the conflict took place at the local precinct house and involved police officers. Over the course of the conflict, police became as intimately acquainted with the boycott as any of the other public officials who intervened. To monitor the conflict, the NYPD assigned a community relations officer who was "totally familiar with all the demonstrators, the Koreans—he knew everybody" (DeLeon 1996).

Over the entire course of the boycott, the police presence was enormous, involving the mobilization of hundreds of officers. Even more remarkably, it was also restrained. The likelihood of physical confrontations between demonstrators and officers was minimized because boycott organizers and police officials actually sat down together to exchange information and lay ground rules. A number of meetings took place before, during, and after police enforcement of the court injunction keeping protesters fifty feet from the store (Lucas 1995). Boycott leaders even went so far as to praise the "reason and restraint" of police commanders, their longtime archrivals (Lucas 1990a).

The conduct of police during the boycott was especially surprising given the public perception—and often the reality—of extreme hostility between the NYPD and black activists. Police resisted a number of opportunities to inflame the conflict. In May, they refused to enforce the state Supreme Court injunction ordering picketers to stay fifty feet from the two stores, arguing that the matter was a civil case.[46] Remarkably, this resistance came from the police command (headed by Lee Brown, the city's second African American police commissioner), not City Hall (DeLeon 1996)—although typically in New York City, the police commissioner answers directly to the mayor, and the move probably had Dinkins's approval. Still, police resisted enforcement of the injunction because they feared that physically forcing demonstrators to move across the street "would probably cause a violent confrontation that could prolong the boycott" (Roberts 1990), a reasonable assumption.

Moreover, when homemade bombs were found on a rooftop near the Red Apple in September, police quickly announced that no evidence could be found linking the bombs to protesters. And when a Vietnamese man was seriously beaten by black youths one night in the neighborhood of the stores, police retracted their initial pronouncement that the assault had been a hate crime after finding new evidence to the contrary. The point here is not that police were sympathetic to the boycotters—they most certainly were not. Critics contended that Commissioner Brown (and by extension, Mayor Dinkins) had ordered officers to "go easy" on the protesters—an unlikely possibility, given the frequency of arrests.[47] Actually, the NYPD had a long, acrimonious relationship with the December 12 Movement.

More likely, police commanders were interested in preserving public order, just as Mayor Koch's police commissioner, Benjamin Ward, had been during the Tropic boycott in 1988, when he recommended against court intervention. Importantly, the NYPD not only had the will to ensure public order without resorting to extreme measures, it also had the way: the department had 27,000 sworn officers in its ranks, and it had community connections to public officials and neighborhood activists, which helped it monitor the boycott. Of course, police officials also recognized that dealing with demonstrators the wrong way could lead to violence: remarkably, of all the arrests, none exploded into mass violence. Boycott leaders, who wanted to preserve their control over protesters and over the goals of the boycott, likely shared the concern for order.

The persistent and overwhelming presence of the police, however, also helped boycott leaders maintain high levels of support for the boycott. Instead of having to transport marchers to police headquarters in downtown Manhattan or gather at a precinct station, the boycott brought the police—a frequent target of the December 12 Movement—to the neighborhood. This gave boycott leaders yet another target against which to channel anger and build support.

The massive, continuous, and orderly intervention by police thus influenced the conflict in several ways. By maintaining a presence—and at times outnumbering picketers—they gave boycott leaders a bigger target; but by coordinating their actions in ways that did not conflict with the aims of protesters, they contained the potential for violence.

The Role of the Media

Too often, critics of the news media homogenize it, assigning a single motive and reporting style to a wide range of separate news outlets. For instance, political scientist Claire Kim writes that "White opinionmakers of all political persuasions talk about Black-Korean conflict in a similar way"

(Kim 1999). Kim further argues that the news media in New York City was part of a larger, racially ordered social structure that actively worked against the protesters. Sociologist Pyong Gap Min does not make such a sweeping condemnation, but observes that "the major media in the New York area, with the exception of the *Amsterdam News,* were extremely critical of the boycott leaders and highly supportive of Korean merchants. . . . [Korean community leaders] generally were satisfied with the mainstream media's treatment of Korean merchants as innocent victims and of Black boycott leaders as political opportunists" (Min 1996, 107). Much of the major media did appear to side with Korean merchants against the black boycotters, and this probably had much to do with the fact that media outlets respond to similar social, commercial, and professional incentives and constraints (Kaniss 1991).

Homogenizing the media and simplifying its role, however, overlooks two important points about the media's impact on the conflict. First, as Min acknowledges, the attention and the criticism given to the boycott by the media may actually have prolonged it by energizing and unifying its supporters. As political scientist Michael Lipsky observed in his analysis of protest politics, protesters depend on media exposure for their success (Lipsky 1968). Second, those whom Kim calls "White opinionmakers" differed to some extent in their reporting of the boycott. *New York Newsday,* which began covering the conflict the earliest, provided the most balanced and informed coverage of any major newspaper.[48] It certainly published the most articles on the conflict: *Newsday* carried fifty-five stories and columns on the boycott, whereas the *New York Times* printed forty-one and the *Amsterdam News* (a weekly paper) published fifteen. More than the other papers, *Newsday* provided context to both the black boycotters' demands and the Korean merchants' dilemmas. Reporting in the *Amsterdam News* varied—at times it was balanced and objective, at others less so. The *New York Times,* the *Daily News,* and the *New York Post* were the most critical of the boycott. Newspapers in other cities (such as Los Angeles) have been less critical of Korean store boycotts than these papers (Min 1996), suggesting that the imbalance in news coverage of the Red Apple boycott may have more to do with the local context than with a universal tendency.

The editorial boards of newspapers, very much actors on the political scene in any city, took sides in the conflict as often as activists and politicians.[49] The *New York Times* published an editorial titled, "These Boycotts Are Racist, and Wrong," which not only criticized boycott leaders but also Mayor Dinkins for inaction and a failure to denounce the boycott: "The longer racism is appeased by weak leadership, the more embattled will be New York's already ragged race relations" (Amsterdam News 1990b). The editors of the *Amsterdam News* neither denounced nor supported the boy-cott in explicit terms, choosing instead to call for a mutual resolution between the storeowners and boycott leaders. However, they roundly crit-icized a black schoolteacher for leading his students across the picket lines to shop at the Red Apple and charged the white-run media with using him to ease the conscience of whites (Amsterdam News 1990b). Significantly, though, the *Amsterdam News* published features and guest columns by writers—including Korean Americans—with a wider variety of perspec-tives than other newspapers.[50]

The most outrageous reporting on the boycott came from television news. The four major local stations—WABC, WCBS, WNBC, and WNYW—began covering the conflict in May (during a news vacuum in the middle of sweeps month, when audience ratings are used to determine advertising rates), repeatedly broadcasting live scenes of loud, angry crowds. Journalist Alex Jones described the television coverage this way:

> On May 8, WNYW's segment about the boycott was dominated by fu-rious face-to-face simultaneous harangues through bullhorns as each side tried to drown out the opposition, leading the reporter to observe that "Brooklyn could blow up." But that assessment, repeated in vari-ous forms on other stations, seemed based on the behavior of several dozen loud and furious demonstrators who generally refused to explain themselves. Gabe Pressman, on WNBC, observed ominously that the "gorgeous mosaic may be falling apart." (Jones 1990)

Charges of inflaming racial conflicts may thus be most accurately leveled at television news, given the lack of time and interest most local stations de-vote to providing background in their reporting. Differences in reporting clearly existed between the print and broadcast media, and among print outlets, and the media's overall impact was far from simple and straight-forward.

AFTERMATH: SMALLER BOYCOTTS IN THE 1990S

Four other black-led boycotts of Korean stores took place between Jan-uary 1990 and April 1991, dwarfed by the ongoing conflict over the Red Apple, and three more took place in its wake. None, however, lasted nearly as long or galvanized anything close to the same amount of support (or op-position).

The Red Apple boycott had barely gotten underway when Kevin Coohill, a twenty-year-old black man, was shot and killed at the Blue Rib-bon, a market in the Bay Ridge section of Brooklyn, during a struggle with the store's Korean owner. Black residents of the neighborhood, furious that the merchant (who had been charged with second-degree murder) had been freed on bail, demonstrated outside the store and demanded its closing (McQueen 1990). Despite the severity of the initial incident, demonstrations did not last long.

Later the same year, in August, another conflict broke out in the Brownsville section of Brooklyn. The course of this conflict contrasted markedly with the Red Apple boycott. The Dinkins administration, facing intense criticism for failing to end the Red Apple boycott, scored a victory for itself by intervening and ending this one. The boycott of the R&N Fruit and Vegetable Market began somewhat differently than others. After a fight with three customers—two sisters and their mother—in a dispute over cherries, the owners were robbed and assaulted by a crowd on the street, they told police (Min 1996, 79; Terry 1990a). Witnesses reported that fruit stands were overturned and windows smashed (Baillou 1990a). Almost immediately, the owners closed the store and sold it. When it reopened a couple of weeks later, the new Korean owner (who had hired black and Latino employees) faced a boycott by protesters who believed the store had simply been sold to a relative in order to deflect community opposition (Terry 1990a). Dinkins aides first persuaded the protest leaders and the storeowners to meet at City Hall, and then the mayor visited the black family involved in the initial dispute (Jordan and Flynn 1990). The boycott ended within two weeks, after protesters were convinced that the old and new owners were unrelated (Baillou 1990a).

Then, in February 1991, soon after the manager of the Red Apple was acquitted of assault charges in the initial dispute in Flatbush, black residents of Elmhurst, Queens, led a boycott of a Korean-owned C-Town Supermarket. Protesters charged that an employee had mistreated an eleven-year-old black boy and picketed the store to demand the employee's arrest and prosecution—but not to demand that the store close. As in Brownsville, the boycott in Elmhurst came to a quick resolution (ending after only four days). A well-known community organizer, Rev. Herbert Daughtry, came from Brooklyn to lead pickets at the C-Town, but said he would "move in concert with the community leaders" (Fried 1991). Neighborhood activists who were involved in the protests, fearing potential escalation, met with storeowners to defuse the conflict. Leaders of the tenants association at Lefrak City apartments (where many of the picketers lived) intervened, accompanied by Dinkins aides, police officials, black and Korean representatives from the neighborhood Community Board, and the local State Assembly member (Fried 1991; New York State Advisory Committee to the U.S. Commission on Civil Rights 1994). Following the series of talks and an agreement to fire the offending employee, Daughtry publicly called for an end to the pickets (*New York Times* 1991; Browne 1991). With the damage done by the Red Apple conflict fresh in their minds, this time the mediators, who were primarily neighborhood-based, shared a desire to prevent the R&N from turning into the Red Apple: said Stephen James (1995), an attorney who had briefly represented protesters in the Red Apple boycott and became involved in the R&N case as well: "One was the teaching tool and one was the result of learning the lesson."

Four more conflicts involving blacks and Koreans occurred over the next several years in Flatbush, Greenwich Village, and Harlem. They were small in size, short in duration, and easily resolved. In the case of a Korean-owned hat store in Greenwich Village in 1995, a Korean trade organization was able to intervene and negotiate with local activists, ending the protests by responding to specific demands concerning the operation of the store. A member of the organization drew on contacts he had established among black activists and politicians in order to quell rumors that threatened to escalate the boycott, including a rumor that Al Sharpton and Sonny Carson planned to join it (Sa 1995).

Some observers have argued that conflicts eased because underlying cultural issues—like misunderstandings and rude behavior—had eased. However, evidence of individual-level tensions persisted: in the mid-1990s, numerous merchant-customer disputes occurred, but there were few boycotts (ibid.). Other factors must have been at work to forestall overt conflict.

Two factors in particular likely combined to reduce the frequency and intensity of boycotts in the 1990s. First, the Red Apple was a turning point. The boycott on Church Avenue had been so expansive and severe that black and Korean civic leaders came to recognize a new urgency for resolving conflicts quickly and locally. As Daok Lee Pak, a Community Board member who helped mediate the Elmhurst boycott, observed, "People had become tired of such unproductive racial disputes" (New York State Advisory Committee to the U.S. Commission on Civil Rights 1994, 19–20). Neighborhood activists became less willing to invite radical activists like the December 12 Movement to take part. Korean organizations became less willing to use merchant-customer disputes to enhance ethnic solidarity.

The second factor that combined—in some cases at least—to produce shorter boycotts was that ties had developed among black and Korean civic and trade groups over the past decade, due to their intervention in overt conflicts, that allowed easier conflict resolution in later years. Such intergroup, interorganizational ties had been rare for most of the 1980s; when ties had existed, usually among clergy, they tended to be ineffective in resolving conflicts. Now, however, thanks to the frequent outbreak of conflicts, black and Korean community leaders had met face-to-face, come to know each other, and sometimes developed working relationships. Also, events like prayer meetings and goodwill trips to Korea, which had done little to solve immediate problems, paid off later by establishing additional long-term ties.

In the years following the Red Apple boycott, public officials and activists found they could build on the new ties with one another that had developed in face-to-face meetings as they responded to conflicts. Mayor Dinkins's human relations staff built on this foundation as well. According to Dennis DeLeon, "There were seventeen [disputes] that we were able to resolve right off the bat—threatened boycotts or boycotts that had been started [between] Koreans and Latinos or blacks. . . . The whole notion of responding quickly and massively is the key" (DeLeon 1996).

THE ABSENCE OF SEVERE VIOLENCE

Remarkably, the tensions that fueled the massive mobilization around the Red Apple boycott and the myriad other conflicts that involved blacks and Koreans in New York City never escalated into severe violence, collective or otherwise. Table 4.3 lists the incidents of violence between blacks and Koreans reported in the press from 1980 to 1995. Only one incident resulted in a death; most cases resulted in injuries, and many involved mere scuffles. Hospitalization of the victim was reported in only a few. Given the high salience of the issue, more severe incidents would surely have been reported, had they occurred. It did not take such incidents to spur activists to action, however. Table 4.3 shows that half the sixteen incidents were followed by boycotts.

One of the most severe (and widely reported) incidents connected to black-Korean conflicts was the assault by black youths on a Vietnamese man they mistook to be Korean. The attack on Tuan Ana Cao, which took place in May 1990 during the Red Apple boycott, was initially labeled a hate crime by police because the attackers shouted ethnic slurs (about Koreans) at their Vietnamese victims, and because it took place in the neighborhood of the boycott. The incident was reported as such by USA Today and by papers in Chicago, Los Angeles, and other big cities, as well as by the major media in New York. Police investigators quickly revised their account, however, and explained that despite the slurs, the attack had been spontaneous and had been triggered neither by the boycott nor by the mistaken ethnicity of the victims (McFadden 1990).

Occasionally, physical violence occurred in front of stores, during picketing. For instance, during the Red Apple boycott, the wife of the manager

Table 4.3. Reports of Violence between Blacks and Koreans
in New York City, 1980–1995

Incident	Date	Neighborhood	Outcome
Altercation at Ike's[a]	Oct. 1984	Harlem	Injury[b]
Altercation at Tropic[a]	Aug. 1988	Bed-Stuy	Injury
Altercation at Koko's[a]	Sept. 1988	Harlem	Injury
Kevin Coohill Shooting[a]	Jan. 1990	Bay Ridge	Death
Altercation at Red Apple[a]	Jan. 1990	Flatbush	Injury
Assault at Church Fruits	Feb. 1990	Flatbush	Injury
Assault at Fancy Foods Deli	April 1990	Manhattan	Injury
Tuan Ana Cao Assault[c]	May 1990	Flatbush	Injury
Altercation at R&N[a]	Aug. 1990	Brownsville	Injury
Bong Jae Jang Assault	Aug. 1990	Flatbush	Injury
Assault at C-Town[a]	Feb. 1991	Elmhurst	Injury
Altercation at Lee's Fancy Fruit[a]	April 1991	Flatbush	Injury
Looting at Sneaker King	Aug. 1991	Crown Heights	Damage
Second Bong Jae Jang Assault	Oct. 1991	Bay Ridge	Injury
Assault at Lee's Fancy Fruit	Dec. 1991	Flatbush	Injury, Damage
Lee's Fancy Fruit Arson	Feb. 1992	Flatbush	Damage
Assault at Hong's Fruit	Dec. 1992	Flatbush	Injury

[a]Incident was followed by a boycott.
[b]Most injuries were minor (required no hospitalization).
[c]Victim was mistaken for Korean (see text).

of Church Fruits was assaulted by a demonstrator, and arrests followed. Police and demonstrators engaged in occasional scuffles. But incidents like these were rare, especially given the magnitude of the conflict—thousands of demonstrators and police officers faced each other during the course of the Red Apple boycott. Despite fears of riots, the long, hot summer of 1990 did not end in fire. The scarcity of violence begs explanation.

Activists who lead protests in a competitive field of neighborhood organizing are more likely to try to avoid violence than to provoke it, even when they are inspired more by self-interest than by moral philosophy. In fact, self-interest itself is a powerful motivator. For organizers, the degeneration of protest into violence can mean loss of control over followers and agendas. Moreover, when protesters engage in violence, they risk losing broader legitimacy and incurring a repressive response by police (Eisinger 1973, 13–14). Of course, leaders may lose control of crowds if tensions overwhelm their capabilities—or the capacities of neighborhoods or cities—for organization. However, in New York City, the dense networks of neighborhood organizations make protest virtually routine, and the competitive context among them shapes the interests of organizers.

Certainly, protesters can be extremely disruptive, and even threatening. For instance, during the Koko's boycott in the late 1980s, shoppers reported harassment by protesters marching in front of the store (Browne 1988; Mwalilino 1988). But reporters at the scene observed a difference between marchers supporting the boycott and leaders organizing the protest. One marcher yelled, "Let's burn it down!" (Mwalilino 1988) Organizers, however, used their bullhorns repeatedly to try to cool outbursts.[51] Importantly, protest leaders organized tensions so that they were channeled into protest rather than violence. One need not see this as a moral obligation felt by boycott leaders. Maintaining control over the tenor of protests is in the interest of community organizers simply because it better enables them to realize their goals. Once violence occurs, community organizers can no longer exert control. In a competitive field, their reputations suffer, and they risk losing support to other activists.

The evidence from New York allows me to make preliminary observations regarding the four questions that remained from the national-level analysis of black-Korean conflicts. First, what role do tensions play in producing nonviolent conflict? Tensions alone may not have been enough to activate black residents to boycott. Even if certain objective conditions (such as the factors associated with competition theory or middleman minority theory) must be present for conflicts to occur, neighborhood residents are not likely to mobilize for conflict unless convincing subjective interpretations of those conditions are available. Activists provide those interpretations. For instance, boycott leaders in New York City made frequent attempts to link the contexts of individual merchant-customer disputes to larger concerns like economic control of black neighborhoods and respect for black communities. The role of tensions may thus be linked to the strength of black nationalism, which offers appealing interpretations of the apparent disparities between blacks and Koreans and explanations for the disrespect black customers perceive. In other words, one might find evidence supporting a relationship between the sociological forces that produce tensions and the occurrence of boycotts in places where black nationalism is more prevalent among activists. Other studies of black-Korean conflicts have noted the role played by black nationalism (Kim 2000; Light, Har-Chvi, and Kan 1994; Min 1996). Black nationalism, however, is not a monolithic category—different styles exist, with different emphases. For now, suffice it to say that the community organizers in New York City who led boycotts often practiced a highly activist, radical, and antiestablishment form of black nationalism. As the next chapter shows, the characteristics of the movement in Los Angeles were much different.

Second, if traditional-style political institutions increase the propensity for nonviolent conflict, do they also dampen collective violence? Minor incidents of violence involving African and Korean Americans were common in New York City, but more severe incidents were rare and collective violence was nonexistent; thus, political institutions may only be effective at preventing these latter, more damaging, forms. Also, the participatory impact of political institutions and their impact on community organizing may provide only half the answer. The behavior, degree of involvement, and structure of police departments may provide the other half. In New York City, protest leaders and police worked to the common end of controlling picket lines. For different reasons, both sought to maintain relative order; moreover, both had the resources to do so.

This relationship among police and activists in New York City has extended to racial confrontations other than black-Korean conflicts. For instance, during a 1997 march protesting the police torture of Haitian immigrant Abner Louima, police conferred with leaders of the march to keep the event orderly (Kifner 1997). In 1999, during demonstrations against the police shooting of Amadou Diallo, an unarmed black man, protest organizers and high-ranking police officials met often, as reporter Dan Barry explained, "to confirm ground rules established in earlier negotiations" in a "cordial choreography of street theater that has come to define many demonstrations." On that occasion, exchanges between protesters and police appeared exceptionally cooperative:

> The police politely explained that to get arrested on charges of disorderly conduct the demonstrators would have to block both entrances to the building. In turn, the demonstrators promised not to resist arrest. At times the organizers have even provided the police with the names of those planning to be arrested—a thoughtful act designed to expedite warrant checks and, ultimately, the release of the conscientious scofflaws. (Barry 1999)

Of course, police and activists do not always keep each other so well informed during protests. The extent of coordination may vary among different sets of protesters. Moreover, providing police with too much information can mean that protest leaders sacrifice some control over demonstrations. The line is a fine one and the balance delicate—both sides desire control. And police may not always reciprocate. The conditions under which police choose to cooperate are worth discovering, a matter I discuss in chapter 6.

Cooperation between police and black activists in New York City has not meant that riots will never happen, just that they are less likely to happen and smaller when they do. Police enjoy the formal resources and backing of city governments; protesters, however do not. Even when spurred by the political context to mobilize neighborhoods, most activists make do with meager resources in the face of broader social and economic forces, which place barriers in the way of their efforts to mobilize. Consequently, plenty of potential protesters remain unreached (or unreachable) by community organizers. Rev. Herbert Daughtry admitted as much in his "painful" reflections on the 1990 rioting in Crown Heights:

> Let me emphasize that the people, mostly youth, who were engaged in the eruption were unknown to me. Everybody agreed that these youths, mostly of Caribbean background, were alienated, angry, and fearless. A statistic worth noting is that . . . of the 90 odd people arrested, 60 or so gave no place of employment. These young people did not belong to anybody's anything. I have criticized Black leadership, myself included for allowing such a large segment of our community to be unattached. (Noel 1992, 32)

The failure of activists to reach young people hardly means that all thanks go to the police. In response to a state report that charged the NYPD with a "leadership vacuum" during the Crown Heights rioting, former Commissioner Lee Brown claimed credit. "We avoided, with the action we took, a Los Angeles-type riot," Brown said (Verhovek 1997). Brown's response overstates the case. But the size of the NYPD and its relationship with activists, both consequences of New York's political structure, are partly responsible for the absence of conflagrations the size of the Los Angeles riots. Thus, the New York City case demonstrates that political institutions may dampen violence by impacting two separate factors: the depth of community organizing and the practices of the police. Even more crucial, perhaps, were the ties between the two. In large protest situations, community organizers and police commanders were experienced at working together.

Third, what exactly is the relationship between the two forms of conflict? Did boycotts lead to violence? Dennis DeLeon recalled an increase in "anti-Asian bias incidents" after the Red Apple boycott began (DeLeon 1996). However, no increase in severe racial violence resulted from the massive mobilizations on Church Avenue, or from any other black-Korean conflicts in New York City. Instead, reports of violence frequently served as opportunities for activism; as Table 4.1 shows, eight of the fourteen boycotts followed reports of violence.

Finally, why are boycotts more intractable in some places than in others? The protracted nature of most black-Korean conflicts in New York, at least prior to the Red Apple boycott, clearly had something to do with the multiple, uncoordinated responses of third parties. The actions of the mayor were important, but not solely determinative of the course of the conflict. Interventions by other public officials and institutions and by black and Korean organizations also mattered. The intervention of certain public institutions—the courts and the police—served to prolong the Red Apple boycott in particular. Finally, the strategies of boycotters and Korean trade organizations—and their unwillingness to negotiate—precluded quick resolutions.

Chapter 5

Los Angeles: Fire without Smoke

The sheer scale of the violence in 1992 took Los Angeles by surprise. Previous racial and ethnic conflicts had been relatively easy to resolve, and practitioners of ethnic peace could breathe a sigh of relief when they heard about events in New York City. During the 1980s, New Yorkers had become accustomed to hearing repeated, dire predictions that their city would explode; Angelenos, however, saw or heard little to suggest that a major conflagration lay ahead—much less one that would involve Korean Americans and African Americans.

Just twelve months before the riots, a column in the *Los Angeles Times* reported that a "group of business, religious and community leaders has been successful in avoiding the acrimonious boycotts that characterize Black/Korean relationships in New York City" (Fairchild 1991). As the city would learn in 1992, however, the absence of overt conflict did not mean the success of race relations; it just meant that existing tensions had failed to take visible, collective form.

To be sure, signs of tensions were present, and astute observers noticed them. But Los Angeles had been home to one of the nation's longest-lived biracial political coalitions, which had put Mayor Tom Bradley in office in 1973 and kept him there until 1993. Relations among racial and ethnic groups may not have been perfect, but they appeared far better than in New York. Consequently, the city was ill prepared for the severity of the violence in 1992. One might have expected mass violence to be preceded by telltale signs: when one sees smoke, fire is not far behind. In Los Angeles, however, the fire came with little warning.

Long before the riots, frequent, organized protest was conspicuous by its absence from the streets of Los Angeles. Like New York, the city was rife with opportunities for local organizers to mobilize their communities around individual disputes in order to advance causes and build organizations. Unlike New York, however, few boycotts materialized. Instead, violence became the currency of conflict. Violence was the focus of mediators who hoped to ward off conflicts, and during the 1992 riots violence was the outlet for tensions. Reports of violence rarely provoked community mobilization by neighborhood activists.

An analysis of the development of intergroup relations in Los Angeles during the 1980s and 1990s demonstrates that the nature of conflict in Los Angeles arose from the city's political and community organizational context, which also shaped the pattern of intervention by third parties. As in the Red Apple protest in New York, Los Angeles's most protracted boycott, which targeted a store called John's Liquor[1] in 1991, began with a report of violence and attracted the attention of public officials and other third parties. But due to the differing political and organizational context in Los Angeles, it was far shorter and ended in a negotiated agreement between the boycotters and Korean merchants.

The 1992 riots in Los Angeles represented both the culmination of tensions and a turning point in relations between blacks and Koreans, as the Red Apple boycott had in New York. In the aftermath of the riots, community organizers pursued a third path, between boycotts and violence, by mobilizing the residents of riot-torn neighborhoods in a campaign against the rebuilding of liquor stores—many of them owned by Koreans. These events, viewed in the context of prior black-Korean relations in Los Angeles and in contrast with the development of conflicts in New York, provide important evidence needed to solve the puzzle of politics and conflict.

THE EARLY 1980S: TENSIONS AND A CALL TO BOYCOTT

As in New York City, public attention to black-Korean tensions in Los Angeles began with a series of stories published in the city's major black readership newspaper, the *Los Angeles Sentinel*.[2] In late summer 1983, these front-page features reported anger and frustration among African American residents who had encountered mistreatment by Korean storeowners (Cleaver 1983b, 1983c, 1983f, 1983g).[3]

The *Sentinel* did not stop at merely reporting the emerging tensions, however. It took a stand. Its counterpart in New York City, the *Amsterdam News*, had begun its reportage by condemning blacks who had expressed ill will toward Koreans. The *Sentinel*, however, did the opposite, condemning Korean merchants for mistreating black customers. James Cleaver, the *Sentinel*'s executive editor, pointed out that the "essential anger" was directed not only at Korean merchants but also at "the banking and business system," which he claimed routinely provided Asian entrepreneurs with loans for business start-ups while systematically denying them to blacks (Cleaver 1983c).[4] But Cleaver apportioned the blame to "Asian merchants" as well, accusing them of dismissing black employees, treating customers in a "cold, distant and . . . disrespectful manner," simultaneously charging customers high prices and undercutting competitors' prices, laughing at blacks behind their backs, and mistreating patrons (Cleaver 1983b). As evidence of the "documented amounts of forceful and illogical behavior" of Korean merchants, the paper quoted black businessmen, readers who had written letters to the editor, and residents of Crenshaw—a middle-class district that was to be devastated in the riots a decade later (Ivory 1983).

Interviews and letters-to-the-editor had shown a propensity for violence: one reader wrote to the paper that, if an Asian merchant "ever puts his or her hands on me, they'd better be prepared for another version of the Vietnam War" (Ivory 1983). However, the *Los Angeles Sentinel* denounced violence as a solution to the problem. Instead, it called for blacks to boycott offending stores. "It doesn't have to be an organized effort," the paper told black Angelenos. "It just has to be one family after another deciding they have been abused enough." To spur readers into action, the paper invoked the memory of the most celebrated of black protests: "Remember the Montgomery bus boycott?" (*Los Angeles Sentinel* 1983b).[5]

The *Sentinel*'s reportage drew harsh reprimands from the L.A. County Human Relations Commission, whose director, Eugene Mornell, castigated Cleaver for his "inflammatory" use of "racial stereotypes" and "implications of racial exclusion" (Mornell 1983). Responding to the commission's broadside, the paper claimed that public opinion was on its side. Cleaver's series on black-Korean tensions had "drawn more favorable letters than any other article or series of articles in the past 10 years." In one such letter, a reader supported the *Sentinel*'s proposal for action: "We need to be networking among ourselves and discovering those merchants who have abused us, and then quietly, without any fanfare or picket lines, start boycotting those stores" (Cleaver 1983d). The call to boycott had been issued. In coming years, however, there would be much fanfare, but few picket lines.

The earliest sign of what lay ahead came several months later. The *Sentinel* reported "a proliferation of assaults" against Asian merchants in Crenshaw and repeated its condemnation of violence (*Los Angeles Sentinel* 1984b). Two organizations met to defuse tensions—the Black Agenda, founded by two clergy members, and the Southern California Korean Grocery and Liquor Retail Association (Cleaver 1983e). The association donated 250 Thanksgiving turkeys to the Black Agenda, which distributed them to local churches (*Los Angeles Sentinel* 1983a).

THE MIDDLE TO LATE 1980S: TENSIONS WITHOUT BOYCOTTS

If we are to believe accounts by the city's oldest black newspaper, tensions between African Americans and Korean Americans were rampant in black neighborhoods. The *Sentinel* was not alone in this perception, however; similar observations came from other quarters. Even before the *Sentinel* published its controversial series and called for boycotts, the county Human Relations Commission had held a public hearing to address "the very evident tensions" between members of the two groups (Mornell 1983). In 1986, the Los Angeles chapter of the NAACP announced a "selective buying campaign" to encourage blacks to avoid stores that treated them disrespectfully or that had no black employees (Hernandez 1986). In short, the atmosphere seemed full of opportunities for protest.

When few boycotts actually materialized during the 1980s, observers commonly assumed that African Americans and Korean Americans in Los Angeles had been able to overcome tensions and were enjoying better relations than those in less fortunate cities, such as New York. The strongest evidence for this assumption was the fact that Los Angeles experienced fewer and shorter boycotts than New York City. Blacks led only four boycotts of Korean stores through 1990 (all at the end of the decade), and three thereafter, all in 1991 (see Table 5.1). Most of these were short-lived, last-

Table 5.1. Black-led Boycotts of Korean Stores in Los Angeles, 1980–1995

Store (Neighborhood)	Date[a]	Duration[b]	Peak Size[c]
Finest Market (South Central)	Jan. 1987	3	30
Crenshaw Swap Meet (Crenshaw)	May 1987	8	20
Village Inn Café[d] (Crenshaw)	Aug. 1988	28	20
L.A.-Slauson Swap Meet (South Central)	Dec. 1989	30	20
Empire Liquor[d] (South Central)	Mar. 1991	7	150
La Fiesta Food Warehouse (Watts)	June 1991	55	200
John's Liquor Store[d] (South Central)	June 1991	110	150

[a]Indicates month in which boycott began.
[b]Number of days.
[c]Number of protesters.
[d]Boycott followed a report of violence.
Notes: Some dates, durations, and peak sizes are approximate.
Two additional boycotts took place in nearby cities in Los Angeles County.

ing little more than several weeks. New York City had experienced twice as many boycotts, with an average duration of several months.

Favorable assessments of intergroup relations in Los Angeles, however, mistook the absence of collective action for the successful resolution of tensions. Overt, organized conflict is an inadequate yardstick for measuring tensions. As we saw in New York City, boycotts resulted from more than just tensions—there, they were also fueled by competitive pressures that were present in politics and in neighborhoods. Similarly, tensions alone will not produce boycotts, if the capacity and will for mobilization are missing, as they were in Los Angeles.

Four Brief Boycotts

The first boycott of a Korean store in Los Angeles, in January 1987, was short-lived and quickly resolved. It targeted a store called Finest Market in South Central Los Angeles and was led by Verma Foreman, a former employee who charged that the owner engaged in "discriminatory practices"—not against herself, she said, but against black customers. As many as thirty marchers gathered outside the store on at least one day of the boycott, which lasted a single weekend. The demonstrations ended with a written agreement in which the owner, Young Kim, agreed to hire black employees, donate money to local charities, stock better quality fresh food, reduce prices, and ensure that employees did not abuse customers. Kim acted on several of the promises within a week (Bailey 1987a, 1987b).

The quick success of the boycott prompted a reporter to ask Foreman whether she would "take her fervent campaign and personality to other neighborhoods and stores." Indeed, the *Sentinel* ran a second story on the boycott after receiving more than a dozen telephone calls from readers who expressed support and wanted to know more. But no such large-scale campaign was in the offing. Foreman had no connections to existing community organizations that could aid her in such an effort. As she told the paper, "I've thought about it but I really don't know who or what the powers that be are so I wouldn't even know where to begin" (Bailey 1987b). Despite the *Sentinel's* characterization of the event as a "citizens' uprising" that had "awakened a sleeping giant," the boycott was no more than a minor conflict with little chance of spreading. The newspaper itself, rather than networks of neighborhood residents, had served as a link to potential participants. Without leaders interested in mobilizing them, however, the conflict fizzled.

The next two boycotts in Los Angeles targeted swap meets, huge warehouse buildings that housed scores of stalls rented to individual vendors. Like traditional outdoor markets, swap meets drew customers shopping for bargains and discounts. Swap meets were becoming ubiquitous in Los Angeles, and many had not only Korean owners but Korean vendors renting stalls as well (Thom 1996). The stalls sold a variety of wares: clothing, appliances, cosmetics, records, and videos. The two boycotts at swap meets—at the Crenshaw Swap Meet in 1987 and the L.A.-Slauson Swap Meet in 1989—failed to attract the attention of local elected officials but did draw federal mediators from the U.S. Justice Department's Community Relations Service (CRS).[6]

In the Crenshaw case, black business owners from the neighborhood mounted the boycott, saying that the owner of the swap meet refused to rent stalls to black merchants. Protesters actively demonstrated for a little over a week. Charles Cook, leader of a group called United Black People of America, charged the owners with exploiting residents and "draining what little financial resources exist" in the neighborhood (McRae 1987). According to the swap meet's own figures, five out of the fifty-two stalls were rented to African American vendors; the remainder were rented to Korean Americans (Thom 1996).

Cook, who ran a beauty shop next door to the swap meet and ran the pickets between appointments (ibid.), told reporters that he attempted to contact Mayor Bradley, State Assembly member Maxine Waters, and City Council member Pat Russell (McRae 1987). Unlike in New York City, where the multiplicity of responses crowded out efforts by federal mediators to intervene in boycotts, the general inattention from local officials in the Crenshaw boycott left ample room for staff from the Community Relations Service to step in. The mediators helped the protesters and the owner reach an agreement, although not until nearly a year later (due partly to the complication of a change in management at the swap meet). A written agreement resulted in changes in the swap meet's policies. The following year, the Crenshaw Swap Meet was upholding its end of the bargain, in part by donating money to two neighborhood social service programs (Thom 1996).

In December 1989, a group known as the Organization of Mutual Neighborhood Interest (OMNI) boycotted the L.A.-Slauson Swap Meet. It rallied a larger number of community residents at the outset, but the size of protests dwindled quickly. "The staying power was difficult," said Stephen Thom, the CRS mediator who intervened (Thom 1996). Once again, with the assistance of CRS mediators, boycotters reached an agreement with the swap meet that resulted in policy changes there. In addition, Jay Lee, L.A.-Slauson's manager, hired a man of black and Korean parentage to handle disputes (Dungee 1991).

At about the same time as the L.A.-Slauson conflict, OMNI boycotted another swap meet in the neighboring city of Inglewood, home to a black middle-class population.[7] Ward Wesley, the community activist who led OMNI and owner of a janitorial service, targeted Korean stores that showed disrespect to black customers. Wesley not only organized the boycott; he acted as a voice of moderation as well. Concerned about the potential for blacks to react violently to Korean merchants, he saw a need to channel tensions peacefully:

> Some (black) people, after years of struggle are making $70,000. They may stop in a Korean merchant's store, get disrespected, called a name, and, after years of all that hard work, you really feel ready to kill somebody. We are already killing each other in the black community. . . . I don't want to see anything bad like that happen. . . . But that's how bad the sentiment is running. I know these young Crips running around feel that way, and, as dangerous as they are, no telling what they may start doing. (Njeri 1989)

Ironically, shortly after the L.A.-Slauson boycott, Ward Wesley and Jay Lee were among the 150 black and Korean businesspeople and community leaders attending a dinner and forum sponsored by organizations hoping to foster better relations (Dungee 1990).

One more boycott took place in the 1980s, at a restaurant called the Village Inn Café in Crenshaw. The conflict was sparked by a dispute between two black customers and the Village Inn's owner over an order of french fries. One of Los Angeles's more protracted Korean store boycotts, it lasted nearly a month, although demonstrations may have taken place only on certain days during that time. Officials from two local NAACP chapters "endorsed" the boycott and joined the picketing, which involved some twenty demonstrators. Police called to the scene refused to arrest the owner on assault charges, but after one of the customers sent a letter to city officials, the owner was charged with misdemeanor assault by City Attorney James Hahn. Other officials who were sent copies, including Mayor Tom Bradley and City Council members Nate Holden and Ruth Galanter, took no action (McRae 1988).

Intergroup Harmony or Collective Passivity?

Black-led boycotts of Korean stores in Los Angeles were few in number, short in duration, and small in size. Does this mean black-Korean relations were better than in New York City? A number of observers have compared Los Angeles favorably with New York City in their relations between blacks and Koreans. Sociologist Pyong Gap Min makes the strongest case, offering three reasons for the scarcity of collective action in Los Angeles during the 1980s: first, black nationalists had less influence in Los Angeles than in New York; second, Tom Bradley, a black mayor, was able to influence black leaders to resolve conflicts more easily than Ed Koch, a white mayor; and third, in Los Angeles a biracial organization called the Black Korean Alliance (BKA) was able to prevent conflicts (Min 1996, 83–84).

This explanation correctly identifies the realms of politics and community organizations as holding the answer. On the particulars, however, it is mistaken on each point. First, black nationalists did not have less influence in Los Angeles than in New York. Instead, black nationalism assumed a different dominant form—one that did not promote protest. Second, although Bradley mediated one boycott effectively in 1991, he did not work extensively to prevent conflicts during the 1980s. Third, the BKA was more reactive than preemptive in its efforts, meaning it did not prevent conflicts so much as it attempted to shape the public dialogue surrounding conflicts. Each of these points speaks to the nature of black-Korean conflicts in Los Angeles and the context that shaped them.

Black Nationalism in Los Angeles

For decades, Los Angeles has been fertile ground for black nationalism. The Black Panther Party, for example, "bloomed" in the aftermath of the 1965 Watts riots, partly as an organized resistance to the Los Angeles Police Department (Horne 1995, 13). The Panthers put together a highly influential black nationalist organization that had a revolutionary, internationalist tinge—and a short life span, as the party was "virtually extinct about five years after their 1966 founding" (Horne 1995, 197). Its legacy in Los Angeles was limited (for the most part) to only one part of its program: an emphasis on black pride. In fact, as historian Gerald Horne argues, political repression of left-wing activism and the subsequent decline of working-class organizations in postwar Los Angeles narrowed the scope of black community activism in general. Instead of the Panthers' "revolutionary" brand of black nationalism, which had a more politically oriented, outwardly focused style and aimed at direct confrontation of the state, black communities were left mainly with another strand: a more passive "cultural" nationalism.

Cultural nationalism stressed inwardly focused solutions such as self-improvement and identity; and it was conservative, in the sense that it did not challenge the foundations of American politics (democracy) or economics (capitalism) (ibid., 199). Instead, it promoted coexistence with these institutions. The dominance of cultural nationalism left its imprint on Los Angeles in two ways. First, it facilitated the rise of street gangs, which offered violence as a means of building racial pride.[8] Second, it fed the growing influence of the Nation of Islam.

The strength of the Nation of Islam in Los Angeles exemplified the brand of nationalism most widely available to black communities. In New York City, the prominence of the December 12 Movement reflected the availability of a radical form of black nationalism, which kept alive the confrontational, antigovernment style of the Black Panthers. In Los Angeles, however, no "militant substitute" had arisen since the 1960s to challenge the Nation's influence. An inward focus on black pride and economics not only promoted middle-class values but also fueled the growth of street gangs (Horne 1995, 362); Louis Farrakhan became the one national black figure that the Bloods and Crips "seem to take seriously," as Mike Davis (1992a, 99) argues. Black nationalism's more conservative orientation in Los Angeles made that city "a center of NOI influence." As Horne points out, "weekly figures showed that its newspaper, the *Final Call*, usually sold more copies there than in New York City, where the black population was more substantial and had deeper roots" (Horne 1995, 362).

As the *Los Angeles Sentinel* was reporting tensions between blacks and Koreans in the early 1980s, it was also documenting the huge crowds attending temple dedications by Louis Farrakhan (Cleaver 1983a). The turn to a conservative nationalism in Los Angeles likely derived at least in part from the black population's lack of experience with strong political organizations, a consequence of reform-style government. Consequently, African American activism in Los Angeles did not acquire the more outward, political orientation of its East Coast counterpart.

One result of the Nation of Islam's influence was its impact on community organizations—and one in particular that became involved in black-Korean conflicts. Unlike the December 12 Movement in New York City, which considered the Nation of Islam a bitter rival, an organization in Los Angeles known as the Brotherhood Crusade, which launched boycotts of Korean stores in the city, was led by an ally of Louis Farrakhan. Danny Bakewell, a millionaire businessman, activist, and philanthropist, stood with Farrakhan on the stage at the Million Man March in Washington in 1995 and appeared frequently with him at speaking engagements in Los Angeles. Although not a "practicing Muslim," Bakewell had been a member of the Nation during the 1970s and continued to embrace the Nation's self-help philosophy and acceptance—even advocacy—of capitalism (Njeri 1997, 120–27). Bakewell also maintained ties to the city's political establishment, including Mayor Bradley (*Los Angeles Sentinel*, 1991a; Njeri 1997, 124).[9]

If New York City's December 12 Movement was "underground" in its orientation, the Brotherhood Crusade was anything but—it received funding from the United Way for its charity activities, and Los Angeles city and county government workers could choose to have a portion of their paychecks automatically deducted as contributions to the organization (*Los Angeles Sentinel* 1991a; Njeri 1997). Bakewell himself owned residences in Pasadena and Santa Barbara and a ranch north of Los Angeles; he commuted to work in a chauffeur-driven car (Njeri 1997, 119–20). Despite his wealthy lifestyle, however, Bakewell was one of the few major black figures in the city said to have "street" credibility and who could get significant media play—a phenomenon that he and others attributed to a leadership void in the black community (Aubry 1996; Njeri 1997, 124, 138–39).

Perhaps even more interesting was the way Bakewell and the Brotherhood Crusade reflected the organization of interests in reform-style cities, which tend to advantage political influence by growth-minded corporations. Bakewell's influence was fed and enhanced not only by his ties to public officials but also by his lucrative investment activities and by the Crusade's corporate sponsorship. Bakewell had been an investor in downtown development projects, apartment buildings, and a shopping center, and was president of a downtown municipal securities firm for several years (Freer 1994, 194; Njeri 1997, 123–24). The Crusade's corporate sponsors included Coors, ARCO, Northrop, Lockheed, Coca Cola, and Sony. It would be difficult to imagine Bakewell's organization challenging either the economic or the political status quo (Freer 1994, 194–95). Indeed, that orientation accorded not only with his own economic interests but also with the conservative values promoted by the Nation of Islam.

The Decline of the Bradley Coalition

Although Mayor Bradley was able to use his influence with black community leaders to mediate the 1991 John's Liquor boycott effectively—helping to manage and contain it—there is little evidence that he was able to use his influence with black community leaders to *prevent* boycotts or to resolve other conflicts.

During the late 1980s, when most of Los Angeles's Korean store boycotts occurred, Bradley's biracial coalition experienced a "breakdown of consensus," diminishing the political capital with which the mayor might have influenced conflict-minded activists. Previously, the coalition had experienced a twelve-year period of growing strength. But then the coalition began to show cracks. In 1985, Bradley found himself caught between blacks and liberals over a controversial visit by Louis Farrakhan. In 1987, two Bradley allies lost bids for seats on the fifteen-member City Council. In 1989, Bradley was challenged by a strong mayoral candidate for the first time. Bradley won, but the challenge revealed new vulnerabilities. Finally, in 1989, a financial scandal rocked his administration (Sonenshein 1993, 191–209).

More seriously, Bradley began to lose support among black voters, a major part of his previously rock-solid base. In a 1989 poll that asked about alternative mayoral candidates, "a surprisingly large minority" of black respondents chose Maxine Waters (ibid., 208). Bradley's influence with black community leaders actually declined, as they saw him being increasingly linked to downtown development interests more than to black neighborhoods. Mike Davis argues that Bradley's regime was "little more than catastrophic for inner-city residents" and rewarded blacks with "largely symbolic goods" (Davis 1987, 70). That assessment may be too harsh; Raphael Sonenshein points out that the Bradley coalition was powerless to stop larger, nation-wide forces leading Los Angeles to greater economic polarization. Regardless, Bradley's policies began to draw skepticism. Black community organizers became further disillusioned with the mayor when Bradley disbanded the city's Community Development Advisory Committee (Freer 1994, 185). A black newspaper columnist reflected this when he wrote that Bradley had "rebuilt downtown, the westside, the valley, the whole city, while his own beginnings turned to blight and despair" (Sonenshein 1993). In short, Bradley was hardly in a position to be pushing black activists to halt divisive Korean store boycotts—the very tools that activists were using to highlight the lack of investment in and respect for black communities, which they laid at least partly at Bradley's doorstep.

Moreover, during the 1980s, other black leaders in Bradley's political circle refrained from loudly or publicly opposing Korean store boycotts. Instead, some voiced support for them, at least in principle, as an alternative to violence. For instance, before his election to the City Council in 1991, Mark Ridley-Thomas—then the executive director of the Los Angeles chapter of the Southern Christian Leadership Conference (SCLC), and later a close Bradley ally—expressed support for the concept of boycotts:

> By all means, if any Korean-American merchant is treating customers unfairly, employ every nonviolent means of direct action to put that particular business out of business. . . . But the same standard needs to be applied to others, irrespective of ethnicity. (Njeri 1989)

Ridley-Thomas later sponsored negotiations in the John's Liquor Boycott, and (along with other black politicians) enjoyed good relations with the boycott's leader, Danny Bakewell. Given these tendencies, it is difficult to substantiate the claim that Los Angeles experienced few boycotts because Bradley or other black leaders opposed them.

The comparison of Bradley's leadership in Los Angeles with the lack of an equivalent figure in New York City as an explanation for the lack of conflict breaks down further when one considers that other leaders were available in New York City besides Mayor Koch. Politicians with greater grassroots support, most notably Brooklyn's State Assembly Representative Al Vann, mediated conflicts in New York during the 1980s, but their interventions did not reduce the level of overt conflict. Moreover, the New York case showed that black mayors do not automatically possess the limitless capacity to influence black activists. Just months before New York's Red Apple boycott began, for instance, Mayor Dinkins had enjoyed the support of black community organizers across the city to an unprecedented extent; however, that support failed to translate into political capital in black neighborhoods that might have enabled him to end the boycott quickly. At bottom, mayoral leadership can be effective, but not as much as is often imagined. More generally, nationwide a higher proportion of black elected officials is associated with more frequent boycotts of Korean stores, not less, as the analysis in Chapter 3 established.

The Black-Korean Alliance

The Black-Korean Alliance (BKA), established after the shooting deaths of four Korean merchants in 1986, was a unique biracial organization. Its members made noble attempts to channel tensions and shape dialogues among blacks and Koreans in productive ways. As such, hopes ran high. In 1991, a column in the *Los Angeles Times* declared that the BKA had been key to the city's success in avoiding conflicts: "the alliance succeeded in getting Korean merchants and their protesting customers to talk to each other, thus defusing a potential confrontation" the previous year (Fairchild 1991). However, contrary to this common assumption—that it successfully prevented overt conflicts and thereby eased black-Korean tensions—the BKA functioned mainly in a reactive manner. It was ill-equipped to strike pre-emptively to prevent conflicts, because its members had few resources, little political support—and most important—few grassroots community ties.

At its peak, the BKA consisted of about fifteen individuals who met once a month in different locations, rotating among the organizations to which its members belonged (such as the SCLC, black and Korean churches, and the University of Southern California). There were always two cochairs, one black and one Korean. Many of the members had been recruited into the organization by friends or via previous involvement in joint efforts with other members. As Jan Perry (1996), at the time an aide to council member Michael Woo, put it, "They're already part of a network. . . . Everyone knew each other." Some members who had not previously known each other developed lasting relationships.

In spite of its committed leadership, the organization lacked extensive community ties. Larry Aubry, a community activist who cofounded the

BKA, was keenly aware of the problem: "At the very outset, there weren't a hell of a lot of grassroots there. . . . That was a fairly impressive group of folks, [but] they had no immediate stake. . . . There was concern, they had an interest, but I mean they weren't stakeholders, real stakeholders" (Aubry 1996). For most of the Alliance's life, according to member Bong Hwan Kim, "the BKA was largely individuals" (Kim 1997). The consequences of the organization's lack of strong ties to the grassroots and its members' lack of strong ties to the organization itself meant that it could rarely follow up healthy dialogues between its members with decisive action that would impact race relations. "When a lot of bad things started happening, the members weren't able to, first of all, agree on anything, and then second of all, if it did agree, the members didn't represent any particular segment of either community, or were not connected into the power structure," recalled Alliance member Jerry Yu (1996).

Beyond meager funding from the Los Angeles County Human Relations Commission, the Alliance had little assistance or support from local government. This presented a serious problem, more fundamental than the organization's own deficiencies. Aubry (1987) wrote that "a small group of concerned people is attempting to deal with problems far beyond the scope of their resources. Widespread rhetoric of concern . . . has not been translated into broad-based action." The lack of official support was due in part to the failure of public officials to respond constructively to the BKA's efforts. Moreover, established community leaders did not invest in the organization. "The BKA wasn't really an accepted, valid vehicle, for either community, by the leaders on both sides," said Bong Hwan Kim (1997). "We never really had any of the established leaders come to BKA and play a significant role—the Urban League, the NAACP, the traditional civil rights organizations never joined," the one exception being Joe Hicks, director of the local chapter of the SCLC.

Successive Alliance leaders tried hard to enhance the organization's legitimacy with community institutions, but in the end their repeated efforts met with resistance or, more often, indifference. For many black organizations, its mission simply was "not high on their priority list" compared to more pressing issues such as drugs and poverty (Kim 1997).

The BKA's internal and external problems made it difficult to sustain a consistent, active membership. Not until late 1991—less than a year before it disbanded, and perhaps too late to make a difference before tensions erupted into mass violence—was the BKA able to restructure itself to incorporate community-based groups (Yu 1992, 126). Participation in the organization intensified at this point as reports of violent incidents between blacks and Koreans began to multiply. But by May 1992, just after the riots, the BKA consisted of just four members and two staff (Kim 1994, 106). Its support exhausted and its mission unclear, it soon disbanded.

While the organization existed, its members occasionally tried to respond to merchant-customer disputes before they developed into fullblown conflicts, but according to Aubry (1996), "it was not set up to do that kind of work." Other organizations were better equipped, such as the county Human Relations Commission, which had a larger staff. The commission, however, was not that much larger and dealt with a wide range of other problems as well. Chung Lee, a cochair of the BKA in the late 1980s and president of the Korean Small Business Association in South Central Los Angeles, identified a key consequence of the group's limitations that hindered its capacity to quell conflict: the Black Korean Alliance was not well known, so people in the midst of disputes were not aware that they could seek help from the BKA (Njeri 1989).

Consequently, the BKA did not stop boycotts before they happened. "We were never that proactive," said Bong Hwan Kim (1997). "We were purely reactive." By the time the riots came, the BKA worked "largely in response to the divisive coverage by the media," holding forums, community meetings, and press conferences in response to incidents of violence (Kim 1997). It spent its time trying to mend fences rather than build bridges.[10]

Other organizations besides the BKA, such as the Asian-Pacific American Dispute Resolution Center (under Director Marcia Choo, who would intervene in developing disputes) and the Martin Luther King Jr. Dispute Resolution Center (coordinated by Avis Ridley-Thomas), attempted to ease tensions. The Korean American Coalition sometimes received complaints from black residents about stores, but simply lacked the resources to respond (Yu 1996) Another was a joint effort by black and Korean churches to "promote understanding" using "the common bond of Christianity" (Johnson 1985). Begun in 1985 by ministers from both communities and a black state representative, Mervyn Dymally, the group sponsored scholarships for black students funded by Korean churches, and ministers held joint services.[11] Assessing the success of the ministers' efforts is difficult. In 1986, however, Rev. Huey Rachal pointed out that they were not reaching as many people as he had hoped:

> We have thousands of young men and middle-aged men walking the street. . . . They're tired, they're bored, they're disgusted. . . . How can the churches keep the lid on that? . . . Everything is in one jug, and it is fermenting. Any day someone is going to shake that bottle and that top is going to fly off. They thought they had a lid on it in '65. They didn't. (Hernandez 1986)

In Los Angeles, churches were among the few community institutions available for organizing and channeling tensions. Another type of organization with the potential to channel tensions, the labor union, was becoming less effective at that task as unemployment rates soared and young black men lost their jobs (Davis 1987, 74–76). Moreover, unions were based in the workplace, not the neighborhoods, limiting their potential to contain community conflicts.

THE COURSE OF A CONFLICT: THE JOHN'S LIQUOR BOYCOTT

Unlike New York City's longest black boycott of a Korean store, which defied mediation for more than a year and mobilized thousands of protesters, counterprotesters, and police, the longest boycott in Los Angeles lasted only three months, attracted far fewer protesters and third party interventions, and ended with the closing of the targeted store via a negotiated settlement. Political institutions in Los Angeles made the boycott of John's Liquor both less contentious—by precluding the kind of competitive organizational context native to New York—and easier to resolve—by centralizing informal power among a smaller circle of political and community elites.

The Incident

As the summer of 1991 began, the local news media in Los Angeles was becoming saturated with reports of violence between blacks and Koreans. Against this backdrop, a shooting took place that was not initially as widely reported as other incidents, but which attracted attention for the boycott that followed. Within a week-and-a-half of the shooting, protests commenced at the store where it had taken place, and the *Los Angeles Sentinel* issued an ominous declaration: "Many are afraid that these incidents and those like them will eventually erupt into violence in the multi-ethnic area" (Mitchell 1991b).

Lee Arthur Mitchell, a forty-six-year-old former boxer and resident of South Central Los Angeles, rode his bicycle down Western Avenue the evening of June 4. His ride ended at John's Liquor, a small Korean-owned shop he frequented near the corner of Seventy-ninth Street. After parking his bike outside, Mitchell entered the store to buy a beer, or perhaps a wine cooler. He was not armed.

What happened inside John's Liquor we know mainly from the account of the store's owner, Tae Sam Park, and his wife; it was empty of customers. The Parks told police that Mitchell at first offered to pay less than the sale price for the beverage—although police later found adequate change on his body. When Mrs. Park refused, Mitchell asked if he could make up the difference with a gold chain he produced, and after a second rebuff, stuck his hand into his jacket pocket to simulate a gun. After that, it was said that

Mitchell tried to take cash from the register but was prevented by Mr. Park, who rushed out to his wife's screams. After Mitchell allegedly broke three of Park's ribs in a fight, the merchant grabbed a handgun he kept behind the counter and shot five bullets into him (Dungee and Mitchell 1991; Mitchell 1991b).

Protesters and Mitchell's friends and family later raised doubts about the Parks' story. Activist Danny Bakewell charged that the store's security camera, which might have captured the incident, had been tampered with (Dungee and Mitchell 1991; Njeri 1997, 132). The fact that Mitchell rode a bicycle to the store suggested that he had not intended to burglarize it (Gardner 1996), and neighbors who knew him argued that he "didn't have a violent bone in his body" (Dungee and Mitchell 1991).

Law enforcement responded to the incident with a low profile. After an investigation, and in light of the Parks' testimony of self-defense, police cleared Tae Sam Park in the killing.[12] Similarly, the district attorney's office did not file charges. (Protesters later called for the district attorney to reopen the case, making it a condition of the boycott's resolution, but it never happened.)

Who Were the Boycotters?

Within a week, members of Bethel A.M.E. Church—located directly across the street from John's Liquor—began the boycott. The church, led by Rev. Edgar Boyd, was joined by the Brotherhood Crusade, led by Danny Bakewell. These two groups not only spearheaded the boycott but provided the bulk of demonstrators.[13] From the beginning, their aim was simple and clear: to close the store and force Park to leave.

According to church officer and protest organizer Joseph Gardner (1996), the Mitchell incident "sparked something that hadn't occurred in the community before, and that was a unity of purpose." Neighborhood residents were not accustomed to organizing protests, and the boycott helped to solidify and extend that unity. During the boycott, Bakewell took a hard line, vowing not to negotiate with anyone for ninety days (Mitchell 1991a). For Rev. Boyd and the church organizers, however, it was a different story: they met with the Korean American Grocers Association (KAGRO), Mayor Bradley and his staff, and other public officials, all of whom tried to persuade them to end their picketing. The protesters refused. "When you're standing on the right side of the issue, you have no problem," said Gardner. "The mayor's office and the Korean grocers and the community at large did not think we were going to stay on the firing lines as long as we did. But through perseverance and dedication of community residents, we did manage to stay" (Gardner 1996).

Picketers marched on the sidewalk in front of the store for 110 days, every day, from the time John's Liquor opened to the time it closed (ibid.). With a base of operations not fifty feet away (in the church across the street), it would have been surprising if protesters had not been able to maintain a continuous presence—the store's location allowed boycott leaders to surmount logistical obstacles, such as transporting marchers or monitoring the scene. Danny Bakewell referred to John's Liquor as "well situated" (Njeri 1997, 122). Consequently, as many as 150 marchers gathered outside the store during the early stages of the boycott. Church organizers considered the option of expanding their protests to the office of the district attorney in order to press the call for a prosecution of Tae Sam Park. However, leaders decided against the move for logistical reasons: as Gardner (1996) stated, it would have been "too difficult to do that." Even from across the street, however, maintaining a presence became difficult as the boycott wore on. In its final days, the number of protesters dwindled to about half a dozen (Gardner 1996; Mydans 1991a).[14]

Like in New York's Red Apple boycott, the boycotters at John's Liquor tried to deflect charges of racism in selecting a Korean-owned store. Church members claimed Park sold liquor to minors, and they disliked the availability of pornography in the store. Moreover, according to Gardner, Park "didn't have a history of getting along with the community." In order to demonstrate that the boycott was not racially motivated, Rev. Boyd pointed out that demonstrators routinely shopped at another Korean-owned store nearby (Mitchell 1991a). Bakewell issued a somewhat enigmatic declaration meant to buttress Boyd's point: "Although the campaign could be termed racial in composition, the campaign is definitely not racist in nature" (Mitchell 1991a).

On the picket lines, demonstrators chanted "Stop the killing" and "Get out of our community" and carried placards with statements like "This store is deadly" and "Respect us or leave us" (Dungee and Mitchell 1991; Schatzman 1991a). For the most part, marchers resisted explicitly racial content in their cries. Keeping the protests calm evidently took some work by protest leaders. Shortly after the initial incident, Black-Korean Alliance member Larry Aubry visited the scene and observed the level that tensions had reached:

By the next day there were flyers coming out of [Bethel A.M.E.]. Very inflammatory. I mean they were clearly something about, we're being abused, clearly the implication was cutting it along the Korean-black lines. . . . They initially had signs up there, "Go Back to Korea." They had to take those down. They took them down. They got other signs. So bad, even Bakewell couldn't support it. (Aubry 1996)

But potential volatility came not just from the crowds of protesters—Bakewell was responsible too. The Brotherhood Crusade leader gave the conflict a racial spin with his fiery demeanor: "This was an extremely emotional thing. Bakewell was . . . heavy, heavy rhetoric. You know how he started off? He says, 'We are here to protest the murder of our brother.' That kind of tone set it." Bakewell may have inflamed tensions at the same time as he "played the press" with color-blind rhetoric (ibid.), but he also helped contain tensions to some extent—perhaps because he wanted to avoid criticism for appearing too anti-Korean, but also because violence would not serve his purpose. For instance, the Nation of Islam contributed marchers to the picket lines, and even expressed a desire "to play a major role" in the boycott. Boycott organizers ruled that out, however, deciding to retain the protest's neighborhood orientation (Gardner 1996)—and also, no doubt, to retain control of the conflict and its agenda.

The success of the boycott in attracting attention and support led Bakewell to propose organizing a "flying force of picketers," with the help of black churches and community organizations, that would target and shut down stores throughout South Central if they failed to respect black consumers (Mydans 1991a; Njeri 1997, 122). He announced the formation of the group, called the African American Honor Committee, just before the end of the boycott. And the Brotherhood Crusade did lead a couple of brief boycotts of Korean stores later: Don's Market, a Korean grocery in the nearby city of Hawthorne, in 1991; and a Korean hat shop in 1996 (Min 1996; Mydans 1991b). But a well-organized "flying force" never materialized on the scale Bakewell proposed.

Responses by Black Organizations and Public Officials

Unlike the Red Apple boycott in New York City, the John's Liquor conflict failed to stir divisions among black Angelenos or to draw public officials into the fray. On the one hand, black community organizations and leaders in Los Angeles offered little explicit support for the boycott. On the other hand, they also refrained from any vocal opposition. The Southern Christian Leadership Conference allowed mediators the use of its offices for negotiations, but the organization's headquarters were hardly neutral ground—Mark Ridley-Thomas, the SCLC's local director, appeared with Bakewell when the Brotherhood Crusade leader announced plans for an expanded "selective buying campaign" (Mitchell 1991a). Some organizations, such as an association of L.A. County black government employees, did declare support for the boycott (Min 1996, 87).

Larry Aubry appealed to Mayor Bradley and others (such as the Urban League's John Mack and council member Mark Ridley-Thomas) to take a strong stance against Bakewell's boycott, but to no avail. Instead, black community leaders were largely passive and did not rally support for a more "evenhanded" approach than Bakewell's (Aubry 1996). Jerry Yu, executive director of the Korean American Coalition, contended that "for the most part, city officials didn't want any part of it. And they withheld making any comments or statements for a long time" (Yu 1996).

City Council members were involved, but not centrally. For the office of Michael Woo, who became a mediator, the boycott "wasn't the biggest thing going on" (Perry 1996). Still, Woo reportedly tried to get other black leaders to persuade Bakewell to talk to Korean merchants (through KAGRO) during his ninety-day moratorium on negotiations. According to a source quoted in the *Los Angeles Times,* however, black community leaders were hesitant to oppose him: "Privately, they loved to criticize him, but publicly, they were afraid to cross him. . . . There were a lot of leaders who felt that this [the boycott] was the wrong way to go, but they felt paralyzed" (Stolberg and Clifford 1991). The scenario could hardly have been more different than the one a year earlier in New York City. Characteristic of black-Korean conflicts in Los Angeles, and unlike in New York City, public officials neither played a major role in mediating a resolution nor intervened significantly in any other fashion. And black leaders were unwilling to risk squandering political capital in opposing a popular activist.

Closing the Store: The Mixed Response of Korean Organizations

The boycott of John's Liquor proved a watershed for Korean community organizations. Prior to the boycott, they had rarely coordinated formally on issues of intergroup relations. Jerry Yu recalled (1996) that the boycott "was one of the reasons why our community, the Korean American community, got together and started trying to deal with it [black-Korean tensions] in a coordinated fashion." These efforts meant that, to some extent, resources had to be withdrawn from other efforts—including Korean participation in the BKA. During the boycott, even the younger Korean members of the BKA, many of whom felt that they understood the underlying black resentment but believed that Bakewell was "trampling on the civil rights" of Tae Sam Park, "retreated back into the Korean community" (Kim 1997).

As in the Red Apple boycott, the chief activity that united Koreans in their response was a fundraising effort to support the beleaguered store. During the boycott, business at the store slid to a minimum, but Koreans raised nearly $50,000 to keep it open (Min 1996, 87). At first, there was broad agreement. Many Koreans interested in the conflict felt the store should be kept open, consciously echoing the response to the Red Apple boycott in New York. As Bong Hwan Kim asserts (1997), "It had important symbolic meaning to the Korean community in terms of not being continually scapegoated unfairly. It was like our attempt to draw a line in the sand and say, this is it, we're not going to take it any more." Storeowner Tae Sam Park himself believed Koreans should take a stand: "If we walk away from this, they'll find reasons to pick on more Korean markets. It won't end with us" (Freer 1994, 191).

Unlike in New York's Korean community, however, mixed feelings eventually surfaced over the appropriateness of the strategy: "On the one hand, . . . merchants wanted the boycotting to end because they didn't want the boycotting or picketing to spread to other stores. . . . But on the other hand, they didn't want them to give up and close down the store because what if their store is picketed and boycotted, then it's almost like terrorism in a way" (Yu 1996). The split that emerged reflected, more than anything else, a generational divide. Older, first generation Koreans—especially members of the Korean American Federation—tended to respond with greater outrage and communal feeling. The conflict heightened the racial prejudices often felt by the older generation toward blacks (Abelmann and Lie 1995, 150–51). Younger Koreans—often those born in Korea but raised in the United States—popularly dubbed the 1.5 generation—tended to respond more cautiously.

However, divisions also became apparent among younger Korean activists along ideological lines. According to Bong Hwan Kim (1997), "We didn't necessarily all agree on the direction that we had to move in. It was a real hodge-podge group of individuals." Kim emphasizes that he and other progressive Korean BKA members attempted "to work within the community and try to educate them about the larger issues and not to give into the reactionary divisiveness." These progressives formed their own organization, dubbed Korean American Racial Equality (KARE), which focused on racial conciliation and broke with the policy of supporting John's Liquor financially.

More conservative members of the 1.5 generation agreed that the older generation's fierce, reactive solidarity was inappropriate, but disagreed with the progressives that Koreans should pursue strategies of ethnic peace and conciliation. Charles Kim, a founding member of the Korean American Coalition, made the following recommendation (1996): "We should not get involved. They [the merchants and customers] have to solve it by themselves." Annie Cho, executive director of KAGRO, gave similar reasons for why her organization did not expect public officials to intervene heavily in the John's Liquor boycott: "What can the mayor do over problems that the actual customers and businessmen were having? They had to work it out themselves" (Freer 1994, 193). These Korean Americans believed that third-party intervention might simply racialize tensions further.

With Korean leaders uncertain on a common strategy, negotiating an end to the boycott was left to a single organization: the Korean American Grocers Association. KAGRO, however, had few personnel and had no interest in being on the "front lines" of conflicts (D. Kim 1996). It also did not have strong roots in the vicinity of the boycott; the association's membership was spread throughout Southern California, with only a small proportion in South Central Los Angeles (Thom 1996).[15] KAGRO's leaders did recognize, however, that protecting John's Liquor might enable it to fortify a positive image of Korean merchants more generally, which would serve its membership in the long run.

David Kim, KAGRO's president, sided with those who preferred a cautious response. When visiting chapters of KAGRO's national organization in other big cities, he advised them to avoid attracting attention from the press (which he warned would worsen their problems) and to resolve conflicts quickly and quietly instead of waiting for them to resolve themselves.[16] In the John's Liquor boycott, where he developed this strategy, Kim met with church members several times throughout the summer, but he did not meet with Bakewell until the end, when they reached a settlement. Kim had more frequent contact with Mayor Bradley—via a Korean American liaison at City Hall.

Around the same time that Bakewell announced his "flying force," David Kim and Yang Il Kim, KAGRO's national president, began suggesting to Bradley's office that they would be willing to persuade Tae Sam Park to close his store in exchange for an end to the boycott (Stolberg and Clifford 1991). Their efforts, in conjunction with those of the mayor, led to the conflict's conclusion. David Kim reasoned that the Korean community would not be able to support Park forever. "We don't want to use him as a scapegoat," Kim told people, but he argued that closing it would be best for the community, for black-Korean relations, and for Park's own peace of mind (D. Kim 1996). The mindsets of Koreans who intervened in the Red Apple boycott in New York City and the John's Liquor boycott in Los Angeles were like night and day.

After convincing Park to close and signing the agreement that resolved the boycott, KAGRO leaders were "severely criticized" by other Korean community leaders for capitulating to boycotters' demands (Min 1996, 88). David Kim even got threats from other Koreans. "I had a very difficult time," he recalled (1996), although he felt KAGRO ultimately "did the right thing." Kim was not completely alone in this assessment. "This is not the best deal," said Duk H. Kang, president of the city's Korean Chamber of Commerce, at the time. "But what can be done? We have no choice. We have to stop it, this boycott, right now. We don't want it to go to another store and another store" (Stolberg and Clifford 1991). No doubt, in the back of his mind, Kang was thinking of Bakewell's threat—hollow as it may have been—of a flying force of picketers.

The Mayor's Response: Quiet Mediation

In New York City, observers and participants pushed for Mayor Dinkins to take control in the Red Apple conflict, whether that meant forcefully denouncing the boycott or investing the effort it would take to bring the rival parties together. In the end, no one was satisfied with the mayor's performance. In Los Angeles, by comparison, Mayor Bradley drew favorable reviews. However, the milieu could hardly have been more different. To his credit, Bradley acted as a go-between for the merchants and the protesters and helped to end the boycott with some gentle pushing of his own. But he was hardly in control of events, and his stands were hardly more decisive or forceful than Dinkins's.

In formal terms, the mayor of Los Angeles is a weak executive; the city charter provides for powerful rivals, such as a strong city council and highly independent city agencies (Saltzstein, Sonenshein, and Ostrow 1986). However, the centralizing tendencies of the city's reform-style political institutions allow a mayor to amass power informally, as Bradley did successfully during his first decade in office. Bradley built a solid, biracial electoral base and combined it with a policy focus on downtown development that guaranteed stable support from business leaders. Like any mayor, however, Bradley's influence was subject to the continued reliability of his electoral support. In the late 1980s, of course, Bradley faced challenges from rival politicians, and cracks began to emerge in his electoral base. In the early 1990s, Bradley saw a political recovery, as the Rodney King beating case "breathed new life" into his biracial coalition (Sonenshein 1993, 211). Bradley's recovery was underway just as the John's Liquor boycott was beginning, giving the mayor a measure of political capital that had not been available for resolving conflicts just a few years earlier.

Bradley's direct intervention consisted of arranging private meetings throughout the summer with KAGRO leaders and organizers from Bethel A.M.E., as well as with the Community Relations Service and black and Korean community leaders (Sauerzopf 1991a). As for public actions, he held a press conference in front of another store that had been gutted by arson—thought to be gang-related, unlike a similar incident that happened around the same time at John's Liquor, which was thought to be the work of protesters. Bradley condemned the firebombings, but spread the blame:

"These tragedies must stop, and I am here today to demand that some members of the African American and Korean American communities stop engaging in actions that are detrimental to both groups" (Njeri 1997, 113). As for the John's Liquor boycott, the mayor remarked that it hurt attempts at intergroup reconciliation, but—like David Dinkins—he did not explicitly denounce it. Instead, Bradley refused to oppose "any peaceful organized efforts" (ibid., 113): "I'm not one who says people's right to demonstrate peacefully should be abrogated. I simply believe there are better ways to achieve their goals and ours" (Sauerzopf 1991a).

Naturally, Koreans opposed to the boycott were not pleased. Jerry Yu of the Korean American Coalition expressed a common view (1996): "As a public servant, he should have come out against people like Danny Bakewell. . . . I don't remember him doing that." Unlike in New York City, however, where Koreans were able to force the mayor's hand with a massive rally and the support of outspoken conservative white politicians, Koreans in Los Angeles could not change Bradley's stance. Several factors explained their ineffectiveness. First, Koreans in Los Angeles were not as well organized or as experienced with conflict as Koreans in New York City, who had been responding to black-led boycotts and other threats for years. Second, the only significant pressure that Bradley felt during the summer of 1991 came from black leaders—who either supported the boycott or refused to oppose it publicly. Black and Korean members of the BKA appealed to the mayor to use his public stature to "neutralize" Danny Bakewell's influence, but "Bradley wasn't interested in doing that, because Danny had a pretty solid following in the black community that Bradley didn't, among the disenfranchised," according to Bong Hwan Kim (1997). Kim continued, "The black leadership implicitly supported [Bakewell] but would never do it explicitly. . . . None of them ever criticized his actions."

Consequently, Bradley had more room to maneuver—allowing him to ignore those who explicitly opposed the boycott, most of whom were Koreans. The mayor did not entirely lack ties to the Korean community; he used a Korean American liaison in his office, Yoon He Kim, to communicate directly with KAGRO (Kim 1997; Song 1996; Yu 1996). Bradley's choice to work with it rather than other Korean organizations partly explains why KAGRO ended up representing the Korean side at the negotiating table—to ill effect, in terms of its reception by many Koreans afterward. KAGRO had relatively weak roots in the city of Los Angeles, meaning that its leaders would be less responsive to community pressures.

In the fall, after the end of Bakewell's moratorium on negotiations, Bradley's efforts to bring the groups together bore fruit: KAGRO and the Brotherhood Crusade held talks that spanned a week and a half, ending in early October. The mayor's role, however, was purely "facilitative"—no one expected substantive contributions from him (Freer 1994, 193). With the assistance of Deputy Mayor Mark Fabiani, Bradley's key negotiator, the parties soon consented to a deal. Black protesters heralded the agreement, but Korean representatives merely accepted it—with reactions ranging from resignation to disappointment.

Reflecting the frantic state of the negotiations, each side rushed to announce the resolution on its own, and each reported a slightly different interpretation of the terms. Bakewell told the press that the end of the boycott (and the prevention of future boycotts) was conditioned on all stores in South Central agreeing to a ten-point "code of ethics," which included hiring at least one black employee. Bakewell also said the protesters planned to continue demanding that the district attorney reopen the case in the Mitchell shooting that had sparked the boycott. KAGRO officials said neither of these two points had been part of the negotiated resolution: they claimed that the code of ethics was something that was to be worked out jointly in the future (Stolberg and Clifford 1991).

The two sides agreed to other major points: the store would be closed and offered for sale to a black buyer, if one came forward; the sale would not include the store's existing liquor license; both sides would work together to set up a center to resolve disputes before they became boycotts; and Korean merchants would work together with the Urban League, other black organizations, and the mayor's office to provide 100 jobs for South Central residents (Freer 1994, 192; Mitchell 1991d; Stolberg and Clifford 1991).[17] Danny Bakewell had the last word, ending the conflict with a declaration of victory. "What is significant about today is that we are winning," he told a crowd of celebrating protesters outside John's Liquor. "We have brought home the bacon" (Stolberg and Clifford 1991).

Not only were Mayor Bradley's words and actions no more forceful than David Dinkins's the previous summer; he also did not feel compelled to make the symbolic move of shopping at the beleaguered store—the litmus test of leadership that critics in New York City applied to Dinkins. Despite the similarity in their stances on boycotts, Bradley felt nothing like the storm of public criticism that rained on Dinkins. The two mayors followed similar paths, but Dinkins paid the higher price.

THE 1992 CIVIL UNREST

The most severe conflict involving blacks and Koreans in Los Angeles was not a protracted boycott that drew multiple, organized interventions, of course, but its polar opposite: a brief, unorganized, devastating explosion of violence. Thus, it makes sense to compare New York's Red Apple boycott not only to the boycott of John's Liquor but to the 1992 civil unrest as well. In making such a comparison, I do not mean to provide a full-blown analysis of the rioting—such an effort is beyond the scope of this book. Instead, I draw mainly on existing research to identify the roles played by black-Korean tensions, public institutions, and community organizations.

Down the Path to Violence: Latasha Harlins and Soon Ja Du

As received wisdom tells it, the acquittals of four white police officers in the Rodney King beating case triggered the 1992 riots. There is no doubt that the acquittals fueled a sudden fury among black Angelenos, who had already endured a long history of injustices by police. However, the Rodney King case was not the sole trigger: the shooting of a black teenager by a Korean merchant—and the case's ultimate outcome in the courts—was at the same time galvanizing blacks against the injustices of white-dominated institutions. Just one week before the riots, an appeals court upheld a reduced sentence for the convicted shooter, generating a wave of anger that set the stage for the riots. This incident led the city down the path to the riots; so in order to put the riots in context, it is necessary to backtrack in time to a few months before the boycott of John's Liquor.

On the morning of March 16, 1991, just two weeks after Los Angeles police officers assaulted Rodney King, fifteen-year old Latasha Harlins walked into the Empire Liquor Market Deli in South Central to buy an orange juice. Within minutes, the plastic container she chose from the store refrigerator became the object of a dispute. Soon Ja Du, the forty-nine-year-old Korean woman behind the counter, accused Harlins of shoplifting; Harlins had put the juice in her backpack, but it was sticking out the top, and she denied the accusation. The dispute turned physical: Du was smaller than Harlins, but despite her size, she grabbed her. Harlins replied with three punches to Du's face, which knocked her to the floor, and then the older woman threw a chair at Harlins. When Du pulled a gun from under the counter, Harlins put the juice on the counter, turned around, and walked away. As the teenager left the store, the merchant braced herself and fired—directly into the back of Harlins's head, killing her (Cannon 1997).

We know exactly what happened because the action was caught on videotape by the store's security camera. However, Soon Ja Du told both her husband (who ran into the store immediately afterward) and the police (who arrived shortly) that a robbery had occurred. Du's lie in the face of concrete evidence gave black activists reason to doubt the similar testimony of Tae Sam Park in the Mitchell shooting, which was not caught on camera. As with the tape of the King beating, the tape of the Harlins shooting was later broadcast repeatedly on local television.

The very next day, the Du family closed their doors and Mayor Bradley met with members of the BKA and other black and Korean leaders. The group issued a statement calling for calm to prevail and emphasized that the incident had not been racially motivated (Min 1996, 85). The same day, Bradley personally called David Kim, KAGRO's president, and recommended that city government and KAGRO buy the store together to use as a job training center for South Central residents. Kim, in turn, contacted Hung Ki Du, Soon Ja Du's husband, who expressed interest. Later, however, after speaking with his attorney, Du called Kim and refused the deal (D. Kim 1996).

After these unsuccessful attempts to quell tensions, protests began. In two days, Bakewell and the Brotherhood Crusade led demonstrations at the closed-down Empire Liquor, which took place for several days across the span of a week. About 150 people marched. Adopting the position he would use again in the John's Liquor boycott, Bakewell played down the racial aspect of the shooting but played up the call for blacks to mobilize. He also stressed that protesters were advocating peaceful solutions, not violence. A new organization called Mothers in Action joined Bakewell in the protests (Min 1996, 85; Mitchell 1991c).

Given the senselessness and severity of the shooting, the size of demonstrations seemed small and their duration short, even for a city as unaccustomed to protest as Los Angeles. Empire Liquor's immediate closing was one reason—but not the only one—why extended picketing did not take place. Another was strategic. A boycott of Tae Sam Park's store, which came a couple of months later, made more sense to the Brotherhood Crusade president: "We may not get the best deal trying to buy that store [Empire Liquor, which was larger than John's Liquor]," Bakewell said. John's Liquor, on the other hand, "is perfectly situated. It's the right size and we could get it for $200,000, probably less" (Njeri 1997, 122). Moreover, authorities had been quick to charge Du with murder, and, given the videotaped evidence, "even blacks who were skeptical about the fairness of the legal system assumed Du would be convicted and sent to prison" (Cannon 1997, 111).[18]

By October, passions in South Central had cooled somewhat, aided by the agreement in the John's Liquor boycott. But court proceedings in the Du case stirred new anger, which generated renewed protests. On October 11, just a week after the John's Liquor truce, the jury in the Du case (which included five black members) returned a guilty verdict. However, it had rejected a charge of second-degree murder, finding Du guilty only of voluntary manslaughter.[19]

The jury may have reached its decision out of sympathy for Du, who maintained that the shooting had been accidental, and who had expressed fears because her store had been robbed repeatedly and on one occasion her son's life had been threatened. Du faced up to sixteen years in prison, but was freed on bail (Ford and Wilkinson 1991). This was the first blow to Harlins's family, community activists, and others who were outraged at the case's outcome.

The second blow—and the more severe—came in November, when Superior Court Judge Joyce Karlin reduced the sentence to five years' probation, a $500 fine, and payment for Latasha Harlins's funeral (Cannon 1997, 172). Some believe that Karlin was trying to reduce tensions with her ruling (Min 1996, 86). Karlin may have been taking into account Du's reported emotional problems. But the reduced sentence, combined with insensitive comments about the case that Karlin issued from the bench, spurred an outburst of anger in South Central.[20]

Over the next few weeks, church leaders and community organizers tried to channel the rage of South Central residents (Cannon 1997, 171–72). Perhaps recognizing that tensions might surpass their limited capacities, Danny Bakewell, Mayor Bradley, and other black leaders came together to denounce another shooting death, of a nine-year-old Korean American girl during a robbery in South Central in late October (Malnic 1991). In response to Judge Karlin's reduced sentence for Du, black and Korean ministers led a peace rally that drew 400 supporters to the steps of Los Angeles City Hall. City Council members John Ferraro and Nate Holden—neither of whom had been active in past mediation efforts—addressed the crowd. In the city of Compton, where part of the Du case had been tried, Mayor Walter Tucker, City Council member Patricia Moore, and other local black politicians led rallies, and 300 protesters marched on the courthouse (Sauerzopf 1991b). Demonstrators emphasized that their protests were not meant to escalate ethnic tensions but to target public officials and the legal system. Indeed, for many blacks, the conflict had moved to this new level entirely, leading activists to launch a recall campaign to remove Karlin from the bench. (She was later reassigned to juvenile court, but the recall campaign failed.) Still, the damage was done. As Korean activist Bong Hwan Kim recalled (1997), "That probation decision just drove a deep wedge right between the black and Korean communities. There was no middle ground; you were either for us or you were against us."

Black activists, along with District Attorney Ira Reiner, both worked to appeal the reduced sentence. But on April 21, 1992, just a week before the riots, the state court handling the appeal upheld Judge Karlin's decision, affirming Karlin's right under California law to wide latitude in sentencing. Ironically, the Black-Korean Alliance issued a statement blaming the justice system, and urged Angelenos to seek legal reform instead of engaging in intergroup conflict (Kim 1997; Wagner 1992). But the bid for peace came too late. The twin injustices of Latasha Harlins's fate and the courts' rulings guaranteed that African Americans would respond in some fashion to express their anger. The outrageous outcome of the case did not guarantee that the response would take the form of mass violence, rather than nonviolent protest, however; that was determined by the political context in which the fury developed.

Reports of Violence Grow

Because boycotts were rare in Los Angeles during the 1980s, many local observers refused to believe tensions were serious. This changed with the Latasha Harlins incident: "Some were of the mind that what was happening in New York wouldn't happen in L.A., because there hadn't been this open conflict," recalled Bong Hwan Kim in 1997. "But knowing [now] that there were these tensions, I think that the Latasha Harlins incident just blew the lid off . . . what had been underneath the surface for a long time."

Although few boycotts took place, newspapers began reporting more incidents of violence between blacks and Koreans. Fifteen shootings, five assaults, and five incidents of arson were reported between 1980 and 1995, most of them during 1990 and 1991 (see Table 5.2). In most of these, blacks were the perpetrators. Later, attorney Angela Oh, who became a media spokesperson for Korean Americans after appearing on *Nightline* after the riots, tried to counter the popular image that Koreans were shooting blacks—which happened much less often, but seemed to be promoted more by media reports—by issuing annual press releases that listed Korean merchants who had died or suffered injuries while tending their stores (Seo 1993).

An analysis of police data on hate crimes by Nadine Koch and H. Eric Schockman concluded that attacks by black perpetrators against Korean merchants correlated with "media-driven exposés about tensions/flare-ups between the two communities" (1994, 76). However, they did not correlate neatly with protest activity, suggesting that violence did not represent the escalation of tensions from boycotts but rather a separate path. Ten incidents were reported by the police in February 1990, a month that was free of boycotts. Then, after a year with no reports of hate crimes, six were reported in April 1991, the month after the Latasha Harlins shooting. During the summer of 1991, while the John's Liquor boycott was taking place,

Table 5.2. Reports of Violence between Blacks and Koreans
in Los Angeles, 1980–1995

Incident	Date	Outcome
Shootings of 4 Korean merchants	April 1986	Deaths
Village Inn Café Assault[a]	Aug. 1988	Injury
Shooting/beating of Korean man	June 1990	Injury
Assaults of Korean merchants	Aug. 1990	Injuries
Firebombings of 2 Korean stores	Late 1990–Jan. 1991	Damage
Latasha Harlins Shooting[a]	March 1991	Death
Lee Arthur Mitchell Shooting[a]	June 1991	Death
John's Liquor Firebombing (twice)	June & Aug. 1991	Damage
Empire Liquor Firebombing	Aug. 1991	Damage
Shooting of 2 Korean merchants and 1 black customer	March–Sept. 1991	Deaths
Dennis Lee/Young Song Shooting	Sept. 1991	Injury
7 Days Food Store Altercation	Sept. 1991	None
Juri Kang Shooting	Oct. 1991	Injury
Century Liquor Store Shooting	Nov. 1991	Injury
Paul Park Shooting	Dec. 1991	Death
Yong Tae Park Shooting	Dec. 1991	Death
Hyung Hsu Kim Assault	Feb. 1993	Death
Ja Suk Sim Assault	Aug. 1993	Injury

[a]Incident was followed by a boycott.
Note: Five additional incidents were reported elsewhere in Los Angeles County.

there were one, two, or three per month, suggesting a possible relationship with protest activity. After the boycott ended, however, reports actually increased: in October, five incidents were reported. This was around the time a jury convicted Soon Ja Du on lesser charges and freed her on bail. In November, when Judge Karlin reduced Du's sentence to probation, seven incidents were reported (Koch and Schockman 1994, 66–68). Notably, the increases came immediately after the Du incident and then, later, after the two court rulings. During the John's Liquor boycott, the number of cases actually *declined*.

The Los Angeles Police Department's hate crime data did not include a couple of severe incidents that took place in late 1990 and early 1991: two Korean stores were destroyed by arson, thought by police to be the work of black gang members (Min 1996, 84) but not formally declared bias cases. Also, in the summer of 1991, two stores targeted by protesters

(John's Liquor and Empire Liquor) were firebombed: as in the previous cases, no perpetrators were positively identified. In one case at John's Liquor, however, the suspect was believed to be a gang member who had had a dispute with Tae Sam Park, the store's owner. Authorities believed the incident was unrelated to the boycott (Njeri 1997, 113). Although all the firebombings were probably unrelated to protests, some Korean observers nevertheless saw them as a violent reaction to longstanding tensions (Dungee 1991).

With the rise in tensions accompanying increasing reports of violence in the press, those interested in mediating conflicts recognized the need for a new approach, different from the reactive approach that had characterized typical efforts in the past. For instance, the Community Relations Service appealed for greater resources from the federal government. As mediator Stephen Thom recalled, "We were getting too many of these small incidents occurring, and we had asked our agency whether they would give us backing to send more mediators in, so that we could pro-actively work through the communities and the different storeowners so we could get some communication going" (Thom 1996). The CRS failed to get all it wanted. But even if it had, it probably could not have prevented the escalation in attacks on Korean stores that culminated in the 1992 unrest. In a city that lacked extensive networks of neighborhood organizing and strong connections between community activists and residents, tensions were not easily channeled into nonviolent, organized forms.

Many Riots, Not One

Because of the Rodney King case, it was easy to see the 1992 civil unrest in the mirror of past American race riots—as a "traditional" conflict between blacks and whites. However, the riots represented much more. Participation crossed lines of class, race, and ethnicity, involving blacks, whites, Asians, and Latinos, in poor and middle-class neighborhoods. Author Mike Davis (1992b) called it a "postmodern bread riot"; historian Peter Kwong (1992) called it the "first multicultural riots."

The complexity of the events that took place during the six days of rioting cannot be understated, and my focus on the role of black-Korean tensions should not be taken as an attempt to locate a single cause or to suggest that other causes were less important. Raphael Sonenshein puts the point most aptly when he writes that "there will be a tendency to attach a single definition to the 1992 violence, but that search for simplicity may be misplaced. Perhaps the most accurate assessment would be that it was several different, overlapping riots" (1993, 222). Social scientists have emphasized the roles of racial attitudes, poverty, and immigration. Law enforcement has blamed street gangs; others have blamed an inadequate response by the LAPD. However, as journalist Lou Cannon writes: "In their origins, the riots were neither a gang conspiracy nor a revolt against harsh conditions but a cry of black rage," provoked by both the Rodney King and the Latasha Harlins cases (1997, 282). Certainly the unrest was many things, but one inescapable facet was the expression of tensions between African Americans and Korean Americans.

The Targeting of Korean Stores

The ubiquity of Korean businesses in Los Angeles, especially in black and Latino neighborhoods, meant that rioting for any reason would put them in harm's way. However, Korean stores did not merely fall in the path of a rage that had little to do with them. Instead, they were often targeted by rioters and were especially likely to suffer severe damage. The evidence is not always clear cut, but, as Kathleen Tierney concludes, "The riot damage data make a strong *prima facie* case for the selectivity hypothesis" (Tierney 1994, 155).[21]

At about 6:00 P.M. on April 29, violence erupted at the corner of Florence and Normandie Avenues in South Central—a scene that came to be known as the flashpoint that triggered broader violence (Useem 1997). However, events had actually been set in motion two hours earlier, just after the verdicts in the Rodney King case were announced, a few blocks west on Florence. This was close to two former boycott sites: John's Liquor and Finest Market. There, after hearing the verdicts, five young black men robbed a Korean-owned liquor store, struck the owner's son on the head with a beer bottle, and threw more bottles at the floor. One yelled, ironically, "This is for Rodney King." Police arrived and chased one of the looters to the intersection of Seventy-first Street, where black residents began to form a crowd—one block from the soon-to-be-famous flashpoint. From there, people in the crowd moved to Normandie and began attacking Asian, Latino, and white motorists (*Frontline* 1993; Cannon 1997, 281). Rioters continued to invoke the name "Rodney King," but they also spoke the name "Latasha Harlins"—the two had become intertwined via twin perceived failures of the justice system (Cannon 1997, 282).

Once the violence began to spread, black business owners labeled their establishments in order to avoid damage. Those near Korean stores were sometimes spared (Morrison and Lowry 1994, 34). Korean merchants reported that bands of young black men, possibly members of street gangs, "tagged" Korean shops with spray paint and then torched them (Casuso 1992; Domanick 1992, 37; Min 1996, 91). In testimony at hearings after the riots, African Americans indicated that the sentence in the Soon Ja Du case had contributed to the targeting of Korean stores (Min 1996; Tierney 1994, 155). Foreshadowing the type of violence during the riots, targeted firebombings had taken place at Korean stores in 1991. Rioting took place in the same locales where handfuls of protesters had boycotted stores: Finest Market, on West Florence Avenue, was ten blocks from the flash-point of Florence and Normandie; the L.A.-Slauson Swap Meet, on West Slauson Avenue, and John's Liquor, on South Western Avenue, were not far; the Crenshaw Swap Meet and the Village Inn Café, both near the intersection of Crenshaw and Martin Luther King Jr. Boulevards, were near the heart of destruction in the city's Crenshaw district.

Ultimately, one-third of all the businesses damaged in the city of Los Angeles were Korean-owned, according to city government records. Moreover, those hit the hardest were more likely to be owned by Koreans: they accounted for nearly half of the 400 or so businesses that suffered total destruction rather than partial damage or looting (Tierney 1994, 151–52).[22] Insurance claims, which suggest significant damage, indicate an even higher proportion. Koreans made up three-quarters of all business owners reporting damage to the California state insurance office (Ong and Hee 1993a, 9).[23] Also, about three-quarters of all business owners who received state Disaster Unemployment Insurance were Asian American, most of them Korean. And about 60 percent of business owners who applied for federal relief were Asian, again mostly Korean (ibid., 10).

Korean businesses in South Central Los Angeles were hit especially hard. Koreans owned 1,600 of the 2,411 businesses in South Central (Koch and Schockman 1994, 51; Min 1996, 67). More stores there were torched and suffered massive damage (defined as greater than $100,000 in losses) than either in Koreatown—a business district for Koreans, but home to many Latinos—or in all the other parts of the city combined, according to data collected by the *Korea Central Daily* newspaper. In Koreatown, stores were looted, often by recent Central American immigrants (Kwong 1987; Rutten 1992). South Central also suffered the biggest total dollar losses of the three areas (Ong and Hee 1993a, 11, 12). For Ivan Light, Hadas Har-Chvi, and Kenneth Kan, the higher incidence of arson and total destruction in South Central indicates that "rioters evidently had a stronger component of hatred of and revenge against Korean merchants" there than in Koreatown or in other parts of the city (1994, 80–81).

Attempts to Contain the Violence: The Absence of Police and Community Organizations

Much has been made of the lack of preparedness by the Los Angeles Police Department, a factor that undoubtedly helped propel the unrest to its enormous scale. But the problem of the department's response went beyond a lack of preparation for handling riots—it went deeper, to the very structure of the LAPD as a police organization. The LAPD's highly insulated, professionalized character, rooted in Los Angeles's reform-style political institutions, prevented it from either preparing for or responding to the unrest adequately.

Like the rest of Los Angeles local government, the LAPD was designed with efficiency in mind, making it small, centralized, and highly insulated from political pressures. The city of Los Angeles has 349 residents per sworn police officer, giving it barely more officers per capita "than the average rural county" (*Los Angeles Times,* 1998). The resident-officer ratios in other big cities, especially cities with long histories of traditional party organization, are much lower. New York City, for instance, has only 198 residents per officer (not including its transit and housing police, which lower its ratio even further). Chicago, which has about the same population as Los Angeles, has roughly the same ratio as New York: 210 residents per officer.

The organization of police departments is closely tied to the context of local politics. Most important, the presence or absence of machine politics greatly influenced the development of urban police forces over the course of the twentieth century. As James Wilson explains (1998):

> In cities such as Chicago and New York, party organizations often dominated police departments. This did not happen in Los Angeles. Most Angelenos thought that this was a good thing, because it spared the city a tradition of corrupt officers and a massive influx of organized crime. . . . [However,] the lack of parties meant that . . . there were no mechanisms for inducing the police to pay much attention to ethnic differences and neighborhood concerns. When good chiefs were in office, the police attracted able officers, but each of them quickly learned to respond to orders from above and not to cues from outside.

In 1978, Proposition 13 (a tax-limiting law passed by ballot initiative) curtailed new revenues that might have allowed the police to hire more officers. The result, by the 1990s, was "a heavily overworked, poorly equipped" police department. Furthermore, Mayor Bradley and various police chiefs had opposed transitioning the force from a "military paradigm" to a community-policing model, meaning that by the time of the 1992 unrest, "it had also lost much of its connection with local neighborhoods" (Wilson 1998; see also Cannon 1997, 89–91).

Ill will between police and minority communities—another factor affecting police performance—had existed in Los Angeles long before the Rodney King incident. Thus, in April 1992, Mayor Bradley and City Council member Mark Ridley-Thomas had been told by community leaders to expect the worst if the Rodney King case delivered acquittals. Both Bradley and Ridley-Thomas—believing that a large show of force by the police would exacerbate violence—objected to a highly visible police presence while the city awaited the verdicts. They met with little opposition from Police Chief Daryl Gates, who saw no need for preparation: he did not expect a crisis. Gates believed, along with many others, that the officers in the King case would be convicted. Instead, Gates took two relatively minor steps: he allocated an extra $1 million for police overtime, and he recorded a videotape that was shown to officers across the city. In a telling move, Gates's recorded message told officers to ignore community leaders who had warned of "very serious uprisings" (Cannon 1997, 252–53). Those very individuals might have provided police with greater knowledge about South Central and increased the police department's capacity to control the violence, but the LAPD had not cultivated much of a relationship with them in the past. Gates, by discrediting community leaders, essentially negated any possible use that police could have made of them during the unrest.[24]

The inadequate response of law enforcement certainly contributed to the scale of rioting. But the great untold story of the riots has got to be the tale of what community activists attempted to do—in vain—to channel tensions in the early hours of rioting. Little information is available on such efforts, which were likely scarce, but we know something about a few of them. Immediately after the verdicts were issued, demonstrators mobilized at the Parker Center, the LAPD's downtown headquarters. The protesters were initially mainly white radicals, but the group soon became more racially mixed. Organizers were not able to keep marchers peaceful, if they tried to do so—within a few hours, the protests turned violent (Crogan 1992, 35–36).

Another instance, which took place in South Central, involved efforts by a church—not, notably, a neighborhood organization. The First African Methodist Episcopal Church was the city's biggest and oldest black church, with 8,500 members. The evening of the riots, Rev. Cecil Murray—who was joined by Mayor Bradley and other black leaders and politicians—urged residents to maintain calm in case the jury returned acquittals in Simi Valley (Cannon 1997, 252–53, 325). During the riots, First A.M.E. provided "a safe haven in the war zone. . . . Overnight, the church became a makeshift center for local activists trying to control the disturbances" (Smith and Cannon 1992). Even as churchgoers urged peace inside, however, demonstrators outside the church expressed anger over the verdicts. As the riots began, neighborhood residents began to mill outside the church, at first merely protesting the verdicts (Frontline 1993). However, for the First A.M.E., even with its vast size, the burden of channeling the rage ultimately proved too weighty.

Activists in South Central were doubly handicapped: first by the lack of dense organizational networks available to them in Los Angeles neighborhoods and, second, by the lack of assistance from police. The police had equally handicapped themselves by not maintaining ties with community activists in the past. Such ties, if they had existed, would have been reinforcing in both directions.

Later, Mayor Bradley and City Council member Mark Ridley-Thomas received criticism for their objections to a visible police presence in South Central before the verdicts. Their belief that lines of officers would lead to violence in black neighborhoods was probably accurate. Such a presence would have been provocative anywhere. The question, rather, is *what* kind of behavior it would have provoked: in Los Angeles, where police lacked any ties to community activists with whom they could cooperate and share information, the only possible path was violence.

Actually, in one sense, there was "organizing" going on during the riots, but its thrust was not to facilitate peaceful demonstrations. Instead, it was organizing for violent ends: gangs roved and marked their targets, police officers mobilized to fight rioters, and Korean merchants armed themselves and rallied to defend their stores.

Latino Rioting in Koreatown

Academics, community leaders, journalists, and even Korean merchants themselves were shocked to find that stores in Koreatown were attacked by Latino rioters. Prior to 1992, researchers had found no evidence of "public demonstrations" of "overt hostility" between Korean merchants and Latinos. At least two arguments have been offered for the lack of overt conflict: Lucie Cheng and Yen Le Espiritu argue that a shared belief in the American dream had muted tensions (1989, 523–24). Light, Har-Chvi, and Kan (1994) argue that Latinos lacked an ideology equivalent to black nationalism that targeted "outsiders." Both base their explanations for the lack of overt conflict on differing belief systems between blacks and Latinos.

Although "acquisitiveness" may have been the primary motivation for many Latino residents of Koreatown and neighboring districts to loot stores (Light, Har-Chvi, and Kan 1994), there is evidence that intergroup tensions existed as well. In Koreatown, Latinos served as a source of cheap labor for Korean merchants, whose profit margins were often thin. A study of public opinion in Los Angeles around the time of the riots revealed evidence of hostilities between Koreans and Latinos and called it a "hidden conflict" due to its lack of public expression (Bobo et al. 1994). As Peter Kwong writes, "Until the riots, the tensions between the Latinos and the Korean Americans went unarticulated, smothered at least in part by the struggle both immigrant groups were mounting to survive and prosper" (1992, 90).

Reflecting on American proclivities to focus on black-Korean conflicts, Nancy Abelmann and John Lie ask why there was never as much "media coverage of the 'Korean-Latino conflict,' especially given that so many Latinos work for Korean American businesses and industries" (Abelmann and Lie, 1995, 161). The answer may simply be that there were few overt, recognizable signs that such a conflict existed. Instead, the manner in which Latino rioters acted on antagonisms might be explained by the lack of organizational resources available to them for alternative means of action, such as protest. No doubt, black nationalism played a role in producing a distinctive reaction by African Americans. However, patterns of community organizational activity—independent of ideology—also played a role: ethnic groups tend to have particular "repertoires" of action unique to their communities (Tilly 1984). African Americans have a more developed tradition of political mobilization and protest than Latinos, especially more recent immigrants: "Unlike black workers, they do not aggressively militate for higher wages, and they have no organizations to represent their interests" (Kwong 1992, 90). Like African Americans, Latinos may have harbored grievances, but blacks were more likely to mobilize for protest in reaction to those grievances.

Aftermath: Rebuilding and Not Rebuilding

Post-riots Los Angeles, like pre-riots Los Angeles, was remarkably devoid of organized, public demonstrations. Few protests took place in black neighborhoods; and aside from a march by sixty protesters through South Central demanding "amnesty" for arrested rioters and a series of pickets led by Danny Bakewell at construction sites that employed Latinos rather than blacks, most of the demonstrators in rallies that took place in the years immediately following the riots were Korean Americans. Relying on extensive organizational networks that had gone unused for race-relations ends in the past, Koreans from across the greater Los Angeles area responded to calls to gather in Koreatown—most notably in a three-hour march of 30,000 people (Chang and Krikorian 1992)—but also for smaller protests. Korean rallies focused on relief for merchants and on interethnic peace; smaller numbers of blacks and whites joined them.

The sudden, massive mobilization of Korean Americans derived from their sharp losses, especially in Koreatown, a center of community life for

Koreans throughout Southern California. During the boycott of John's Liquor, Koreans had begun to coordinate across previously splintered organizations; now, they continued those efforts on a much larger scale. For many, it was a rude awakening to the importance of politics. As Jerry Yu (1996) recalled:

> Korean Americans . . . saw just dramatically . . . how much we as a community here lacked any sort of political power—the ability to influence things that are impacting us, whether those are getting the LAPD to come out to protect a store, or the National Guard to come down here, when all this stuff's going on, when there's an emergency, or even being able to call up a city councilman.

Some Koreans in Los Angeles—especially those already involved in politics and community organizations—became more active in public life. The Korean American Coalition actually recorded modest increases in voter turnout after the unrest. Other Korean residents of Los Angeles, however, went in the opposite direction and withdrew even further from public involvement (Yu 1996).

The chief response of local government to the civil unrest—the Rebuild Los Angeles foundation—was a classic instance of the reform-style approach to governance that had long characterized Los Angeles politics. Mayor Bradley called on former baseball commissioner Peter Ueberroth to chair the organization, which, at least initially, consisted of business leaders and experts in their fields, individuals considered to be "above the fray" and with few ties to the grassroots. Still, there were signs that things were changing. Community activists redoubled their efforts and undertook numerous initiatives to try to ease tensions created and exacerbated by the riots. Some of these consciously tried to learn from the pitfalls of the Black-Korean Alliance, particularly its lack of grassroots foundations (Regalado 1994).

Only one black boycott of a Korean store took place after the riots: led by the Brotherhood Crusade in 1996, it targeted a hat store in South Central that refused service to a black minister (Kang 1996). Blacks and Koreans continued to meet over the counter, occasionally violently, in Korean stores—at least, those that rebuilt or reopened. What was most noteworthy about relations after the unrest was not the presence or absence of boycotts, however, but the fact that black-Korean tensions were for the first time channeled down a third path.

A Third Path: The Liquor Store Campaign

The chief conflict that involved African Americans and Korean Americans after the riots was a campaign by South Central residents and organizers to prevent the rebuilding of liquor stores. This campaign, led by a federally funded organization called the Community Coalition for Substance Abuse Prevention and Treatment, was unique in a number of ways. Its motives, structure, and strategies were unlike those of any other community organization that became involved in conflicts between blacks and Koreans—in any city, not just Los Angeles.

The Community Coalition's unique role was due in part to the riots themselves and to the response of city government to concerns about the sale of liquor in high-crime neighborhoods—the destruction of so many stores meant that anyone who objected to their previous presence in South Central, for whatever reason, could now oppose their rebuilding. But the Coalition was unique in other ways too: it pursued its aims through a formal political process, mobilizing residents to appear at city planning hearings; it relied on federal funding for its existence, rather than exclusively local or neighborhood resources; and it explicitly avoided targeting Korean merchants by ethnicity, or even referring to the stores it targeted as owned by Koreans. Instead, it identified stores linked to "public nuisance" problems such as crime.

The Community Coalition was founded in 1990 by Karen Bass, an African American University of Southern California researcher who became its executive director, in order to combat the crack cocaine epidemic via community organizing. It owed its existence to a five-year grant from the U.S. Department of Health and Human Services, which it received in conjunction with the university. An organization that partnered academics and activists, it began with a staff of seven and meager resources, but grew "massively" in five years. By 1997, after its first grant had expired, it had a staff of eighteen and new federal funding, it boasted extensive political ties and media exposure, and it was planning the opening of a new community center (Bass 1996; Sonenshein 1996).

After canvassing the community in 1991 as part of the needs-assessment survey required for its federal funding, Bass and the organization's staff "discovered" a widespread concern among South Central residents about liquor stores. Residents complained that liquor stores—which were ubiquitous in South Central—presented a "public nuisance" and "brought down" the neighborhood: they tended to attract crime (a claim that they argued was bolstered by police data), loitering, and drug use (Bass 1996).

The Community Coalition was not the first organization to mobilize residents against liquor stores in Los Angeles. The issue reached back more than a decade, predating overt black-Korean conflicts in Los Angeles. A group called the South Central Organizing Committee (SCOC), affiliated with the Industrial Areas Foundation and closely tied to local churches, had targeted liquor stores in the early 1980s and successfully pressured public officials to limit the sale of new liquor licenses (*Los Angeles Sentinel* 1984a). Bass had not been involved in that effort but sought advice from its leaders. At the same time, however, she found that its tactics had been too "punitive" and "regulatory," and she sought to remake the movement in a new form (Bass 1996).

Coalition organizers only realized that most of the owners of liquor stores they were targeting were Korean after they had decided to follow in the SCOC's footsteps. It was after that realization that Bass began contacting Korean organizations and befriended Korean community activist Bong Hwan Kim, who persuaded her to join the Black-Korean Alliance. Ironically, on the very eve of the riots, Bass and her organization's staff traveled to Mayor Bradley's office in City Hall to discuss strategy on how to shut down liquor stores (Bass 1996; Kim 1997).

The riots gave them their opening. As the fires died down and calm returned to the streets of South Central, hundreds of constituents made phone calls to City Council member Mark Ridley-Thomas, asking him to stop the rebuilding of liquor stores. Ridley-Thomas referred callers by the droves to Bass. "We weren't that well known," Bass (1996) recalled. "So we felt that this was our day. If we did not launch a campaign and respond to the community outcry, we'd be finished."

Occasionally, the Community Coalition organized public demonstrations on the streets or at City Hall. Prior to the riots, for instance, the group had tried to prevent the granting of liquor licenses to new businesses in South Central. In one instance, it joined a local trade union, churches, and other organizations in briefly picketing a new market called La Fiesta, which had applied for a license (Schatzman 1991b; Shiver 1991).

After the riots, however, the Community Coalition made its primary strategy the mobilization of residents to testify at public hearings that had been required by the City Council on the rebuilding of stores with liquor licenses.[25] The Community Coalition did not oppose the rebuilding of every liquor-selling store that applied to the city; instead, it canvassed the neighborhoods around stores and selected sites that had been linked to public nuisances. (If a merchant had merely been rude to customers, Coalition leaders ignored complaints.) In many cases, the organization demanded that stores not be rebuilt at all; in others, however, it demanded that rebuilding only take place if certain conditions were met, such as better security and lighting. Of the 200 stores gutted by the riots, ultimately, only sixty rebuilt. Of those, thirty-one stores reopened with improved security but without liquor licenses (Bass 1996). In new legislation sponsored by Mark Ridley-Thomas and Michael Woo, the City Council offered financial incentives to storeowners with liquor licenses to rebuild as Laundromats, but the program was not successful; only one conversion took place (C. Kim 1996; Seo 1993).

Representatives from the Community Coalition attended 150 hearings from 1992 to 1994 (after which the appeal process ceased). Transporting volunteer residents to scheduled public hearings proved easier than boycotting individual stores, as Bass recalled in 1996:

> One of the pressures [from residents] during the campaign was for us to just boycott stores, and I personally was adamantly opposed to it, mainly because we didn't have the capacity. I don't like boycotts. . . . When you say you're going to boycott a store, that's an incredible amount of resources. You have to have people in front of the store, you have to come up with alternatives for people. It's too much work. A lot of our constituents wanted us to boycott, and we didn't want to that because we didn't think we had the capacity to do it, and also because of the way it would be then lumped together with all the other boycotts.

The strategy reflected the Community Coalition's relative newness to the neighborhoods it served; rather than beginning life with grassroots ties, it had to build them. Growing local roots required a great deal of financial resources—and the Coalition relied on funding from the federal government to do so.[26]

In seeking federal funding, the Community Coalition was following a precedent established by past community organizing efforts in Los Angeles. Networks of neighborhood organizations were sparse in Los Angeles, a situation that generated high start-up costs for new organizations wishing to pursue social change. Unlike in New York City, local government in Los Angeles lacked a political interest in neighborhoods and had few resources of its own to make available to neighborhood groups. In the late 1970s, however, the Bradley administration had used federal funds to incorporate community organizations into the city grants process (Sonenshein 1993, 167). Faced with few options, the Community Coalition adopted Bradley's model and applied for grants from the federal government. When the organization's grants expired in 1996, it succeeded in renewing its funding with the help of former Bradley aides who were experienced in writing grant applications (Bass 1996).

Its very reliance on external sources of funding, however, had the potential to compromise its efforts at constructing grassroots ties. As Doug McAdam has argued, heavy reliance on external resources carries the risk of co-optation by elites (McAdam 1982). In fact, for this reason, Saul Alinsky had opposed relying on outside resources for his own work and was suspicious of governmental aid (Alinsky [1971] 1989). Community groups in Los Angeles in the 1970s had faced a similar dilemma, as Sonenshein points out: "The danger arose that these groups would become too adept at working the system, and lose touch with their obligation to serve the community. Moreover their skills in manipulating the grant system would be less useful if external funds were removed—which, of course, is what happened" (1993, 167). The Community Coalition managed to evade this particular pitfall, at least in the short term, and maintained close ties to the grassroots—largely due to the high priority its leaders placed on grassroots connections.

Its success was explainable by the priorities of its leaders, who focused their attention on close connections to the neighborhoods it served. It also received political support from Mark Ridley-Thomas, who stressed neighborhood connections in his own relations with constituents. Ridley-Thomas had established his own network of neighborhood-based constituent service centers in South Central, and he helped the Community Coalition set up similar stations so it could amass signatures for petitions (Cannon 1997, 364).

Dilemma of the Third Path

The Alinsky method of community organizing requires activists to discover local concerns without imposing their own agendas and then to employ confrontational tactics in order to achieve social change and build stable organizational resources. As the Community Coalition found, "liquor stores were a serious pulsating issue," and residents vented to the activists about their concerns that liquor sales were generating crime and "bringing the community down" (Bass 1996). Those concerns, however, were intermingled with longstanding tensions between blacks and Koreans. Karen Bass made it the group's mission to avoid racializing the liquor store campaign. Although the Coalition did not explicitly oppose boycotts that black organizations had led against Korean stores in the past, it did seek to distance itself from them. The Coalition, however, faced an important dilemma. It sought to channel tensions into a nonracial movement, even as those tensions were fueled by intergroup antagonisms.

The Community Coalition's leaders attempted to alter the discourse of conflict and tried earnestly to avoid making the liquor stores an issue between blacks and Koreans (Aubry 1996; Sonenshein 1996). "I don't like this issue," Bass (1996) said. "It was never where we were coming from" Actually, although the liquor store campaign involved blacks as the major players on one side and Koreans as major players on the other, the conflict did not involve just blacks and Koreans. The Community Coalition had

Latino members and staffers; at the same time, black merchants as well as Korean ones wanted to rebuild their liquor stores (Moffat 1992). Instead of escalating tensions among ethnic minorities, the organization sought to channel them into more productive ends.

However, as much as Coalition leaders disliked racial antagonisms, ill will toward Koreans lay at the roots of support for the campaign. As Bong Hwan Kim (1997) put it, the neighborhood fervor of the campaign was

> driven by the same emotions and perceptions, that the same Koreans who kill our kids are also trying to feed us these substances that are bad for us. Koreans were painted in the same light. In some ways, also, the issue became liquor stores. But a lot of people in the Korean community felt liquor stores were just another code word for "get Koreans out of our neighborhoods." So the community sentiments were identical.

Bass and the other Community Coalition leaders thus had to walk a fine line. "Divisiveness was not part of her strategy," Bong Hwan Kim said. "It was a completely different approach [from Danny Bakewell's] to dealing with the issue. But you can't ignore the fact there was this anti-Korean sentiment that was being leveraged to fuel a lot of that liquor store stuff." Bass herself acknowledged the presence of divisive attitudes among black residents: "Community members fall into these pitfalls all the time. If we had not constantly, religiously, educated community residents to look at the issue objectively, we could easily have made this a black-Korean issue. That could absolutely have been the case. It was a conscious decision on our part not to concede that."[27] At the Coalition's meetings, longtime residents pointed out to newer and younger ones that whites had owned the neighborhood stores before Koreans, and that the problems had been similar. Older generation residents of South Central, in fact, formed the core of the Coalition's membership (Sonenshein 1996), and may have been more willing to accept the Coalition's nonracial premise. As the Community Coalition expanded, it consciously added new programs to draw youths into the organization.

Ryan Song, executive director of KAGRO at the time, applauded the Community Coalition's efforts to deracialize conflicts and expressed great respect for Bass, his rival in the rebuilding effort. However, he could not agree with the Coalition's strategy: "The target, I thought, was quite cowardly because instead of going to the liquor companies or politicians directly, they were targeting storeowners who can't really provide anything, other than the fact they would just disappear and the business would go away and the community people would suffer because they don't have any store to go to" (Song 1996). Actually, Bass agreed with Song on at least this: the source of South Central's problems with liquor and crime lay outside the neighborhood, and in deeper problems of racism and economics. As she put it, Korean merchants were "ruthlessly used" by the alcohol industry, which aided Korean merchants in legislative battles at the State Assembly in Sacramento (Bass 1996).

The Community Coalition's choice of targets merely reflected the dilemma facing neighborhood-based organizations more generally: too often, the institutions responsible for social inequities are located outside the neighborhoods—and even the cities—that they victimize. Alinsky, who inspired so much of that organizing, believed that activists had to use local concerns to stir up conflict and to inflame passions if they were to strike at community apathy and achieve social change; connecting the neighborhood to a well-defined, broader social agenda at the national level, however, eluded him. The problem was compounded by the frequently parochial nature of neighborhood concerns: what if those very genuine concerns were entangled with racial prejudices? Alinsky did not favor changing people's prejudices or views; he believed people would rise above them if given the chance. Bass argued that this was the case in South Central; Korean activists were not so sure.

The problem was that Alinsky's method constrained activists' options in a context of racial segregation and economic disinvestment. Bass said blacks were incorrectly and unjustly portrayed as "victimizers" and Koreans as "victims." Bass was right. However, equally so, the reverse was not the case. Korean merchants may have had greater economic resources than many residents of South Central, but the institutions with the real resources—such as the alcohol industry, which profited from having Korean merchants sell their products in the inner city—simply were not available as targets in minority neighborhoods.

Constrained in the their options, Community Coalition leaders nonetheless made choices that had important implications for the alignment of interests in the liquor store conflict. In a number of instances, police officers served as "tactical allies" in the liquor store campaign, testifying along with residents at public hearings. They stated that their interest was in reducing crime (Bass 1996). KAGRO, which helped storeowners get through the rebuilding hearings and permit process, objected to this assistance from police officers as well as to the manner in which both attributed crime to the presence of stores.

To Korean merchants, it appeared that the LAPD was being pressured to cooperate by black elected officials (Song 1996). This was insult added to injury for many Korean Americans, coming just months after the ransacking of Koreatown, which they explained as the failure of the LAPD to protect a politically powerless immigrant community. In the liquor store campaign, black and Latino activists ended up allying with police against Korean merchants, when, under different circumstances, blacks and Koreans might instead have allied against police on the issue of adequate police protection. As in New York City, such an alliance never materialized.

Korean Americans who opposed the City Council's rebuilding hearings also argued that black politicians had been the ones who, in the 1980s, had allowed liquor licenses to spread throughout South Central (C. Kim 1996). At the same time, some Korean activists refused to blame the Community Coalition and instead sympathized with its leaders. As Jerry Yu (1996) explained:

> I might not have liked it—I fought against it actually. Our organization led a campaign against theirs, and we fought. But I respect what they did, and I understand what they did. And I think they were working on behalf of the community, in the proper way of community organizing, through all the political channels. So I don't see a problem with what they did. And I actually have a relationship with those people.

However, even as the Community Coalition tried to defuse racial tensions, and as similarly minded Korean American leaders reciprocated, media outlets—especially television news programs—often tried to play up the racial composition of the conflict. At times they tried to pit black and Korean leaders against one another. For instance, a joint appearance by Bass and KAGRO's Ryan Song on a local news program that employed an adversarial format reveals a media bias that favored intergroup confrontation. The producers objected to them talking casually before going on the air, which led them to agree on more than they disagreed—to the producers' disappointment (Song 1996; Bass 1996). Moreover, Bass recalled an instance when a *Los Angeles Times* reporter neglected to cover a rebuilding hearing in which the Community Coalition opposed a black-owned store, even though Bass urged the reporter to do so. And when the Community Coalition offered its associate director, Sylvia Castillo—who was not black, but Latino—as a spokesperson for a television news program, its producers refused, insisting on Karen Bass instead (Bass 1996).

The Community Coalition faced larger dilemmas that might have been insurmountable, but it can be credited for giving black-Korean tensions a new outlet. One wonders what might have happened if the Coalition and other organizations like it had been prevalent before the riots. In some respects, the Community Coalition's creative organizing and its reliance on external sources of funding calls to mind Boston's Dudley Street Neighborhood Initiative (DSNI), a highly successful community organization active in the late 1980s and 1990s. DSNI focused on neighborhood planning and affordable housing and never became tagged with interethnic conflict. But like the Community Coalition, DSNI took advantage of opportunities in the urban planning process to mobilize residents for social change. After the riots in Los Angeles, a Boston city official close to the organization remarked that, "If there were more DSNIs, L.A. wouldn't have happened" (Medoff and Sklar 1994, 247). More DSNIs or more Community Coalitions might have prevented the riots, or at least reduced their intensity, but there could hardly have been more such grassroots organizations in a city where the political system had long discouraged them.

The evidence from Los Angeles can now be gathered to complete the puzzle of politics and black-Korean conflicts. Recall the four questions posed at the end of chapter 3: First, what role do tensions play in producing nonviolent conflict? Second, what role does the political process play in preventing violent conflict? Third, what is the relationship, if any at all, between the two forms of conflict? Fourth, why have boycotts been far more intractable in New York than in Los Angeles?

Take the fourth question first. The short and relatively mild nature of Korean store boycotts was explainable by the political and community organizational context of Los Angeles. Protests against Korean stores—whether the boycotts or the liquor store campaign—can be understood as having served the same purpose as their equivalents in New York City: they allowed black activists to build organizations, strike at community apathy, and pursue larger causes. As Bong Hwan Kim (1997) observed, strategy was everything: "The more the conflict, the better, for the black community. They had nothing to lose but everything to gain by heightening awareness of the joblessness, the poverty, in the South Central community. If they had to use Koreans to get to the media to highlight that point, then so be it."

However, the number of activists willing and able to engage in collective, organized conflicts were few, and the kind of dense organizational networks that might have facilitated extended mobilization were rare. This also made boycotts relatively short-lived. As CRS mediator Stephen Thom (1996) put it, boycotts in Los Angeles simply did not have the "staying power" that would have made them a more prominent feature of intergroup relations. Mobilizing people was difficult. Unlike in New York, organizers could not rely on sizeable crowds to march for them: when they talked about strategy, they referred to the logistics of protest as if protesters were in short supply (Bass 1996; Gardner 1996). Without neighborhood organizations, they could turn to churches. Activists could "piggyback" on a church for support, as in the John's Liquor case, but churches were no substitute for the politically oriented and protest-hardened neighborhood organizations of New York City. All in all, logistical difficulties help to explain why boycotts in Los Angeles were not only short-lived but also relatively moderate in their demands compared to those in New York. Activists mounting boycotts with only a handful of supporters posed small threats; as such, they could hardly make big demands.

However, the difficulties confronting community organizers were not the only factor shaping black-Korean conflicts. The responses—or, rather, the lack of responses—by public officials and third parties also mattered, often allowing quicker resolutions to conflicts. When public officials intervened in boycotts, the interventions were few in number and well coordinated. By design, the city's reform-style political system insulated city leaders from the grassroots and discouraged conflict among them, making close bonds possible at the level of political and community elites. Consequently, community leaders and activists in Los Angeles traveled in relatively tight circles. Moreover, their relationships often cut across racial and ethnic boundaries. Black and Korean community leaders and activists on opposite sides of conflicts often met at functions and frequently enjoyed collegial relations (Aubry 1987; Bass 1996; Kim 1997; Song 1996; Yu 1996). The Black-Korean Alliance was the most visible sign of this. At the level of political and community elites, racial boundaries in Los Angeles were "fluid."[28] This atmosphere was also reflected in the common progressive racial ideology shared by members of Tom Bradley's biracial coalition (Sonenshein 1993).

But the good relations enjoyed among elites across racial lines did not extend to the grassroots. Raphael Sonenshein (1993) characterizes the problem as an abundance of interest conflicts, but it also reflects the disconnection of political elites from their constituents. The relatively cooperative relations among elites did not even hold within groups. Interestingly, strategies for handling intergroup conflicts met with greater divisions among Korean Americans than among African Americans—the opposite from what happened in New York. Even before the riots, Koreans community leaders were divided doubly: by generation and by ideology.

Although interventions on the part of local elected officials could be effective in ending conflicts, more often they were simply nonexistent. When local officials failed to step in, federal mediators went to bat. Although tensions between Korean merchants and black customers and activists were receiving little attention from local officials and community organizations, they were receiving federal attention in at least two ways. First, federal attention came from the Community Relations Service, the Justice Department agency that mediated several boycotts. In contrast, CRS mediators had been somewhat crowded out of the action in New York City. And second, federal attention came in the form of funding for the Community Coalition.

Notably, in the conflicts that were resolved most easily, one particular public institution was conspicuously absent: the courts. Courts only became involved in one case of conflict involving blacks and Koreans—the Latasha Harlins case. That case proved the most difficult to mediate (similar to the extremely intractable Red Apple boycott in New York, which also attracted court intervention), and had the most severe consequences. Courts have long played a role in racial controversies in the United States; their suitability as effective mediators of group conflict may be worth questioning.

Returning to the first of the four questions, the relationship between tensions and boycotts can be addressed by looking to the style and form of black nationalism. The predominant form in Los Angeles was a cultural black nationalism, espoused and spread by the Nation of Islam, which coexisted comfortably with the political and economic status quo and resisted outwardly focused, organized confrontations. Unlike in New York, black nationalist activists were thus not accustomed to mounting public protests to achieve their aims. The dominance of this form of black nationalism in Los Angeles was probably facilitated by the lack of residents' experience with strong grassroots political organizations. In other cities, one can imagine other combinations of political context and forms of black nationalism.

The second question, concerning the role of politics in preventing violence, can be addressed (like in New York City) by looking to the structure and policies of the city's police. Police did not maintain a presence at protests against Korean stores. In some cases, police officials may have decided that boycotts did not merit their attention because of the small size of crowds. However, LAPD officers did not see themselves as conflict mediators, like the NYPD did. Officers were not at the scenes of larger protests either, like the ones at John's Liquor or Empire Liquor. If police did oversee those boycotts, they were so few as to escape notice by reporters. More important, however, the relationship of politics to violence can be seen in the limitations that the LAPD—a police force crafted and developed under a reform-style politics that devalued the importance of neighborhood and ethnic attachments—faced during the 1992 civil unrest. Like other big cities, New York and Los Angeles both had histories of bad relations between police and minorities. Despite such antagonisms, the structure of the NYPD allowed officers to maintain ties to the activists whom they confronted regularly. The structure of the LAPD did not.

With respect to the third question, concerning the relationship between the two forms of conflict, we can compare the types of incidents reported. In New York, many more minor assaults and altercations were reported between 1980 and 1995—quite possibly because they were followed by boycotts, which served to publicize the initial incidents. In contrast, many such minor clashes might not have been reported in Los Angeles because boycotts did not follow them. In Los Angeles, community activists were less likely—and less available—to see minor disputes as opportunities for mobilizing communities. If there had been more boycotts, and they had mobilized greater numbers of people, especially as the number of violent incidents reported in the media grew in 1990 and 1991, then the tensions that eventually exploded might have been channeled more effectively—producing *less* violence and destruction in 1992.

Chapter 6

No Fire Next Time

Appearances can be deceiving. Before 1992, incessant conflict in New York City made Los Angeles look like an oasis of ethnic peace. We find it easy to condemn conflict that polarizes people, but hindsight shows that its absence can be worse. In New York, frequent, contentious protests channeled intergroup tensions; without those protests, Los Angeles suffered on a larger scale. A comparison of the experiences with black-Korean conflicts in the two cities suggests that conflict can actually be desirable, if it comes in the right form: in fact, turning up its volume may prevent mass violence.

If boycotts of Korean stores helped New York City to avoid one fate, however, they were unproductive in achieving an even more desirable goal: the joint pursuit of worthwhile, long-term, political goals. Black-Korean conflicts failed along these lines in both cities because they engaged the wrong adversaries: they took place in the streets rather than in and around the halls of government, and they targeted actors that were too far removed from the sources of underlying problems. The primary lesson of these cities' experiences, then, is not that conflicts should be eliminated entirely, but that tensions should be channeled into the most productive forms. Finding the means to channel conflict effectively requires first understanding its causes. Comparing black-Korean conflicts allows us to untangle the relationships among politics, protest, and violence. Even more importantly, it points to ways for thinking about appropriate remedies.

THE CAUSES OF BLACK-KOREAN CONFLICTS

Tensions among African Americans and Korean Americans have had as much to do with economic interests as with ideas. Racial stereotypes and an American ideology pitting a model minority against an underclass certainly have helped to generate ill will between blacks and Koreans. However, tensions emerged first among business owners, when black merchants began to face growing competition from Korean entrepreneurs. As tensions spread, community organizers saw their potential for fueling neighborhood activism and adopted the cause, which fit well with the rhetoric of black nationalism. Later, boycotts and rioting took place as much in middle-class black neighborhoods as they did in impoverished communities. To be sure, these conflicts took place in a context of limited economic opportunities; however, opportunities were limited for both groups, and the conflicts were not clear-cut cases of haves versus have-nots.

Boycotts of Korean stores became the dominant expression of inter-group tensions, but they derived neither wholly nor solely from such tensions. They also owed their existence to the larger context of the times in which they arose. During the 1970s and 1980s, the civil rights movement had slowed and fragmented, and a new wave of black activists became oriented toward local rather than national goals. The focus on local politics led to an extraordinary rise in the number of black elected officials in city governments, but at the same time it generated a dilemma for community organizers. These cadres of neighborhood activists had helped put blacks in public office, but neither was able to dispel the most serious social and economic afflictions in black neighborhoods. Protest movements, the tried and true path to political mobilization and social uplift, began to search desperately for targets at the local level. At that moment in time, due to the end of restrictive immigration laws and the exodus of business from cities, Korean merchants appeared.

Thus, blacks and Koreans became intertwined in overt conflicts for political and organizational reasons as much as anything else. From the point of view of black activists seeking to mobilize their neighborhoods, whether they were advancing their own positions or larger causes, Korean stores were neighborhood institutions in neighborhoods that often lacked bigger targets. Korean merchants were not the architects of a racially oppressive environment, but they served as symbols of it for the sake of protest. They differed from other ethnic merchants in that they were not only ubiquitous but well organized as well, making them appear to be part of a highly networked and successful chain of ethnic establishments and not just another brand of mom-and-pop grocers. The ethnic support networks on which individual Korean merchants relied were often fragile and tenuous, but conflicts with blacks led them to strengthen their networks and increase their solidarity.

Violence was a different matter. Isolated shooting incidents may have had little connection to more generalized tensions, and even less connection to political institutions. The mass violence that took place in Los Angeles, however, was tied to both. In New York City, there were certainly enough raucous, crowded protests to provide the setting for violent outbursts, but none occurred. Rounding up the usual suspects in explanations of rioting—crime rates, unemployment, poverty, segregation, racial injustice—fails to differentiate the two cities. These factors underlay the rioting, but they could not explain why it happened where it did.

The answer to the puzzle of politics, protest, and violence in black-Korean conflicts—why tensions assumed the form of mass violence in one city but not the other—has several parts. First, due to the structure of political institutions in Los Angeles, there was a paucity of neighborhood organizations willing and able to launch boycotts and channel tensions. Tensions were more likely to be channeled into protest in cities with strong legacies of traditional political organization and high levels of black political representation. Where political organization was scarce, boycotts occurred only in small, fitful bursts, leaving tensions unorganized and creating the potential for mass violence. Local political institutions also made a difference via their impact on the form of black nationalism. The fragmented nature of the Black Power movement that took hold in the wake of the civil rights movement meant that strategies pursued by black nationalist organizations were influenced more by local political contexts than by a single, overarching, national agenda. In New York City, a more politically active, outward-oriented form of black nationalism helped channel tensions. In Los Angeles, black nationalism adopted a form that was not only more middle-class oriented, but also more politically passive. Finally, political institutions shaped the policies of police departments, the governmental agencies with the most direct roles in shaping conflict. The LAPD lacked the structure and capacities that the NYPD had for maintaining ties to neighborhood activists and for monitoring crowds during demonstrations.

Some observers of conflicts argued that boycotts stirred up tensions that promoted incidents of violence. However, incidents of violence actually preceded boycotts more than they followed them; activists used the incidents as triggers for organizing protests. Reports of violence had higher potential for emotional content, making them a useful tool for mobilizing protests. If boycotts led to violence at all, it was only when they stopped short of their potential and intensified tensions without fully organizing them. This notion is supported by the fact that large-scale violence was precipitated in the city that experienced fewer boycotts, not in the one that experienced more.

THE LIMITS OF LEADERSHIP

Political scientists have longed viewed the management of conflict as a principal function of urban government (Banfield and Wilson 1963, 18). Numerous conflicts make their way into the chambers of city councils; issues such as economic development and education find a place on the agenda in no small part because the political system has formal channels for their expression. Other conflicts, including the most divisive, do not make it into the halls of government: these are fought on the streets instead of in voting booths or council chambers. Although the political system lacks formal avenues for managing such conflicts, governments are expected to resolve them.

The burden of public expectations inescapably falls on the shoulders of mayors, the officials with the broadest mandates from city electorates. Supporters, rivals, and critics all call on mayors to employ "moral leadership" to end difficult social conflicts—a demand that requires them to take a straightforward moral stand and communicate that position to the public, who are expected to listen and act accordingly. This logic makes two flawed assumptions, however: first, that mayors' formal powers over the machinery of government translates into equal power over conflicts that take place outside the formal political system; and second, that mayors' electoral victories automatically reward them with an unbounded reserve of legitimacy that allows them essentially to dictate to their supporters. In fact, mayors operate under great constraints, and even the strongest tend to be weak players when compared with economic actors and other informal forces in urban politics. Moreover, because they win elections on the crests of coalitions that are frequently rife with internal contradictions, their legitimacy even among ardent supporters can easily turn sour as they juggle competing demands.

Actually, mayors vary in their capacities to mediate and resolve difficult social conflicts. Ultimately, they can only resolve conflicts by persuading other actors in the political system to mobilize in ways that favor their course of action or by preventing the mobilization of those in opposition. As Charles Levine has noted, the effectiveness of mayors in managing divisive conflicts depends on both "contextual forces and purposeful choices" (1974, xi). Consequently, the same mayoral leadership style can be highly effective in one city but less so in another.

One constraint has to do with the complex social and political dynamics of intergroup relations. When social scientists investigate conflict, they typically look to the structure of relations between racial and ethnic groups. Rarely, however, do they pay comparable attention to the structure of relations within groups, that is, among subgroups. In fact, what we think of as intergroup conflict—or intergroup cooperation—more often consists of interactions between factions of different ethnic and racial groups, not between entire groups. Factions within communities compete or cooperate with one another, invoking their own or another group's ethnicity, and thereby influence the nature of larger intergroup relations.

The pattern of support and opposition within black communities and within Korean communities figured importantly in shaping boycotts. Interventions by black community organizations in the Red Apple boycott were divided: some organizations supported the boycott, but many opposed it. Interventions by Korean organizations were unified in purpose, and trade organizations even competed to capitalize on the community's solidarity. In contrast, interventions by black organizations in the John's Liquor boycott were few and unified, with virtually no vocal opposition. The Korean community, however, was divided in its response, with its leaders uncertain over whether to support the store or allow it to close. Community activists were central to such dynamics; those seeking to understand intergroup conflict would do well to pay more attention to this strata of political actors—who are too often neglected by social scientists—and, more important, to the role played by political context in facilitating or constraining their activities.

The structure of political institutions also plays a role in the development of conflicts, making them more or less intractable and thereby limiting the impact mayors have. Consequently, different contexts demand different responses. In both the Red Apple and the John's Liquor boycotts, each mayor preferred to pursue a "quiet," behind-the-scenes strategy. However, it proved easier to apply for Tom Bradley in Los Angeles, with its relatively insulated reform-style politics and its tight circle of elite actors involved in matters of intergroup relations. In New York City, the structure of government, the fragmentation of political organizations, and the high level of mobilization made political battles highly competitive and less conducive to a quiet strategy. Ironically, David Dinkins had been elected as an alternative to his more vocal and racially insensitive predecessor, Ed Koch, but a quiet strategy simply became untenable in New York's more competitive, pressure-group-oriented system. As Dinkins's critics would have it, he simply stood by and watched for too long. However, even if the mayor mishandled the conflict somewhat, to a greater extent he was hamstrung by forces beyond his control. Too many actors responded for any single one to have his way—the fragmented local political system made this outcome likely. Coalition management, already a difficult task in a highly competitive political setting, became impossible.

Just as mayors get shouldered with the blame when something goes wrong, they often get the credit when something else goes right. When the Rodney King verdicts were announced in 1992, no violence broke out in

New York City; instead, there were large public demonstrations, and the mayor got credit for keeping the peace after he and his staff toured neighborhoods urging calm. "Thank God, the people of New York, and most of all the Mayor," Governor Mario Cuomo told an audience of New Yorkers (Sims 1992). "Take a Bow, Dave," wrote the *New York Post*, a paper that had been highly critical of the mayor in the past. Similarly, Rudolph Giuliani, Dinkins's successor, received credit for the significant decline in violent crime that New York City experienced in the 1990s—a trend that paralleled a nationwide decline. David Dinkins did not single-handedly prevent rioting in New York City in 1992. Nor could he have prevented the Red Apple conflict in 1990.

If there were too many cooks stirring New York's pot of ethnic tensions, spoiling the soup, in Los Angeles there were too few, and it boiled over. Mayor Tom Bradley faced little pressure to denounce boycotts and none to shop at boycotted stores. However, even in this context, it was not the moral weight of the mayor's office that ended boycotts (as boycott critics in both cities would have liked), but the balance of political power and the effectiveness of elite ties. To generalize, when too many officials intervene without coordination and under tremendous public pressure, as they did in New York, they end up working at cross-purposes and extending conflict. When too few officials feel public pressure to intervene, as in Los Angeles, a resolution may be reached quickly, but the brevity of conflict may fail to adequately channel tensions or to represent the interests of enough players.

The public officials best able to mediate conflicts, however, may not be the ones with the broadest mandates. Racial and ethnic conflicts often involve disputes at the grassroots, meaning that the success of mediators depends on their legitimacy in the eyes of participants at that level. The only public official (and possibly the only third party) in either New York City or Los Angeles who was able to end a boycott without granting the core demands of protesters was Al Vann—not a mayor, but a state assembly representative. Vann represented a relatively small, neighborhood-sized constituency in Brooklyn and shared the grassroots, insurgent origins of the boycott leaders—allowing him to steal their thunder and resolve the conflict by end run.

However, events in Los Angeles—and specifically, the liquor store campaign—show that only good leadership has the potential actually to transform tensions, by deracializing them. Conflict can be most constructive if the responses to it help lay the groundwork for future coalition-building. New York's incentives for activists and neighborhood organizing promoted greater grassroots involvement in politics, but the conflicts such involvement generated created problems for progressive coalitions, hindering their development. On the other hand, the boycotts established ties among activists who had genuine grassroots connections, laying potential groundwork for new kinds of coalitions in the future. Mayors interested in cross-racial coalition-building might have the greatest impact on unproductive conflicts by successfully coordinating with the activists, third parties, and other officials who have such ties and who possess greater local legitimacy in the eyes of conflict participants.

In many ways, the patterns of intervention in both contexts were analogous to recent understandings of the workings of interest group politics in national policy-making arenas, particularly with regard to the role of political elites in maintaining networks of communication. Elites can be seen either as comprising a single cohesive community—a "central circle"—that mediates conflicts among organized groups, or as comprising a network of "adjacent, politically-compatible interest groups" that "deal with their allies, not their adversaries," exhibiting a "hollow core." When networks of community leaders have hollow cores, the potential exists that "government officials act as the mediators who bind the system together" (Heinz et al. 1990, 381–82).

In cities, the ability of public officials to provide an "inner circle" of effective mediators depends on the structure of the political system. In reform-style cities, institutions have been designed to discourage open conflict, precisely by ensuring that an inner circle would dominate decision-making (Stone 1976, 30). However, the disconnection of inner-circle elites from their constituents has meant that they have been able to resolve open conflicts only in the short term, leaving underlying tensions unresolved. The patterns of conflict intervention in Korean store boycotts suggest that intergroup relations in New York City exhibited a hollow core, whereas in Los Angeles they involved an inner circle.

In a sense, Los Angeles held forth an example of consociational politics, in which "a strong coalition is formed at the elite level, crossing polarized group boundaries" (Sonenshein 1993, 139). By contrast, in New York City a "street-fighting pluralism" (Yates 1977) prevented easy bridging by elites. Elite-level solutions like consociationalism, however, only work well in preventing mass conflict when elites are well grounded in their communities, a relationship that was lacking in Los Angeles. Moreover, elites' attempts to bridge racial and ethnic group boundaries are made difficult by divisions within those groups. African American and Korean American activists never mounted significant attempts in either city to mobilize supporters from both groups around shared interests, such as for adequate police protection or against police abuse. The reason has to do not just with the quality of leaders or the willingness of followers, but with the relationship between the two. In Los Angeles the leadership lacked a base, and in New York City the base lacked leadership.

AVOID FALSE HOPES

Those interested in resolving unproductive conflicts will only find the right tools to do so after they recognize both the importance of relationships between leaders and followers and the constraints on public officials in managing informal social relations. To begin with, would-be mediators should avoid relying on two models of conflict resolution that have gained currency in the wake of the Los Angeles riots, both of which aim to settle group differences in apolitical ways: one emphasizes intergroup dialogue and another looks to the courts. The experiences of black-Korean conflicts, both peaceful and violent, demonstrate the pitfalls of relying on either model.

The dialogue model seeks to engage representatives of conflicting groups in a discussion that will yield mutual understanding and erase hurtful stereotypes. In the late 1990s, President Bill Clinton launched the most well-known example of this approach, the President's Initiative on Race, which sought to draw Americans into an "honest dialogue" (White House 2002a). The Initiative on Race defined dialogue as

> a forum that draws participants from as many parts of the community as possible to exchange information face-to-face, share personal stories and experiences, honestly express perspectives, clarify viewpoints, and develop solutions to community concerns. Unlike debate, dialogue emphasizes listening to deepen understanding. . . . Dialogue invites discovery. It develops common values and allows participants to express their own interests. It expects that participants will grow in understanding and may decide to act together with common goals. In dialogue, participants can question and reevaluate their assumptions. (White House 2002b)

In concert with this definition, the Initiative centered around televised town meetings, conducted by Clinton himself, and public hearings held in locales across the nation, moderated by a panel of experts whom he had appointed to a Race Advisory Board. The town meetings served as opportunities for audience members—and, vicariously, television viewers as well—to vent their feelings about race, resembling more than anything else the cathartic group therapy of television talk shows.

Lani Guinier (1995), who advocates reforming politics in order to change the way Americans talk about race, similarly argues that candid conversation among representatives of different groups is the best hope for harmonious intergroup relations. However, talk can be empty if detached from substance and, more important, from government action. As Adolph Reed warns, "the notion soothes and reassures, conveying a sense of gravitas, while at the same time having no clear, practical meaning whatsoever" (1997, 18). Ultimately, the public hearings that were part of Clinton's Initiative on Race became the targets of conservative critics who accused Clinton of failing to appoint members reflecting a diversity of views (Wickham 1997). If the implicit aim of dialogue was to achieve mutual understanding through candid talk and gentle persuasion among a diversity of voices, little was accomplished.

There is perhaps no better evidence for the failure of the dialogue model than the experience of Los Angeles in the years leading up to the civil unrest. Efforts at dialogue took various forms: conferences, seminars, banquets, goodwill trips to Korea, joint prayer sessions, and holiday food donations. The Black-Korean Alliance was central to these efforts and represented the formalization of the dialogue model: it was an organized, enduring, government-sanctioned forum that brought together community leaders in an attempt to process tensions. No one came to realize the inherent problems with relying on dialogue better than the organization's founders and most dedicated members. As the Korean American Coalition's Jerry Yu put it, efforts based on goodwill and cultural exchange are "nice" but need a "mighty disclaimer": "It is easy and has been easy, to fall into a trap of essentially dealing with similar thinking, similar acting people. . . . We have to make a distinction between form and substance" (1992, 35). At best, efforts aimed at dialogue that are neither adequately grounded at the grassroots nor adequately provided for by governments risk wasting the resources of communities and the time and reputation of leaders. At worst, they risk deluding citizens and public officials into believing that race relations are progressing toward greater harmony even as mounting tensions go unnoticed, simply because they lack outward manifestations.

According to a second popular model, the courts are conceived as effective mediators of social conflict. Like chief executives, they are expected to resolve conflicts by drawing on the legitimacy they derive from their formal, constitutional status. The Supreme Court is often thought of in this way, as Charles Franklin and Liane Kosaki (1989) assert: "The conception of the Court as republican schoolmaster generally reflects the notion that the Court, through its explication of the law and its high moral standing, may give the populace an example of the way good republicans should behave." However, with respect to the issue of abortion, the Court is limited in its capacities to resolve conflict by external forces, such as the structure of public opinion, and can even exacerbate it (Franklin and Kosaki 1989). Indeed, in black-Korean conflicts in both Los Angeles and New York City, the involvement of courts made conflicts more divisive rather than less.

Courts are the appropriate venue for deciding questions of law, but we should be careful not to conflate questions of law with questions of politics, especially when the resolution of intergroup conflict is at stake. In order to channel conflicts in a productive direction, elected officials and other mediators should avoid steering public expectations toward the courts. Unfortunately, trends at the local and national levels suggest that politicians have been increasingly using legal institutions to decide matters better left to political bargaining. The decline in political parties as strong organizations and as mobilizing forces has led politicians to seek new weapons for achieving their goals—utilizing courts, as well as the news media and interest groups, in what Benjamin Ginsberg and Martin Shefter (1999) call "institutional combat." Similarly, elected officials confronted with resolving racial and ethnic conflicts, a task for which they often lack the legitimacy and resources, have adopted strategies that hold little promise of success.

Both the dialogue and the court models of conflict resolution eschew politics. The dialogue model abhors conflict, even when it is productive conflict, instead seeking peace through a process of group therapy. However, genuine efforts to build durable foundations for cooperation may require an arduous and difficult process of mobilization and bargaining before yielding fruit. The court model threatens to exacerbate conflict by focusing resolution on an up-or-down judicial ruling, thereby framing the outcomes as zero-sum rather than the product of compromise. And both pass the buck, forgoing action for talk—in the case of dialogue—and leadership for legal solutions—in the case of courts.

Public officials and other would-be mediators who try to shift the arbitration of conflict into these arenas risk raising false hopes because they give the impression that conflict resolution is under way even as tensions continue to mount. Instead, leaders should embrace political solutions and engage their supporters in concrete, constructive projects that build firmly grounded alliances across group boundaries. Broadly participatory projects involving genuine stakeholders in conflicts—such as joint community development projects, as Bong Hwan Kim (1997) has suggested—should be part of the solution. To its credit, President Clinton's Initiative on Race published a list of "Promising Practices"—organizations and activities that brought individuals of different races and ethnicities to work together on common tasks—for local officials and activists to emulate (White House 2002a).

Both the dialogue and court models of conflict resolution make the assumption that conflicts are caused by ideas; as such, their remedies involve persuasion and rely on changing the attitudes or values of people in conflict. If interests are at the root of conflicts, however, as seems more likely, then the remedy must be government action that decreases inequality and increases economic opportunity. If political institutions play any part in causing the conflict, then they must be a part of the remedy too. An institutional explanation suggests that concrete, grounded, participatory projects are the best path to avoiding unproductive conflict. City, state, and the federal governments could facilitate such projects by providing urban neighborhoods with the resources they need to channel tensions.

Resources are most commonly conceived as financial. Funding from the federal government or from charitable foundations can provide individual organizations with the resources to become effective community mobilizers, as was the case with the Community Coalition. However, such sources make weak foundations for revitalizing communities in the long run, because relying on them makes organizations subject to shifting political trade winds in Congress and improves the chances only of organizations lucky enough to win funding—when what is needed is the wholesale retooling of political institutions.

To some extent, local political parties once served the functions of mobilizing neighborhoods and tying leaders to their bases of supporters. Since there is little hope of political parties being rebuilt from the ground up, cities need to look for other ways to restore and maintain these functions. Other intermediary institutions, such as labor unions and churches, hold some potential. Labor unions, long only weak forces in American politics, have begun a revival, but their long-term viability depends a great deal on favorable government policy. Government assistance to churches—as part of President George W. Bush's focus on making faith-based institutions partners in social policy, for instance—may help to build social capital and ease poverty in some urban communities. However, burdened as they already are, inner-city churches will never be as effective at organizing citizens and involving them in politics as would networks of neighborhood organizations. In Los Angeles, activists bemoaned the lack of financial support from city government for coalition-building and mediation activities as an obstacle to achieving better race relations. Underlying this problem, however, was the city's lack of incentives for mass political participation and its need for a system-wide refocusing.

The most basic and effective way to achieve this, in Los Angeles and other cities like it, is for local governments to encourage networks for neighborhood mobilization by restructuring their political institutions. By promoting greater routine citizen mobilization, these networks would help to prevent a recurrence of the large-scale rioting that happened in Los Angeles in 1992. Other reform-style cities that could benefit from greater neighborhood mobilization include Miami, which experienced periodic rioting during the 1980s, or Cincinnati, which experienced riots in 2001. Given the inherent weakness of cities in the face of economic realities, this may be their best hope for preventing mass violence. Local institutional reform and restructuring might have even longer-lasting consequences if they were backed by financial resources from states or the federal government.

Los Angeles has already taken a step down the right path: in 1999, voters approved a package of reforms to the city charter that included a proposal for a system of neighborhood councils to encourage greater citizen participation in local government (Charter Reform Commission 1999). For some, the neighborhood council reform represents the potential to open up an elite-run, politically insulated City Hall and to change the balance of power in Los Angeles. For example, social critic Mike Davis (1992c) envisions a "parliament of neighborhoods" that would not only "abolish the invisible government" but "encourage interethnic unity" as well:

> The fundamental point is that neighborhood government would mobilize the passion and creativity of thousands of ordinary people who want to build true social justice in Los Angeles. The current system merely corrodes their idealism and deters their participation. . . . Moreover, a neighborhood tier would guarantee previously voiceless groups—Central American refugees, Korean merchants, inner-city youth, even the homeless—an immediate, compelling presence in city politics.

A system of neighborhood councils certainly holds great promise and represents the charter's most radical reform. Pinning such high hopes on them, however, especially in the short term, will prove disappointing. Because the neighborhood councils will be advisory bodies rather than hold formal powers, they might usefully be compared to New York City's community boards. The community boards frequently act as lighting rods for community mobilization, drawing residents to vent against city government without having to travel to City Hall.

Still, as D. J. Waldie (1999) points out, "neighborhood councils face many risks, not the least of which is the brittleness of the system in which they would operate." With decades of reform politics behind it, the political system in Los Angeles will likely remain top-heavy, organized to be most receptive to downtown business interests. Elites will likely try to make use of the councils, perhaps by controlling their agendas via appointments. The charter reforms themselves began as an attempt to appease a growing secession movement in the San Fernando valley, one of the city's wealthiest districts. The new charter will not establish patterns of community organization overnight that took decades of traditional politics to build in New York City. Still, if bringing politics into the neighborhood life of Angelenos can create even a trickle of its own activity in the short term, this experiment at decentralization may begin to lay the groundwork for greater community mobilization in the long term.

With the strengthening of local democracy, however, advocates of ethnic and racial peace must remember this: more democracy will not initially mean greater harmony but its opposite. Lani Guinier, who argues that switching to an electoral system based on proportional representation will bring greater harmony, is right to seek an answer in the reform of political institutions; however, her hope that such reforms will usher in racial and ethnic peace is misplaced (Guinier 1995). More democracy inevitably means more conflict. Fundamentally, democratization represents the expansion of the scope of conflict, because it brings to the table the demands of groups that had previously gone unmobilized and unheard (Schattschneider 1957). This means that the most enduring solution will not come by the shortest path; ethnic peace may appear to suffer in the near term. The contentiousness of intergroup relations in New York City seemed undesirable, but in the end it proved preferable to the calm before the storm in Los Angeles. The future will, and should, entail greater conflict. The important task before both cities, and the rest of the nation, is to ensure that conflict takes the right path.

THE FUTURE

The Los Angeles riots represented a failure of ideas—in that prejudice won over tolerance—and they represented a failure to protect the interests of the most vulnerable in society. Equally profoundly, however, they represented a failure of democratic institutions, not only in the modern, liberal sense—in the guarantee of individual liberties and minority rights that were violated in the Rodney King case—but also in the classical sense—in the responsibility that political institutions have to inculcate civic virtue, that is, to draw citizens into the political process and encourage a vibrant political life. As newspaper columnist Tim Rutten wrote shortly after the riots, "It is not only that Los Angeles is a huge place, whose neighborhoods and citizens are even more divided from one another than in other cities, and that we have more foreigners here who cannot vote. . . . It is also that the local political system is an unworkable relic of the progressive era" (1992, 54). Black-Korean conflicts—but especially the riots—were fundamentally problems of political participation, rooted in political institutions. To avoid conflicts like them in the future, cities have to reorganize their political systems in order to encourage the grassroots expression of tensions and to facilitate the growth of leaders who have the capacity to champion coalitions for progressive change.

Black-Korean conflicts may have faded from the headlines since the mid-1990s, but not because they were resolved in any meaningful way. As community activist Larry Aubry pointed out (1996):

> It is no longer a problem not because there has been public resources brought to bear, but rather because the problem has simply receded. . . . People have moved on to other things, so the underlying conditions are still there, and there's been no real governmental response of a positive or lasting nature. . . . It is almost like a pyrrhic victory, it's almost like fool's gold. Like this is what we see, but not what we've got.

Public officials must be taken to task for failures to encourage intergroup harmony and, even more, to pursue solutions for the social and economic inequalities that produce divisions. However, Americans also have to embrace a shift in how they understand race and ethnic relations, so that the terms encompass not only the responsibilities of citizens and leaders as individuals, but the responsibilities of public institutions, which represent them collectively, as well (Jones-Correa 1998, 202). As the years following the civil rights movement proved, "assertive government action can define acceptable practices and behavior, and ultimately change the world in which attitudes are formed" (Reed 1997, 18); in other words, public institutions and public policies can mold intergroup relations. We need government action to remove the sources of injustice that make unproductive conflict inescapable.

Unfortunately, a comparable movement that could compel such policies is lacking; potential supporters are divided not only by race, but increasingly by class and ethnicity as well, introducing difficult hurdles in the form of interest-based conflicts at the grassroots. If citizens wait for policy changes to yield the solutions to resolving intergroup conflict, they may wait endlessly. As William Julius Wilson writes, "unless groups of ordinary citizens embrace the need for mutual political cooperation, they stand little chance of generating the political muscle needed to ease their economic and social burdens" (1999, 123). In short, mobilization for cooperation is a precondition for social change—participation molds policy as well. Resolving unproductive conflicts will help to remove the barriers to cooperation. Then, enduring cooperation among the members of different racial and ethnic groups will come only through their participation in concrete, constructive, and possibly contentious projects at the grassroots, where they are themselves stakeholders in the outcomes—and not through well-intentioned but, in the end, false appeals to ethnic harmony.

Appendix

DATA COLLECTION

In order to identify incidents involving blacks and Koreans, I conducted a search of local newspapers using three electronic databases with national coverage: Lexis-Nexis, Ethnic NewsWatch, and FirstSearch Abstracts. I searched printed indexes and archives to supplement the electronic sources. In addition to overcoming the biases discussed in chapter 1, the method of drawing primarily from electronic databases affords a single researcher an unparalleled level of efficiency and convenience.

By far the largest of the three databases is Lexis-Nexis. While much of the material it covers is oriented to business and legal audiences, it also includes the full text of many general circulation newspapers. Lexis-Nexis contains a number of "libraries," or categorized groupings of publications. My searches were conducted on the "U.S. News" library, which at the time of the search included the full text of about 130 newspapers, and "selected text" (usually business-related) of several hundred more. In another library, Lexis-Nexis also contains abstracts of articles from a few major newspapers for which it does not carry the entire text, and I searched these as well. I determined that the full content (abstracts and full text) of about seventy general circulation newspapers (as opposed to sports papers, trade journals, legal newsletters, financial papers, and so forth) were covered. To determine newspaper types, I used the Gale Directory of Publications (1995), which lists descriptive categories (along with a great deal of other information) for every newspaper in publication in the United States. I conducted separate, individual searches of the library files of each newspaper to ensure that I did not miss relevant stories from them in the initial, larger search.

Ethnic NewsWatch contains the text of several hundred publications, including newspapers aimed at particular ethnic readerships (most of which are published weekly rather than daily). Using the Gale Directory of Publications (1995), I determined that Ethnic NewsWatch covers about thirty newspapers with black, Asian, or Korean audiences.

FirstSearch Abstracts contains only the abstracts of stories from twenty-three major city newspapers (with general or African American reader-ships), five of which were not covered by the other two databases. This database thus both complemented and supplemented the others.

I searched all three databases using the keywords "black" and "Ko-rean," a process that resulted in thousands of relevant and irrelevant sto-ries. I sorted through the results to exclude the irrelevant stories (such as obituaries of black veterans of the Korean war, accounts of searches for the "black box" flight recorder of the Korean airliner shot down in 1983, and innumerable others), and coded the remainder. The time periods of cover-age on these databases varies by publication: some papers are covered back to the early 1980s, and others are covered only for the past one, two, or three years. When possible, I searched the printed indexes of the latter for previous years. My aim was to achieve as much coverage as possible of the 1990s and whatever else I could of the previous decade (the latter gener-ally limited to a small number of larger newspapers).

Once relevant newspaper stories were sorted out, I used a systematic coding scheme to extract specific information on each event found. Events were counted when they pitted members of one group against members of the other, individually or collectively, in a public confrontation. Since I was concerned with the relationship between protest and violence, I distin-guished between these two types of events. (See text for definitions.)

The coding scheme I developed required extracting the following basic information about each event: an identifying label for each event (usually the name of the victim or accuser for incidents of violence and the name of the target for protests); the event type (violence or protest); the event loca-tion (the city and the neighborhood or address where it was centered); and the exact or estimated event date (or, for protests longer than one day, the starting date).

For boycotts, the following additional data was collected: the exact or estimated end date (the last date protesters are reported demonstrating at the scene); the protest target (including the number and type); the precipi-tating event reported to have provoked the protest; the name of the protest organization(s) leading the protest, if any (and whether it existed prior to the protest or formed expressly to lead/organize it); the protest demands made by spokespersons or leaders; the reason why the protest ended; and the concessions to protesters made by the protest target.

For violent incidents, the following information was gathered: the type of violence (usually a verbal assault, physical assault, shooting, firebomb-ing, or looting); the primary result of violence (usually an injury, death, property damage, or none); the ethnicity of the perpetrator or police sus-pect; the ethnicity of the victim; the affiliation of the perpetrator, if relevant (such as the store name, if a merchant); and whether the incident led to formal charges or convictions or was labeled a bias crime by police (as reported by newspapers).

Finally, for both boycotts and violent incidents, I coded the responses of the following public institutions and private interest groups, when they were noted: mayor, city council, courts, police, district attorney, or other public officials; black organizations (such as neighborhood or business organizations) and Korean organizations; black and Korean churches; and other groups. For the sake of reliability, I kept citations of the source newspaper stories on each piece of information collected.

THE SAMPLE OF CITIES

The availability of substantial newspaper coverage in the electronic databases and paper indexes determined the sample of cities used in the statistical analysis in chapter 2. Additionally, cities included in the analysis meet three criteria: first, each city is located in a metropolitan area, defined as a Primary Metropolitan Statistical Area (PMSA) by the U.S. Census Bureau (1990), and served by one of the daily newspapers in the databases; second, each city is covered by at least five years of newspaper content; and third, each has a population of at least 100,000. The result is a sample of thirty-nine cities (see Table 1.1).

This group of cities ranges in population size from 102,724 (Berkeley) to 7,322,564 (New York City), with an average population of 698,370. The sample contains cities from each of the regions of the mainland United States: the Northeast (seven cities), the Midwest (eight), the Southeast (six), the Southwest (eight), and the West (nine).

PROBLEMS WITH THE MEASUREMENT OF INDEPENDENT VARIABLES

The measures for several variables used in the statistical models of boycotts and violence were limited by available data, and therefore could only serve as rough indicators of the theories they were meant to represent. Most important, indicators for three of the idea- and interest-oriented theories— the proportion of non-English-speaking Korean Americans, the ratio of the Korean self-employment rate to that of the general population, and the ratio of black-owned to Korean-owned businesses—used data for census-defined metropolitan areas rather than for cities. City-level data for these measures were unavailable. (All other variables in the analysis used city-level measures.) So it remains possible—and seems likely—that the lack of precision in the measurement of the sociological variables has affected their capacities to explain, and thus is partly responsible for the absence of support for them. Perhaps better data on these measures—at the city level or neighborhood level—would have yielded different results.

Moreover, there is an alternative plausible explanation for the significance of the competition variable: it may merely signal a greater number of locations at which interactions between the two groups can take place. Other things equal, when crime is constant and the ratio of black to Korean stores decreases, incidents that might otherwise have taken place in black-owned stores might take place in Korean-owned stores instead.

If the imprecision of these independent variables provides reason for doubting their lack of explanatory power, however, then the same reasoning testifies to the power of the political variables. The political variables are hardly ideal measures. Traditional party organization (TPO) is used as a proxy for the level of political organization in a city, which should encompass more than formal political parties. Measures of other political activities, such as interest group activity and community organizing, reflect other dimensions of political organization that deserve inclusion in future research. Moreover, this variable is imprecise: its range from 1 to 5 may not adequately reflect the full range of levels of traditional party organization. Additionally, the measure was originally constructed by David Mayhew in the late 1960s to compare average levels of local party organization on a state-by-state basis (Mayhew 1986). For greater precision, however, I use Mayhew's rich descriptions of local party systems to adjust local TPO scores when necessary, such as when a city had characteristics different from other localities in the state.

Still, disparaging the use of Mayhew's TPO score distracts from its benefits. Political process theory makes an argument about the broad nature of politics in cities. To use measures of smaller components of this larger whole would defeat the purpose of testing for the effects of a larger phenomenon. Moreover, Mayhew's traditional party organization is a measure that is meant to say something lasting about the nature of politics in a city, something that does not change from year to year.

Notes

1. Events in which an Asian American victim of a different ethnicity was mistaken for Korean were also included.

2. One boycott also occurred in Hawthorne, California, which is not included because the city's population size (75,000) fell under the threshold of 100,000 used in the statistical analysis. Additionally, a campaign against the rebuilding of liquor stores (many of them Korean-owned) in South Central Los Angeles following the 1992 riots is not included because of its unique nature, which is discussed in chapter 5. For some cities, newspaper coverage was only available for the last five or ten years of the time period surveyed. Thus, the newspaper survey may have missed boycotts during the 1980s. It should be noted that black-Korean conflicts may have happened in places that were not covered by the newspapers searched. For instance, the search did not include any newspapers covering cities in New Jersey that have relatively high concentrations of Korean Americans.

3. Motivations in the nine remaining boycotts could not be ascertained from news sources.

4. Reports of violence also occurred in Hawthorne and Compton, California.

5. A member of the Lexis-Nexis service public relations staff informed me that newspapers are chosen for the database according to the needs and requests of the service's customers.

6. The media oversimplifies conflicts between African Americans and Korean Americans just as it oversimplifies other events. But critics of the media rarely offer more than anecdotal evidence for sweeping charges of systematic, ideologically based exaggeration of black-Korean conflicts. For instance, Elaine Kim writes:

> Korean Americans were used to deflect attention from the racism they [the predominantly white news media] inherited and the economic injustice and poverty that had been already well woven into the fabric of American life. . . . As far as I know, neither the commercial nor the public news media has mentioned the many Korean and African American attempts to improve relations, such as joint church services, joint musical performances and poetry readings, Korean merchant donations to African American community and youth programs, African American volunteer teachers in classes for Korean immigrants studying for citizenship examinations, or Korean translations of African American history materials. (Kim 1993, 221–22)

Actually, although newspapers have indeed focused attention on conflicts, they have also reported just the kind of cooperative efforts to which Kim refers. The headlines of a few news stories testify to this: "Merchants Hope Feast Feeds Spirit of Goodwill: Korean Business Community Serves Free Meals to Homeless, Others in Northeast Washington" (*Washington Post,* November 27, 1992, C4); "Why Can't We All Get Along? Many Blacks, Koreans Find Understanding" (*Philadelphia Tribune,* November 23, 1993, A1); and "Two Cultures, One Goal; Project Targets Concerns of Asians, African-Americans" (*Houston Chronicle,* February 7, 1994, A9). Additionally, there were numerous reports of successful mediation attempts that resolved boycotts. In some cities, such as Baltimore, joint efforts to improve relations by members of both groups were reported even though no major conflicts took place locally.

7. One factor that might distort such comparisons, however, would be the structure of the local news market. Although the print media in major metropolitan areas tends to be converging toward a single-newspaper model, cities do exhibit variation (with more variation in broadcast media than in print) (Kaniss 1991, 35). More competitive news markets may have the effect of exacerbating ethnic and racial conflicts by intensifying the pressures on news organizations to report on such events more aggressively than their competitors. The structure of the news market and its effect on urban society and politics is a topic deserving future research, but it is beyond the scope of this book.

CHAPTER 2. EXPLAINING BLACK-KOREAN CONFLICTS

1. The framework of distinguishing explanations among ideas, interests, and institutions is borrowed from Steinmo 1989.

2. Anthropologist Kye Young Park finds that "Korean respondents most frequently mention . . . loudness, bad language, and shoplifting as inappropriate behavior demonstrated by Black patrons. By contrast, Black patrons [mostly] cite the negative attitudes of Korean merchants and employees, the feeling of being watched constantly, and the throwing [of] money on the counter as inappropriate behaviors" (1992, 43–45).

3. Cheng and Espiritu arrive at this conclusion after surveying local English, Spanish, and Korean-language newspapers in the Los Angeles area from 1972 to 1987 (1989). Light, Har-Chvi, and Kan (1994) follow up by searching issues of Los Angeles' biggest-circulation Spanish-language newspaper, *La Opinión,* and the electronic newspaper database *Ethnic News Watch* for the years 1989 to 1992.

4. Moreover, the immigrant hypothesis conflates the class interests of different groups of Mexican Americans: Korean merchants might be viewed very differently by the Mexican merchants with whom they compete, the Mexican workers they employ in their stores, and the Mexican clientele who shop in them. There may also be a difference between older, more-established Mexican communities on the one hand and the very different groups of newer Mexican and Central American immigrants on the other.

5. The reasons Koreans rarely engage in politics, according to Edward Chang, are their small numbers in the population, their recent arrival to and unfamiliarity with the United States, their negative perceptions of government brought from Korea, intimidation from the Korean government (which monitors the politics of Korean Americans), and their perception that "politics are irrelevant in comparison to their immediate goal of achieving economic security" (1991, 174).

6. Nationalist ideologies exist among Latinos but do not have as strong a following. Moreover, the nature, intensity, and social impact of the ideologies varies among national-origin groups. "Chicano power" ideologies among Mexican Americans, for example, differ greatly from Cuban nationalism.

7. In Claire Kim's account, the exclusion of blacks from politics goes hand in hand with racial segregation and economic marginalization (2000, 21–52).

8. For more studies that support competition theory generally, see Giles and Evans 1986; Giles and Hertz 1994; McClain 1993; McClain and Karnig 1993; McClain and Tauber 1995.

9. In this survey the U.S. Census Bureau (U.S. Bureau of the Census 1987) counts firms that are at least one-half owned by members of minority groups; file tax forms for individual proprietorships, partnerships, or subchapter S corporations; have annual receipts of $500 or more; and are not farms, ranches, railroads, postal services, membership organizations, private households or governments. Data come from tax records, social security records, a mail survey, and economic censuses.

10. Ideally, an index of intergroup business competition would use data collected at the neighborhood level in order to capture the effects of competition in just those parts of a city where black residents predominate. Unfortunately, the Census Bureau does not count Korean firms even at the city level—it only counts them for Metropolitan Statistical Areas. A ratio of firms at the metro level must suffice, although consequently it can only serve as a rough indicator of competition. The most recent data are from 1987. The *Survey of Minority-Owned Business Enterprises* takes place every five years; data on Korean firms are not available in the 1992 edition.

11. Another factor that makes an immigrant group a middleman minority is nonassimilation into the host culture. One measure of this that is available from the census is the degree to which Korean Americans do not speak English "very well," which is used here to indicate cultural differences.

12. Unpaid family workers are included with self-employed persons.

13. Blacks organized politically in a number of northern cities prior to the 1960s, but with few exceptions black politicians had little independent power and their organizations were dependent on white-dominated political machines (Katznelson 1973).

14. Mayhew assigns states higher TPO scores if a state meets five criteria: (1) local party organizations exist autonomously from nonelectoral organizations; (2) these organizations (or patterns of organization) are persistent across time; (3) they have "an important element of hierarchy"; (4) they regularly nominate candidates for public office; and (5) they rely on material rather than purposive incentives as a means of enlisting support. Mayhew's scores are based on local political arrangements in the late 1960s (Mayhew 1986, 19–20). A high TPO score does not necessarily imply that machines in a state *control* the government. The average score for the thirty-nine cities that I surveyed is 2.36.

15. Information on black officeholders comes from *Black Elected Officials* (Joint Center for Economics and Political Studies 1991).

16. It must be remembered that the particular measures I use to flesh out the larger theoretical argument about political institutions are to some extent historically contingent. Their usefulness depends on the time period under examination, which was after the demise of political machines that controlled cities with iron fists and after the end of the civil rights movement. However, the broad contours of the argument apply to other contexts as well.

17. The natural log of the city population is used. This allows the statistical analysis to capture the impact of large differences in population size rather than incremental differences, which would assume greater importance if unaltered population figures were used.

18. Crime statistics come from the Federal Bureau of Investigation's *Uniform Crime Reports* for the years 1980–1995.

19. The total number of data points, or city-years, is 284.

20. Both models use logistic regression to estimate binary categorical outcomes. Probabilities were calculated for variables of interest (with other variables set to their mean values) using CLARIFY, software developed by Michael Tomz, Jason Wittenberg, and Gary King (2001). One-tailed (nondirectional) T-tests were used to determine statistical significance.

21. It has been suggested that the TPO score may be capturing a regional effect that has more to do with the geography of cities than the influence of traditional party organizations. Cities with high TPO scores tend to be located in the North (the correlation is .60), and northern cities tend to have more well-defined neighborhoods and a higher residential density. This may certainly influence the likelihood of community organization and protest. However, the sample also contains cities like San Francisco and Boston, which have distinct and active neighborhoods but little traditional party organization. Moreover, when a variable representing population density is included in the analysis, it does not achieve statistical significance.

22. The coefficients for two other variables, not shown in Table 2.2 because they do not achieve statistical significance, are also not correlated in the expected direction: the percent-

age of non-English speaking Koreans and the relative self-employment rate of Koreans both yield negative associations, whereas the theories they test predict positive ones. The coefficient for competition theory, the ratio of black to Korean-owned firms, does, however, bear the expected negative relationship, although it does not achieve statistical significance.

23. When these tests were performed, the relationships for other variables remained the same. Tests were also performed for the simultaneous occurrence of the opposite form of conflict, in other words, when the two forms occurred in the same year in the same city. Here again, there was no relationship between boycotts and violence.

24. Poisson regression models of the frequency of boycotts and violence, performed on a count of incidents between 1990 and 1995 (the only years for which data on the dependent variable was available for all cities in the sample), confirm these findings. The results of these models are not reported here because they essentially repeat those of the logit regression models and because they use less of the available data due to their limited temporal scope.

25. Survey data on black attitudes toward Koreans are available for only one city: New York (Min 1996). Data from a survey that includes blacks and Asians are available for Los Angeles (Bobo et al. 1994).

26. Seymour Spilerman's original analysis found that the structure of local politics bore no relation to rioting. For this reason, Donald Horowitz, who cited Spilerman's findings, rejected "an explanation based on local sources of grievance" (Horowitz 1983, 196). The reanalysis cited expands the number of cases to include riots in recent decades.

CHAPTER 3. COMPARING NEW YORK CITY AND LOS ANGELES

1. Reliable data on the durations of boycotts was unavailable for many cases in the larger sample of cities, and statistical tests failed to reveal any discernable patterns.

2. These figures only include shooting incidents reported in newspapers in which the full text was available for surveying. However, there were likely many more than fourteen shootings involving blacks and Koreans living in Los Angeles between 1980 and 1995. Korean-language newspapers reported additional incidents. Korean community organizations also kept running tallies of incidents of violence against Korean merchants. In 1993, for instance, a press release issued by one organization reported forty-five incidents in the Los Angeles metropolitan area, most of them in South Central Los Angeles and Koreatown (which are predominantly black and Latino neighborhoods), and all but fourteen of them shootings.

3. Only one assault—on a Vietnamese man whom his attackers mistook for Korean—resulted in a reported hospitalization; the others involved punching, throwing objects, etc.

4. Latinos, mainly recent immigrants, engaged in the looting of Korean stores as well. See chapter 5.

5. Protest and other political activity at the neighborhood level do not necessarily make neighborhood organizations more *powerful*, however (Lipsky 1968). The community boards have little power of their own in planning and development, and serve "advisory" roles at best. Moreover, community-based organizations are incorporated into the policy process less in New York than in certain other cities, such as Chicago, especially in the area of school reform (Gittell 1994). Ironically, the extreme fragmentation of community organizations in New York may hamper their policy effectiveness (Mollenkopf 1992, 91) but increase residents' political participation due to increased competitiveness (Greenstone and Peterson 1973).

6. Robert Caro's depiction in *The Power Broker* (1975) of the sway that Park Commissioner and "master builder" Robert Moses held over successive New York City mayors illustrates this point: the great formal powers that New York mayors wield from City Hall mean little when they are faced with challenges by actors who able to rally powerful forces outside city government.

7. Although Yates meant this description to apply to big cities in general, New York City clearly exceeds Los Angeles (and other cities) in these characteristics.

CHAPTER 4. NEW YORK CITY

1. Alerted to possible tensions, interested officials began attempts at mediation early on. In one instance, the New York State Advisory Committee to the U.S. Commission on Civil Rights invited black and Korean merchants and community representatives to its office in downtown Manhattan to talk about "issues of concern." With the assistance of interpreters, the participants exchanged stories of entrepreneurial and racial struggles. Some black participants at the meeting reported unease with the arrangement, however, and came away harboring suspicions toward their Korean counterparts (Noel 1981b).

2. Carson and a set of activists associated with him became central to accounts of black-Korean relations, and I profile them more fully later.

3. Two of the stores targeted in 1982 had the same names (the Red Apple and Church Fruits) and were at the same locations as the two stores boycotted in 1990, but the Red Apple was under different ownership, and Church Fruits may have been as well. The Jang family, owners of the Red Apple in 1990, did not arrive in the United States until 1985 and bought the market in 1988 (Lee and Goldman 1990, 72). As far as I know, it is not generally known that overt black-Korean conflicts took place at these stores well before 1990.

4. Achieving racial unity across the ethnic lines dividing West Indian blacks and African Americans in New York City has been a complex task. As Philip Kasinitz writes, "They hardly speak with one voice, and political strategies that refuse to recognize this risk irrelevance" (Kasinitz 1992, 254).

5. Two of the three boycotts might have lasted as long as six months to a year each, depending on the account. A fourth, smaller boycott, which targeted a fish store in Jamaica, Queens, was settled "within the neighborhood" (Farber 1990).

6. According to one scholarly account, the boycott was organized by the Afrikan Nationalist Pioneer Movement (Min 1996, 75). In articles about the Ike's boycott in the *Amsterdam News*, however, there is no mention of that organization.

7. Lucas was stripped of his pastorship at the Resurrection Roman Catholic Church in Harlem in the 1980s (Hornung 1990).

8. The rivalry with Al Sharpton had faded somewhat by the late 1990s. In 1997, Carson supported Sharpton's candidacy for mayor (Noel 2001).

9. Sharpton himself put it this way: "The goals sometimes coalesce but sometimes they collide. One crowd wants to be the big guys in the system [incumbents in elected office like Al Vann, Major Owens, and Charles Rangel], another crowd wants to change the system [protest leaders like Sharpton himself, Rev. Herbert Daughtry, and lawyer Alton Maddox], another crowd wants to destroy the system [the December 12 Movement]. That's natural conflict" (Noel 1992, 24).

10. The Tropic agreement stated that Korean merchants would move accounts to black-owned banks in Brooklyn, make donations to community organizations, trade with black-owned businesses, train local residents in entrepreneurial skills, and take part in cultural exchanges (Lee 1988). Korean merchants in Bedford-Stuyvesant did open accounts with the Freedom National Bank, the city's only black-owned commercial bank (Beschloss and McNatt 1989; Min 1996, 76). A year later, however, the branch manager of Freedom National reported that she had yet to see "a stampede of new accounts" (Beschloss and McNatt 1989). Several other items in the accord, such as the agreement to set up training workshops, were never implemented (Min 1996, 76).

11. The debate echoed a distinction Adolph Reed (1986) has drawn between types of

black leadership in American politics. Reed observes that two sets of black elites have competed for leadership in the national arena: on one hand is the traditional protest elite, who rose to power in the civil rights movement and continue to claim an "organic" basis for leadership through their positions in respected organizations; on the other hand is the new political elite, who won elected office in the years after the passage of the Voting Rights Act and became empirically validated representatives through elections. Reed's distinction between organic and empirical leadership makes sense here as well: boycott leaders and elected officials were essentially competing to establish the legitimacy of one type of representation over another.

12. Jim Sleeper, in his book *The Closest of Strangers* (1990), asks "who is stopping Carson and his followers from opening up their own, competing chain of cooperatives, farmers' markets, or stores and urging local residents to 'buy black'?" The Peoples Farmers Markets may not have constituted the traditional kind of entrepreneurship imagined by Sleeper, but the arrangement was no fly-by-night operation—it lasted at least through the Red Apple boycott (Min 1996, 76).

13. After selling his store, the owner of the Tropic Market made his living driving a taxi (Min 1996, 77).

14. In November 1988, a few months into the Koko's boycott, Mayor Ed Koch spoke at a meeting of the Asian Business Seminar in Flushing, Queens, a neighborhood where Korean businesses predominated. Koch lauded the growing importance of Asian Americans in the city's economy, and he acknowledged that they faced "problems of adjustments, of language or of cultural contrasts." An *Amsterdam News* reporter, however, highlighted a notable omission: "Mayor Koch fielded no questions and made no comments on the recent outbreak of problems between Korean merchants and the Black community" (Boyd 1988b). The mayor's omission is significant not only because he chose to avoid public action, despite his staff's quiet recognition of the Tropic boycott, but because two years later Koch roundly rebuked his successor, David Dinkins, for similarly preferring a quiet approach during the Red Apple boycott. (The Dinkins administration's response, in reality, would turn out to be much more active than Koch's, even before public criticism forced a reluctant Dinkins to make public statements about the boycott.) Meanwhile, actions at the state level by Governor Mario Cuomo contrasted with Koch's hands-off approach. Cuomo set up a Crisis Prevention Unit under the auspices of the state's Division of Human Rights, giving it a staff of twelve and a budget of $450,000 to begin a series of dialogues between blacks and Koreans, among other things (White 1988). Although the state's crisis unit did not become known for resolving any particular conflict, by the mid-1990s a report said it had conducted training in "cultural awareness" and conflict resolution in schools and communities inside and outside New York City (New York State Advisory Committee to the U.S. Commission on Civil Rights 1994, 11).

15. The same year as the Tropic boycott, Mayor Koch and Commissioner Ward sent "two thousand police to shepherd an estimated six hundred protesters through the neighborhood [of Crown Heights], . . . intent on limiting the march to a demonstration and not providing any opening for a riot to develop" (Mintz 1992, 245).

16. The store's name itself stirred conflict of another kind. Its legal name was Family Red Apple, which it was forced to use after a court injunction initiated by the Red Apple chain of grocery stores (to which it had no connection) (H. C. Lee 1993, 1–2).

17. My account focuses on the interaction and responses of the various parties involved, rather than on some of the "fundamental bases and processes" preceding the initial dispute, such as the "structural contradictions" of Korean stores in New York. For those aspects, I refer readers to Heon Cheol Lee's fascinating study of black-Korean conflict in New York City (H. C. Lee 1993, 31).

18. Picketers even believed that the Red Apple and Church Fruits were owned by the same merchants (*Amsterdam News* 1990a), though they were not.

19. Although before May, *Newsday* ran its stories deep inside the fold.

20. Jim Sleeper, for instance, called it "Sonny Carson's intimidating, racist boycott" (Sleeper 1990, 300).

21. In his account of the conflict, Heon Cheol Lee reports that "although some local residents joined the picketing, marches and demonstrations, those who 'led' the boycott were not local residents, nor customers, nor local community leaders." Lee quotes an unnamed "prominent local resident" as saying that "the boycott was basically kept alive by people who don't reside there" (1993, 174).

22. Alvin Berk, chair of the local Community Board, may have had a point when he argued that neighborhood activists had "brought in" Carson "to ensure a prominent police presence. . . . They understand how the presence of uniforms validates their power" (English 1990a).

23. Some observers maintained that few locals walked the picket lines. In June, CAMBA's Joanne Oplustil told city officials at a public hearing that most of the demonstrators were not residents: "The people who are out there picketing, we do not see our community people. By and large they are not" (New York City Mayor's Committee 1990a, 37). The composition of demonstrations likely shifted over the course of the boycott.

24. Boycotters with similar goals in Philadelphia called Korean merchants' offers of contributions "bribes to buy peace" (Stone 1993).

25. Some observers, such as Fukuyama (1995) and MacDonald (1995), have mistakenly associated Sharpton with the Red Apple boycott.

26. Peter Eisinger writes that "protest action is frequently successful as a strategy for mass mobilization. Protest may often be undertaken primarily as a recruiting activity for organizations, for it is a way of cutting through communal apathy and attracting membership through its sheer excitement" (Eisinger 1973, 26).

27. Local organizers expressed prejudice toward Koreans as well. Brenda Bell, a local organizer of the Flatbush Coalition, told a reporter: "They have always been rude and disrespectful. That is why they have been singled out. . . . It's not an issue just here in our neighborhood. It's citywide. It's as though someone told them you don't respect black people, because they all seem to have that attitude" (English and Yuh 1990).

28. December 12 Movement member Lawrence Lucas highlighted the competition between the radical clique and other black leaders in a column in the *Amsterdam News*: "One of the primary tools or avenues for keeping African peoples divided, confused, and immobile is the proliferation of 'leaders' or spokespeople in our midst, many of whom are actually enemies of the African community" (Lucas 1990b). Lucas urged black New Yorkers to question the motives of blacks claiming leadership via the white-controlled media.

29. The suit, filed in federal court on behalf of fourteen neighborhood residents, demanded that Mayor Dinkins and Police Commissioner Lee Brown enforce a state judge's injunction to keep protesters fifty feet from the store and sought unspecified damages and a permanent injunction against the picketing (Bowles and English 1990).

30. Other Asian American organizations expressed solidarity with the Korean grocers as well. In one instance, about fifty residents of Chinatown in Manhattan visited the boycotted stores to shop (Browne 1990a). For the most part, however, the lack of involvement by Chinese, South Asian, or other Asian American groups in responding to boycotts challenges Yen Le Espiritu's (1992) model of Asian American panethnicity. Pyong Gap Min expresses a contrary view (Min 1996, 153–54).

31. Korean American associations in New York City have also organized boycotts and demonstrations of their own, most often against city agencies and produce wholesalers. Pyong Gap Min counts at least fifteen such collective actions (Min 1996, 195–97).

32. Ilsoo Kim observed in 1981 that "no centralized ethnic organization or leadership has emerged to integrate, coordinate, and direct the various community activities [of Korean Americans in New York]. . . . Decentralization thus characterizes the Korean community structure" (Kim 1981, 185).

33. Ethnic solidarity among Korean Americans in New York City has long been based on an organizational community rather than a territorial community, the latter being the case with traditional ethnic enclaves (Kim 1981, 185).

34. The third organization was the Korean Association of New York, which joined the fray after the two trade organizations.

35. The notion that the ensuing boycott—which lasted more than a year and drew hundreds of supporters and police officers to the scene—was simply "incident-based" (as the Mayor's Commission concluded) is naïve at best. The protesters themselves ascribed their action to a wide range of complaints against Korean merchants, even if the actual trigger was the report of only a single assault.

36. Dinkins used the televised address and several public appearances soon after to announce policy steps in response to the boycott and other recent racial conflicts. These included pressuring the State Senate to adopt a bias crime bill, ordering studies of discrimination in business lending, creating a bias strike force that would lead to "massive mobilization on intergroup relations," and setting up a "street workers" program for youth based on a similar program used by Mayor John Lindsay in the 1960s (Anekwe 1990, 40).

37. Jim Sleeper suggests a variation on this explanation for what he calls "Dinkins' bizarre indulgence of Carson and his crowd": "It may be that his embrace of the permanent government's fiscal crisis politics left him feeling morally vulnerable to the militants' attacks" (Sleeper 1990, 301).

38. Not surprisingly, given New York City's contentious relationship between blacks and Jews, enduring black-Jewish tensions found their way into the Red Apple conflict. Flatbush had once been a heavily Jewish neighborhood; pockets of Jewish residents remained, and to some extent political representation continued to reflect the past. The boycotters highlighted what they saw as neglect by Jewish officeholders in Congress, the state legislature, and the city council (H. C. Lee 1993, 205). Boycott leaders also believed that Jews owned the properties housing the offending Korean stores (and others in Brooklyn), and that the mainstream media in New York, which often carried negative reporting of the boycott, was run by Jews (Lucas 1995). The charges of Jewish involvement in the conflict reflected the city's older, ongoing conflicts between blacks and Jews.

39. In the spring of 1991, as the Red Apple boycott was winding down, a number of protesters, led by Ernie Foster, an activist involved in the boycott, stormed a board meeting and demanded a plan to increase black representation on the board. Ironically, a ranking official on the Flatbush Community Board by that time was George Dames, one of the original organizers of the boycott (Pryce 1991), reflecting one of the numerous ways in which conventional and unconventional politics continuously spawned connections in New York City.

40. Golden also sponsored a forum in May with black and Korean community organizations held at a high school in Flatbush. This meeting was more like a conference than a mediation attempt; community notables and activists gave presentations on long-term solutions to "achieve positive relations." No boycott leaders were present (McQuillan 1995).

41. The lack of better cooperation—for whatever reasons—was unfortunate, since Golden's and Dinkins's aides later gave very similar interpretations of events and in other circumstances might have seen eye-to-eye on how to intervene.

42. Later, the Community Relations Service set up meetings between Red Apple store-owner Bong Jae Jang and representatives from the Small Business Administration, from whom Jang eventually got assistance for relocating his business (Glenn 1995).

43. Lucas also met privately with Dennis DeLeon and police officials when Korean merchants were not present (Lucas 1995).

44. Assault charges were brought against the Red Apple's owner (later transferred to the manager) and against a protester. The five civil cases included two personal injury claims (par-

alleling the criminal cases), and three suits against the boycotters and city officials to stop the boycott (H. C. Lee 1993, 3–4). In one of the personal injury claims suits, Felissaint sued the Red Apple's owner for $6 million. (Her lawyer, Colin Moore, had represented defendants in the Central Park jogger rape case and other high-profile cases.) Interestingly, neither Felissaint nor Moore were directly involved in the boycott.

45. Boycott leaders denied knowledge of the Molotov cocktails, which a police officer said would have done massive damage if they had exploded (Hornung 1990).

46. State Supreme Court Justice Gerald Held, in one of several rulings on the matter, argued that police duties "are not limited to the enforcement of criminal law. . . . Their role is a multi-faceted one and extends to the enforcement of civil matters as well." He also noted that the plaintiffs had "no other avenue of redress" and "the judiciary does not have a separate arm to enforce its decision" (Hurtado and English 1990).

47. Some of the police arrests of boycotters were marked by physical confrontations with officers. Police arrested: on February 1, a female demonstrator in a fight with employees of Church Fruits (Newsday, May 10, 1990); on March 15, fifty-year-old Rev. Clemson Brown, a boycott supporter who was videotaping conversations with customers; on May 24, Raymond Thompson, for disorderly conduct at a prayer session near the Red Apple (Newsday, May 25, 1990); on June 6, Stanley Pauyo, a protester, in a dispute with a police officer; on June 24, three protesters who fought with police in a scuffle that left an elderly passerby and a police officer injured; on August 22, five protesters; on September 19, five out of the fifteen protesters present; and on September 23, eight persons. Given the size of the police presence and the number of protesters, however, it is remarkable that only one arrest (on June 24) led to a more serious confrontation.

48. New York Newsday's relatively enlightened coverage of the boycott contrasted with the above-mentioned racial slur by one of its top columnists, Jimmy Breslin, against a Korean American reporter at the paper (Hays 1990). Breslin was suspended for two weeks after joking about the incident on Howard Stern's radio program (Curry 1990).

49. I could find no unsigned editorials on the boycott by New York Newsday.

50. In a number of stories that the Amsterdam News ran on previous boycotts, the views of Korean merchants were represented alongside those of protesters (Noel 1981a, 1981b). The paper often ran letters to the editor and guest columns criticizing boycotters and offering sympathetic portrayals of Korean merchants (Boyd 1982; Liu 1988; Shannon 1988). This made it all the more surprising to see a different sort of story appear from time to time. These stories appeared with sensational lead paragraphs that were not only potentially libelous (such as accusing a merchant of a crime for which he had not even been arrested) but also were not backed up by facts in the body of the story (Jamison and Browne 1988). In a few instances, stories consisted of little more than long quotations from Sonny Carson (Jamison 1988a, 1988b).

51. The New York Times quoted boycott leader Sonny Carson as using violent language: "In the future, there'll be funerals, not boycotts" (Farber 1990). Talk like that is certainly inflammatory and potentially inciting. But these words appear to have been spoken to a reporter, not to the crowd of protesters, and the New York Times does not have a wide audience among black New Yorkers. Moreover, these words appear to be an exception: no other violent language by Carson was reported by newspapers during the boycott. Protesters may use an implicit threat of violence to achieve their goals even as they seek to avoid actual violence. By making the threat explicit, however, they risk repressive responses from the police and they lose legitimacy among supporters (Eisinger 1973). Carson and other activists who forecast violence may have strategic aims in doing so. One aim might be to highlight their closeness to supporters—and thus enhance their legitimacy as grassroots leaders—by giving voice to supporters' frustrations; another might be to signal the effectiveness of their leadership skills by demonstrating that they can avoid potential violence.

CHAPTER 5. LOS ANGELES

1. The store's name was also reported as Chung's Liquor in a number of press reports. Koreans, however, more commonly used the name John's Liquor.

2. Another black readership newspaper, *Money Talks News,* also ran stories on black-Korean tensions and was similarly critical of Korean merchants (Light and Bonacich 1991, 319; Min 1996, 83).

3. The stories did not explicitly identify their focus as Korean Americans, but they referred to Korean organizations that took part in mediation attempts and individual merchants who had Korean surnames.

4. Actually, Korean Americans have been more likely to use personal savings or loans from friends and family to buy businesses, whereas African Americans have been more likely to use bank loans (Bates 1994).

5. The *Sentinel* advocated two other strategies as well. The first suggestion was to "repurchase" businesses for black ownership—a strategy that saw some action. An organization called The Black Agenda raised money for this purpose (Cleaver 1983c). Also, Mayor Tom Bradley's Small Business Office held a community seminar to identify businesses blacks could buy. Second, the paper suggested legal action, citing readers who declared intentions to file lawsuits against Korean merchants (although the paper only cited one instance of a formal complaint, which was filed with the Mobil Oil Corporation, not the courts, in response to a dispute at a Korean-owned gas station) (Ivory 1983).

6. At the time, the West Coast operation of the Community Relations Service was based in San Francisco, but its small staff traveled frequently to Los Angeles (Thom 1988).

7. The store OMNI picketed in Inglewood, the Inglewood Department Store, was owned by Paul Cho, who began to aggressively pursue means for smoothing relations with customers and became well known for his efforts. In addition to donating to local charities and changing store policies, one unusual move Cho made was to hire a security guard and a customer relations expert who were both black (Mydans 1990).

8. Interestingly, New York City has a comparatively small street gang presence (Holloway 1998).

9. Bakewell's friendship with Bradley would be strained by his leadership of the John's Liquor boycott in 1991.

10. Even if the most committed members of the BKA recognized the importance of grassroots ties, other members did not. Journalist Itabari Njeri believed the BKA was "loaded with Korean grocers and Black would-be entrepreneurs looking for a deal." One black BKA member told her: "I'm just there to network with some of the Koreans 'cause some joint ventures could come out of it" (1997, 112). Similarly, Charles Kim of the Korean American Coalition believed that representatives of some black organizations belonging to the BKA were more interested in soliciting donations than in solving intergroup problems (C. Kim 1996).

11. Interestingly, the black and Korean ministers involved in the joint effort planned a festival with the Brotherhood Crusade (Johnson 1985), an organization that would in a few years lead boycotts of Korean merchants.

12. The county coroner's office also found traces of cocaine in Mitchell's blood (Dungee 1991). Korean leaders argued that this might explain his behavior that day, but protesters argued that the fact was irrelevant and was only used to make Mitchell look bad.

13. A few other organizations, as well as individual residents from the neighborhood, joined the daily picketing but did not take part in its leadership.

14. The Korean American Coalition's Jerry Yu, who visited the scene of the boycott, said some of the picketers told him they had been paid by the Brotherhood Crusade to maintain a presence (Yu 1996).

15. Moreover, KAGRO was a national organization with duties that corresponded. One

major activity that occupied it in late 1991 was a multi-city boycott by Korean merchants of the beer wholesaler McKenzie River Corporation. The merchants stopped buying from McKenzie River after rapper Ice Cube, who appeared in the company's malt liquor advertisements, recorded the controversial song "Black Korea." KAGRO's coordination of thousands of stores across the nation forced McKenzie River to stop running its ads with Ice Cube, and even persuaded the rapper himself to issue a personal apology (Chang 1993; D. Kim 1996).

16. Note the difference in strategy from the Small Business Service Center's Sung Soo Kim in New York, who tried to attract press attention in the hopes of favorably swaying reporters' perspectives.

17. The store never reopened. The owner sold his inventory, but not the store itself, after the boycott (C. Kim 1996). Eventually Bethel A.M.E. Church bought the property for use as a community center, with the intent to "take this negative influence in our community and turn it into a positive thing" (Gardner 1996). Although the Brotherhood Crusade did not purchase it, as Danny Bakewell had intended, it did open a "mom-and-pop" store elsewhere after the riots (Bolden 1992; Njeri 1997, 122).

18. The Harlins family also filed a $10 million wrongful death suit against Soon Ja Du, who settled out of court for $300,000 after the riots. The store's insurance covered the whole amount (*Los Angeles Sentinel* 1991b; Min 1996, 86).

19. Judge Karlin had reduced the maximum charge from first to second-degree murder after ruling that there was insufficient evidence of premeditation (Ford and Wilkinson 1991).

20. Shock at the sentence came from other places, too: District Attorney Ira Reiner later said that "outrage doesn't begin to describe it" (Cannon 1997, 172). According to data collected by the *Los Angeles Times,* a grant of straight probation for a violent crime was rare (Wilkinson and Clifford 1991). Moreover, Compton City Council member Patricia Moore reported court figures showing that only "one of the 163 individuals convicted of voluntary manslaughter in Los Angeles County received a sentence of straight probation" (Moore 1992).

21. In one analysis of riot damage data, Paul Ong and Suzanne Hee argue that "the losses suffered by Korean Americans had their strongest correlation not to racial animosities but to the special niche occupied by Korean storekeepers in the Los Angeles economy" (Ong and Hee 1993a). They acknowledge, however, that "there is no complete list of all stores in Los Angeles County that suffered losses nor is there a complete list of all businesses (damaged and undamaged) in the riot-affected areas by ethnicity. Without such data, it is impossible to determine unambiguously if Korean stores were systematically and frequently singled out" (ibid., 10). Ong and Hee base their conclusion on the assumption that only Korean-owned *liquor* stores would have been targeted, and reason that since many other types of stores suffered damage, black-Korean tensions did not play a strong role (ibid., 7, 11). However, black-Korean tensions were not limited to the sale of liquor, although that became a focus after the riots. Rather, boycotts had taken place at swap meets, restaurants, and other establishments, and the Brotherhood Crusade's broader "selective buying campaign" had not been limited to liquor stores. Similarly, Nancy Abelmann and John Lie argue that black-Korean tensions played no significant role in the riots. Their evidence consisted of interviews with Korean Americans, however (Abelmann and Lie 1995). In South Central, Korean merchants largely abandoned their stores during the riots and thus were not there to observe attacks on their property (unlike in Koreatown, where they mobilized to defend them) (Tierney 1994, 155).

22. These figures do not include non-Korean, Asian-owned businesses (8% of the total), which may have been targeted by rioters' inability to distinguish Asian ethnicities (Tierney 1994, 151–52).

23. These data include only those businesses that had been insured and whose owners actually filed claims, and they likely underestimate "the number of very low-end enterprises owned by all ethnic minorities" (Ong and Hee 1993a, 9).

24. For a detailed account of the police response, I refer readers to two excellent sources: an article by Bert Useem (1997), who argues that politics inside and outside the LAPD had fractured the department, diminishing its capacity to respond, and journalist Lou Cannon's book, *Official Negligence* (1997).

25. For a full account of the politics that led to the Council's decision, see Sonenshein 1996.

26. Churches also assisted in the campaign, especially in a petition drive that gathered 35,000 signatures (Mosher and Works 1994, 19).

27. For instance, in early Community Coalition meetings, residents voiced anger over the shooting of Latasha Harlins. But as Bass told me in a 1996 interview, "If black folks go after Koreans, based on the Latasha Harlins case, it's misdirected. It needs to be at the criminal justice system. And our folks—just like any other folks—need to be educated to understand where to direct and channel their anger. So in our early meetings when we launched the campaign, plenty of neighborhood residents wanted to get up and talk trash about the Korean merchants. That was not acceptable. . . . If you were hung up on Korean merchants, then you weren't welcome in this environment. But we found that residents moved very quickly out of that [black-Korean] space if you just paid a little attention and said, 'put it in historical context.' . . . There is a real issue of community ownership, and the fact that as a person who's lived in this area, I can go and patronize stores up and down the street, and not be able to speak to anybody. . . . Either people speak Korean, another Asian language, Spanish—and for African Americans, that's a real terrible feeling. However, you can choose to understand the issue [only] on its surface, and vent at the people right in front of you, or you can deepen your understanding of the social and economic inequity and see it as much larger than the person who is beyond the counter."

28. I thank Raphael Sonenshein for suggesting this term during a conversation in 1997 and for pointing out the relative ease of cross-racial relationships in Los Angeles compared to Eastern cities.

References

Abelmann, Nancy, and John Lie. 1995. *Blue Dreams: Korean Americans and the Los Angeles Riots.* Cambridge: Harvard University Press.

Alinsky, Saul D. [1971] 1989. *Rules for Radicals: A Practical Primer for Realistic Radicals.* New York: Vintage Books.

Amsterdam News. 1988. Blacks, Koreans Unite in Food Giveaway Drive. December 3, 11.

———. 1990a. Bklyn [Brooklyn] Group Asks Korean Merchants to Move. May 12, 8.

———. 1990b. Korean Markets Boycott: Our Children as Pawns. May 19, 14.

Anekwe, Simon. 1988. Let's Stick Together, Jesse Tells Korean–Americans. *Amsterdam News,* April 16, 10.

———. 1990. Violence Escalates as Mayor Dinkins Repeatedly Calls for Unity and Calm. *Amsterdam News,* May 19, 3, 40.

Aubry, Larry. 1987. The State of L.A.'s Black, Korean Relations. *Los Angeles Sentinel,* March 26, A7.

———. 1996. Interview by author. December 9, Inglewood, Calif.

Bailey, Ralph. 1987a. Blacks March on Koreans: Demands Met. *Los Angeles Sentinel,* January 22, A1.

———. 1987b. Korean Merchant Signs Pact to Improve Relations; Hires Blacks. *Los Angeles Sentinel,* January 29, A1.

Baillou, Charles. 1990a. Boycott against Brownsville Merchant Is Over. *Amsterdam News,* September 15, 9.

———. 1990b. Rallies for Justice Are Not Anti-Asian but for Justice, Organizers Say. *Amsterdam News,* June 9, 4.

Baldwin, James. 1962. *The Fire Next Time.* New York: Vintage Books.

Banfield, Edward. 1961. *Political Influence.* Glencoe, Ill.: Free Press.

Banfield, Edward C., and James Q. Wilson. 1963. *City Politics: Publications of the Joint Center for Urban Studies of the Massachusetts Institute of Technology and Harvard University.* Cambridge, Mass.: Joint Center for Urban Studies.

Baril, Lynda. 1991. Bruises Heal Slowly at Korean Grocery. *New York Newsday,* November 17, 2.

Barry, Dan. 1999. Civil Disobedience, Negotiated. *New York Times,* March 28.

Bass, Karen. 1996. Interview by author. December 10, Los Angeles.

Bates, Timothy. 1994. An Analysis of Korean Immigrant-Owned Small Business Startups with Comparisons to African American and Nonminority-Owned Firms. *Urban Affairs Quarterly* 30 (December): 227–48.

Beschloss, Steven, and Robert McNatt. 1989. A Broken Trust: Many Black Professionals Are Turning Their Backs on Corporate New York and Changing the Rules of Gain. *Crain's New York Business,* October 30, 31.

Blalock, Hubert M. 1967. *Toward a Theory of Minority-Group Relations.* New York: Capricorn Books.

Bobo, Lawrence, Camille L. Zubrinsky, James H. Johnson, Jr., and Melvin L. Oliver. 1994. Public Opinion Before and After a Spring of Discontent. In *The Los Angeles Riots: Lessons for the Urban Future,* edited by M. Baldassare. Boulder, Colo.: Westview Press.

Bolden, James. 1992. Mom & Pop Store Opens; Bakewell Confident Community Will Embrace No-Alcohol Policy. *Los Angeles Sentinel,* August 20, 1992, A1.

Bonacich, Edna. 1972. A Theory of Ethnic Antagonism: The Split Labor Market. *American Sociological Review* 37 (October): 547–59.

———. 1973. A Theory of Middleman Minorities. *American Sociological Review* 38 (October): 583–94.

———. 1994. Thoughts on Urban Unrest. In *Race and Ethnic Conflict: Contending Views on Prejudice, Discrimination, and Ethnoviolence,* edited by F. L. Pincus and H. J. Ehrlich. Boulder, Colo.: Westview Press.

Bornstein, David, and George E. Jordan. 1990. Firebombs at Grocery; Devices Found on Roof of Boycotted Store. *New York Newsday,* September 24, 2.

Bowles, Pete, and Merle English. 1990. Women Suing to End Boycott. *New York Newsday,* June 26, 19.

Boyd, Herb. 1988a. Finding Common Ground in Black-Korean Conflict. *Amsterdam News,* December 10, 16.

———. 1988b. Koch Ignores Black-Korean Conflict in Asian Seminar. *Amsterdam News,* November 12, 4.

Boyd, Sheila. 1982. Why Be Petty about Koreans? *Amsterdam News,* August 28, 14.

Bridges, Amy. 1984. *A City in the Republic: Antebellum New York and the Origins of Machine Politics.* Cambridge: Cambridge University Press.

———. 1992. Winning the West to Municipal Reform. *Urban Affairs Quarterly* 27 (June): 494–518.

Brittingham, Angela. 2000. *The Foreign-Born Population in the United States.* Washington, D.C.: U.S. Bureau of the Census, Population Division.

Browne, J. Zambga. 1982a. Bronx Pol Deplores Attack on Koreans. *Amsterdam News,* October 2, 3.

———. 1982b. Korean Boycott Call Gets Mixed Reaction. *Amsterdam News,* August 7, 1.

———. 1988. Anti-Korean War Seen Dying. *Amsterdam News,* November 12, 4.

———. 1990a. Alleged Assaulted Woman Files $6M Suit vs. Koreans. *Amsterdam News,* May 26, 5.

———. 1990b. Boro Black-Korean Conflict Does Not Ease. *Amsterdam News,* March 3, 11.

———. 1990c. DA's Handling of Grocery Store Case Appalls Lawyer. *Amsterdam News,* September 22, 11.

———. 1991. Queens Residents End Protest at Korean Store. *Amsterdam News,* February 16, 3.

Browning, Rufus P., Dale Rogers Marshall, and David H. Tabb. 1990. *Racial Politics in American Cities.* New York: Longman.

Bunch, William. 1993. Black-Korean Tension Simmers. *New York Newsday,* July 12, 4.

Cannon, Lou. 1997. *Official Negligence: How Rodney King and the Riots Changed Los Angeles and the LAPD.* New York: Times Books.

Caro, Robert. 1975. *The Power Broker.* New York: Random House.

Carroll, Maurice. 1993. Badillo Campaign: Themes or Dreams? *New York Newsday,* April 25, 24.

Carson, Sonny. 1990. Church Avenue Boycott and African Manhood. *Amsterdam News,* May 12, 15.

Casuso, Jorge. 1992. Black-Korean Hostility Fueled Flames of Riot. *Chicago Tribune,* May 8, 1.

Chang, Edward T. 1991. New Urban Crisis: Intra-Third World Conflict. In *Asian Americans: Comparative and Global Perspectives,* edited by S. Hune, H.-c. Kim, S. S. Fugita and A. Ling. Pullman, Wash.: Washington State University Press.

Chang, Irene, and Greg Krikorian. 1992. A City in Crisis: 30,000 Show Support in Koreatown March. *Los Angeles Times,* May 3, A3.

Chang, Jeff. 1993. Race, Class, Conflict, and Empowerment: On Ice Cube's "Black Korea." In *Los Angeles—Struggles toward Multiethnic Community: Asian American, African American, and Latino Perspectives,* edited by E. T. Chang and R. C. Leong. Seattle: University of Washington Press.

Charter Reform Commission. 1999. Proposed Charter of the City of Los Angeles. Los Angeles.

Cheng, Lucie, and Yen Espiritu. 1989. Korean Businesses in Black and Hispanic Neighborhoods: A Study of Intergroup Relations. *Sociological Perspectives* 32: 521–34.

Cheng, Mae M. 1996. Race for Harrison's Council Seat Sparked by Controversial Remarks. *New York Times,* May 3, B1.

Cho, Sumi K. 1993. Korean Americans vs. African Americans: Conflict vs. Construction. In *Reading Rodney King/Reading Urban Uprising,* edited by R. Gooding-Williams. New York: Routledge.

Clark, Terry N. 1971. Community Structure, Decision-Making, Budget Expenditures, and Urban Renewal in 51 American Communities. In *Community Politics: A Behavioral Approach,* edited by C. M. Bonjean, T. N. Clark and R. L. Lineberry. New York: The Free Press.

Cleaver, James H. 1983a. 2,000 See Louis Farrakhan Dedicate Muhammad's Temple. *Los Angeles Sentinel,* September 15, A1.

——. 1983b. Asian Attitudes toward Blacks Cause Raised Eyebrows. *Los Angeles Sentinel,* August 18, A1.

——. 1983c. Asian Businesses in Black Community Cause Stir. *Los Angeles Sentinel,* August 11, A1.

——. 1983d. Asian Series Brings Official Reprimand: Sentinel Called Racist. *Los Angeles Sentinel,* October 20, A1.

——. 1983e. Black Agenda Hosts Korean Dialogue. *Los Angeles Sentinel,* October 20, A1.

———. 1983f. Citizens Air Gripes about Asians. *Los Angeles Sentinel,* September 1, A1.

———. 1983g. Residents Complain about Alleged Asian "Problem." *Los Angeles Sentinel,* August 25, A1.

Cole, Richard L., Rodney V. Hissong, and Enid Arvidson. 1999. Devolution: Where's the Revolution? *Publius: The Journal of Federalism* 29 (4): 99–112.

Crogan, Jim. 1992. Riot Chronology. In *Inside the L.A. Riots: What Really Happened, and Why It Will Happen Again: Essays and Articles,* edited by D. Hazen. New York: Institute for Alternative Journalism.

Curry, George E. 1990. N.Y. Racial Violence Shatters New Mayor's "Gorgeous Mosaic." *Chicago Tribune,* May 15, 3.

Dalaker, Joseph, and Bernadette D. Proctor. 2000. *Poverty in the United States: 1999.* Washington, D.C.: U.S. Census Bureau.

Danzger, M. Herbert. 1975. Validating Conflict Data. *American Sociological Review* 40 (October): 570–84.

Davis, Mike. 1987. Chinatown, Part Two? The "Internationalization" of Downtown Los Angeles. *New Left Review* (July/August): 65–86.

———. 1992a. Burning All Illusions in LA. In *Inside the L.A. Riots: What Really Happened, and Why It Will Happen Again: Essays and Articles,* edited by D. Hazen. New York: Institute for Alternative Journalism.

———. 1992b. *LA Was Just the Beginning: Urban Revolt in the United States: A Thousand Points of Light.* Westfield, N.J.: Open Media.

———. 1992c. Parliament of Neighborhoods. *Los Angeles Times,* October 4, M1.

DeLeon, Dennis. 1996. Interview by author. March 27, New York.

Domanick, Joe. 1992. Riot Chronology. In *Inside the L.A. Riots: What Really Happened, and Why It Will Happen Again: Essays and Articles,* edited by D. Hazen. New York: Institute for Alternative Journalism.

Douglas, Carlyle C. 1985. Korean Merchants Are Target of Black Anger. *New York Times,* January 19, 23.

Duggan, Dennis. 1990. The Early Signs of a Long, Hot Summer for City. *New York Newsday,* May 10, 3.

Dungee, Ron. 1990. Volatile Mix in the Melting Pot: Blacks, Koreans Meet to Diffuse a Potentially Explosive Situation. *Los Angeles Sentinel,* February 8, A12.

———. 1991. Tensions Ignite: Critical Mass in Melting Pot. *Los Angeles Sentinel,* August 22, A1.

Dungee, Ron, and Marsha Mitchell. 1991. Black-Korean Tension Mounts; Leaders Call for Reason, Calm. *Los Angeles Sentinel,* June 26, A1.

Economist. 1998. More Neighbourly Government. *Economist,* January 3, 25–26.

Eisinger, Peter. 1998. City Politics in an Era of Federal Devolution. *Urban Affairs Review* 33 (3): 308–25.

Eisinger, Peter K. 1973. The Conditions of Protest Behavior in American Cities. *American Political Science Review* 67 (March): 11–28.

Elkin, Stephen L. 1987. *City and Regime in the American Republic.* Chicago: University of Chicago Press.

English, Merle. 1990a. Board Member Irked on Black-Korean Flap. *New York Newsday,* March 7, 18.

———. 1990b. Help End Boycott, Dinkins Urged. *New York Newsday*, February 27, 29.

English, Merle, and Melinda Henneberger. 1990. Korean Rally Jeers Dinkins. *New York Newsday*, September 19, 5.

English, Merle, and Patricia Hurtado. 1991. Cop Contradicts Central Figure in Grocer Boycott. *New York Newsday*, January 19, 18.

English, Merle, and Ji-Yeon Yuh. 1990. Black-Korean Conflict Simmers; Store Protests in Brooklyn Fan Old Flames. *New York Newsday*, February 13, 6.

Espiritu, Yen Le. 1992. *Asian American Panethnicity: Bridging Institutions and Identities*. Philadelphia: Temple University Press.

Fairchild, Halford H. 1991. A Sad Tale of Persecuted Minorities. *Los Angeles Times*, March 24, M1.

Farber, M. A. 1990. Black-Korean Who-Pushed-Whom Festers. *New York Times*, May 7, B1.

Fiske, John. 1994. Radical Shopping in Los Angeles: Race, Media and the Sphere of Consumption. *Media, Culture & Society* 16: 469–86.

Flynn, Kevin, and Pete Bowles. 1990. Curb on Grocery Pickets Upheld. *New York Newsday*, Sept. 18, 21.

Ford, Andrea, and Tracy Wilkinson. 1991. Grocer Is Convicted in Teen Killing. *Los Angeles Times*, October 12, A1.

Franklin, Charles H., and Liane C. Kosaki. 1989. Republican Schoolmaster: The U.S. Supreme Court, Public Opinion, and Abortion. *American Political Science Review* 83 (September): 751–71.

Franzosi, Roberto. 1987. The Press as a Source of Socio-Historical Data: Issues in the Methodology of Data Collection from Newspapers. *Historical Methods* 20 (Winter): 5–16.

Freer, Regina. 1994. Black-Korean Conflict. In *The Los Angeles Riots: Lessons for the Urban Future*, edited by M. Baldassare. Boulder: Westview Press.

Fried, Joseph. 1991. Brooklyn Clash Spurred Queens to End Boycott. *New York Times*, February 12, B1.

Frontline. 1993. *L.A. Is Burning: Five Reports from a Divided City*. PBS Video. Videotape.

Fuchs, Ester. 1992. *Mayors and Money: Fiscal Policy in New York and Chicago*. Chicago: University of Chicago Press.

Fukuyama, Francis. 1995. *Trust: The Social Virtues and the Creation of Prosperity*. New York: Free Press.

Gale Research, Inc. 1995. *Gale Directory of Publications*. Detroit: Gale Research.

Gardner, Joseph. 1996. Interview by author. December 10, Los Angeles.

Gibson, Campbell J., and Emily Lennon. 1999. *Historical Census Statistics on the Foreign-Born Population of the United States: 1850–1990*. Washington, D.C.: U.S. Bureau of the Census, Population Division.

Giles, Micheal W., and Arthur Evans. 1986. The Power Approach to Intergroup Hostility. *Journal of Conflict Resolution* 30 (September): 469–86.

Giles, Micheal W., and Kaenan Hertz. 1994. Racial Threat and Partisan Identification. *American Political Science Review* 88 (June): 317.

Ginsberg, Benjamin, and Martin Shefter. 1999. *Politics by Other Means: Politi-*

cians, Prosecutors, and the Press from Watergate to Whitewater. New York: W. W. Norton.

Girgenti, Richard H. 1993. *A Report to the Governor on the Disturbances in Crown Heights: An Assessment of the City's Preparedness and Response to Civil Disorder.* 2 vols. Vol. 1. Albany: New York State Division of Criminal Justice Services.

Gittell, Marilyn. 1994. School Reform in New York and Chicago: Revisiting the Ecology of Local Games. *Urban Affairs Quarterly* 30 (September): 136–51.

Glenn, Patricia. 1995. Interview by author. September 19, New York.

Goldman, Ari. 1990a. Other Korean Grocers Give to Those in Brooklyn Boycott. *New York Times,* May 14, B5.

——. 1990b. Racial Unity and Dissent in Brooklyn. *New York Times,* May 29, B3.

Gonzalez, David. 1990a. 8 Arrested in Boycott of Brooklyn Store. *New York Times,* September 23, A1.

——. 1990b. Bombs Found on Store Roof in Brooklyn. *New York Times,* September 24, B1.

——. 1990c. Boycotted Store Hires a Black. *New York Times,* September 27, B2.

——. 1990d. Brooklyn Boycott: The Fallout Hurts Others. *New York Times,* September 28, A1.

Goodwin, Charles Stewart. 1996. *The Arc of the Pendulum.* Lanham, Md.: University Press of America.

Greenstone, J. David, and Paul E. Peterson. 1973. *Race and Authority in Urban Politics: Community Participation and the War on Poverty.* New York: Russell Sage Foundation.

Griffin, Hugh N. 1994. *And Justice for Some: The Authorized Biography of Stephen G. James.* New York: Alexander Publishing.

Guinier, Lani. 1995. Democracy's Conversation. *The Nation,* January 23, 85–88.

Gumbs, Maurice. 1990. Dinkins and the Speaker's Backyard. *Amsterdam News,* September 22, 15.

Hall, Robert, Martin Feldstein, Ben Bernanke, Jeffrey Frankel, Robert Gordon, and Victor Zarnowitz. 2001. The Business-Cycle Peak of March 2001. Cambridge: National Bureau of Economic Research.

Hamilton, Hugh. 1992. Blacks, Koreans Claim a Cautious Rapprochement. *City Sun,* November 25.

Harvey, Chris. 1990. Dinkins Urges New Yorkers of All Races: "Come Together." *Washington Times,* May 21, A3.

Hays, Constance L. 1990. Asian-American Groups Call for Breslin's Ouster over Racial Slurs. *New York Times,* May 7, B3.

Heinz, John P., Edward O. Laumann, Robert H. Salisbury, and Robert L. Nelson. 1990. Inner Circles or Hollow Cores? Elite Networks in National Policy Systems. *Journal of Politics* 52 (May): 356–90.

Hernandez, Marita. 1986. Tale of 2 Cultures; Murders Refocus Spotlight on Tensions between Koreans, Blacks. *Los Angeles Times,* May 18, B1.

Hernandez, Mike. 1995. Interview by author. September 19, New York.

Hevesi, Dennis. 1990a. 2 Rallies Are Held over Store Boycott, but All Is Peaceful. *New York Times,* September 19, B4.

———. 1990b. Black Protesters March in Brooklyn Communities. *New York Times,* May 13, 24.

Holloway, Lynette. 1998. The Fear Is Real Enough, the Gangs Are Another Story. *New York Times,* February 15, B1.

Horne, Gerald. 1995. *Fire This Time: The Watts Uprising and the 1960s.* Charlottesville: University Press of Virginia.

Hornung, Rick. 1990. The Making of a Revolutionary: Coltrane Chimurenga and the Struggle for Black Leadership in New York. *Village Voice,* October 9, 26–35.

Horowitz, Donald L. 1983. Racial Violence in the United States. In *Ethnic Pluralism and Public Policy: Achieving Equality in the United States and Britain,* edited by N. Glazer and K. Young. Lexington, Mass.: Lexington Books.

———. 1985. *Ethnic Groups in Conflict.* Berkeley: University of California Press.

Howe, Marvine. 1990. March for Racial Peace Meets Jeers and Praise. *New York Times,* May 20, 1.

Hurtado, Patricia, and Merle English. 1990. Cops Ordered to Enforce 50–Ft. Rule at Groceries. *New York Newsday,* June 28, 39.

Ignatiev, Noel. 1995. *How the Irish Became White.* New York: Routledge.

Iverem, Esther. 1987. Koreans Hold Rally at Precinct. *New York Times,* October 19, B4.

Ivory, Lee. 1983. Asians May Face Lawsuits. *Los Angeles Sentinel,* September 8, A2.

James, Stephen. 1995. Interview by author. September 21, New York.

Jamison, Harold L. 1988a. Group Says No to Korean Peace Effort. *Amsterdam News,* September 2, 1, 42.

———. 1988b. Groups Clash over Peace Meeting with Koreans. *Amsterdam News,* September 24, 3, 49.

———. 1988c. Vann's Try to Settle Korean Fight Hits Snag. *Amsterdam News,* October 8, 3.

Jamison, Harold L., and Zambga Browne. 1988. Anti-Korean Feelings Rise after Attack on Grandma; Merchant Accuses Her, Daughter of Shoplifting. *Amsterdam News,* September 3, 1, 39–40.

Jenkins, J. Craig. 1995. Social Movements, Political Representation, and the State: An Agenda and Comparative Framework. In *The Politics of Social Protest: Comparative Perspectives on States and Social Movements,* edited by J. C. Jenkins and B. Klandermans. Minneapolis: University of Minnesota Press.

Jetter, Alexis, and George E. Jordan. 1990. Brooklyn Judge Blasts Dinkins, Cites Inaction in Grocery Rift. *New York Newsday,* May 11, 5.

Johnson, Harold. 1985. A Common Bond. *Los Angeles Sentinel,* February 21, A10.

Joint Center for Economic and Political Studies. 1991. *Black Elected Officials.* Washington, D.C.: Joint Center for Economic and Political Studies.

Jones, Alex. 1990. Two Weeks' News: Sizzle over Substance. *New York Times,* May 19, 26.

Jones, Angela. 1982. Youth Boycott Korean Traders. *Amsterdam News,* February 6, 3.

Jones-Correa, Michael. 1998. *Between Two Nations: The Political Predicament of Latinos in New York City.* Ithaca: Cornell University Press.

Jordan, George E. 1990. Four Months in Anguishing Boycott. *New York Newsday,* May 17, 3.

Jordan, George E., and Kevin Flynn. 1990. 1 Store Boycott Is Settled. *New York Newsday,* Sept. 7, 3.

Jordan, George E., Alexis Jetter, William Murphy, Merle English, and Bob Liff. 1990. Lawyer for Protesters Quits: Action Jars City-Led Attempt to Settle Grocer Boycott. *New York Newsday,* May 17, 3.

Joyce, Patrick D. 1997. A Reversal of Fortunes: Black Empowerment, Political Machines, and City Jobs in New York City and Chicago. *Urban Affairs Review* 32 (January): 291–318.

Judd, Dennis R., and Todd Swanstrom. 1994. *City Politics: Private Power and Public Policy.* New York: Harper Collins.

Kang, K. Connie. 1996. Black Pastor, Korean Shop Owner Resolve Racial Incident. *Los Angeles Times,* June 2.

Kaniss, Phyllis C. 1991. *Making Local News.* Chicago: The University of Chicago Press.

Kasinitz, Philip. 1992. *Caribbean New York: Black Immigrants and the Politics of Race.* Ithaca: Cornell University Press.

Katznelson, Ira. 1973. *Black Men, White Cities: Race, Politics, and Migration in the United States, 1900–30, and Britain, 1948–68.* New York: Oxford University Press.

Kifner, John. 1997. Angered by Charges of Police Torture, Thousands March in Brooklyn. *New York Times,* August 17, B1.

Kilborn, Peter T., and Lynette Clemetson. 2002. Gains of 90's Did Not Lift All, Census Shows. *New York Times,* June 5, A1.

Kim, Bong Hwan. 1994. Reviewing the Black-Korean Alliance. In *Black-Korean Encounter: Toward Understanding and Alliance,* edited by E. Y. Yu. Los Angeles: Institute for Asian American and Pacific Asian Studies, California State University, Los Angeles.

——. 1997. Interview by author. April 1, Cambridge, Mass.

Kim, Charles. 1996. Interview by author. December 11, Los Angeles.

Kim, Claire Jean. 1999. The Racial Triangulation of Asian Americans. *Politics and Society* 27 (March): 105–38.

——. 2000. *Bitter Fruit: The Politics of Black-Korean Conflict in New York City.* New Haven, Conn.: Yale University Press.

Kim, David. 1996. Interview by author. December 12, Los Angeles.

Kim, Elaine H. 1993. Home Is Where the Han Is: A Korean American Perspective on the Los Angeles Upheavals. In *Reading Rodney King/Reading Urban Uprising,* edited by R. Gooding–Williams. New York: Routledge.

Kim, Illsoo. 1981. *New Urban Immigrants: The Korean Community in New York.* Princeton: Princeton University Press.

Kim, Sung Soo. 1995. Interview by author. October 17, New York.

Kitschelt, Herbert P. 1995. Political Opportunity Structures and Political Protest: Anti-nuclear Movements in Four Democracies. In *American Society and Politics: Institutional, Historical and Theoretical Perspectives,* edited by T. Skocpol and J. L. Campbell. New York: McGraw-Hill.

Koch, Nadine, and H. Eric Schockman. 1994. Riot, Rebellion, or Civil Unrest? The Korean American and African American Business Communities in Los Angeles. In *Community in Crisis: The Korean American Community after the Los Angeles Civil Unrest of April 1992,* edited by G. O. Totten, III, and H. E. Schockman. Los Angeles: Center for Multiethnic and Transnational Studies, University of Southern California.

Kwong, Peter. 1987. *The New Chinatown.* New York: Hill and Wang.

——. 1992. The First Multicultural Riots. In *Inside the L.A. Riots: What Really Happened, and Why It Will Happen Again: Essays and Articles,* edited by D. Hazen. New York: Institute for Alternative Journalism.

Lee, Felicia R. 1988. Brooklyn Blacks and Koreans Forge Pact. *New York Times,* December 21, B1.

——. 1993. For a Korean Merchant, Holding on to Dreams. *New York Times,* July 21, B3.

Lee, Heon Cheol. 1993. Black-Korean Conflict in New York City: A Sociological Analysis. Ph.D. Diss., Columbia University.

Lee, John H., and John J. Goldman. 1990. Boycott Puts Korean Store at Center of N.Y. Race Strife. *Los Angeles Times,* May 20, 1.

Lee, Marie. 1991. We Koreans Need an Al Sharpton. *New York Times,* Dec. 12, A31.

Levine, Charles H. 1974. *Racial Conflict and the American Mayor: Power, Polarization, and Performance.* Lexington, Mass.: Lexington Books.

Levitt, Leonard. 1989. Dinkins Paid a "Paper" Group: No Address for Carson Organization. *New York Newsday,* October 12.

Light, Ivan, and Edna Bonacich. 1991. *Immigrant Entrepreneurs: Koreans in Los Angeles, 1965–1982.* Berkeley: University of California Press.

Light, Ivan, Hadas Har-Chvi, and Kenneth Kan. 1994. Black/Korean Conflict in Los Angeles. In *Managing Divided Cities,* edited by S. Dunn. Keele, Staffordshire: Ryburn Publishing.

Lineberry, Robert, and Edmund Fowler. 1967. Reformism and Public Policy in American Cities. *American Political Science Review* 61 (3): 701–16.

Lipsky, Michael. 1968. Protest as a Political Resource. *American Political Science Review* 62 (December): 1144–58.

Lipsky, Michael, and David J. Olson. 1977. *Commission Politics: The Processing of Racial Crisis in America.* New Brunswick, N.J.: Transaction Books.

Liu, Mini. 1988. Asians against Afro-Americans: Who Benefits? *Amsterdam News,* October 29, 15.

Lodder, LeeAnn, and Curtis Rist. 1990. Violent Faceoff at Boycott Stores Leaves Pair Hurt. *New York Newsday,* June 24, 17.

Logan, Andy. 1992. Two Cities. *The New Yorker,* June 8, 90–93.

Los Angeles County Clerk. 1999. Public Officials Roster. http://www.co.la.ca.us/ROVELEC/scripts/roster.htm. County of Los Angeles.

Los Angeles Sentinel. 1983a. Untitled editorial. September 15, A5.

——. 1983b. The Die is Cast. September 8, A6.

——. 1984a. Liquor Control Won by SCOC. March 22, A1.

——. 1984b. Time for Prudence. March 15, A6.

———. 1991a. Crusade Hits Campaign Trail. October 3, A1.

———. 1991b. Father of Girl Killed by Store Owner Files Suit. May 8, A1.

Los Angeles Times. 1998. Odd Math in U.S. Police Funding. June 7.

Lubasch, Arnold H. 1991. Jury Acquits Korean Cited by Boycotters. *New York Times,* January 31, B1.

Lucas, Lawrence. 1990a. Seeing through the Smoke Screen of the Boycott. *Amsterdam News,* October 6, 13, 43.

———. 1990b. Thoughts on African American Leadership. *Amsterdam News,* May 12, 15.

———. 1995. Interview by author. October 18, New York.

MacDonald, Heather. 1995. Why Koreans Succeed. *City Journal* 5 (spring): 12–29.

Malnic, Eric. 1991. Mayor Seeks Help of Black, Korean Ministers to End Strife. *Los Angeles Times,* October 25, B3.

Mandulo, Rhea. 1990. Police Enforce Court Ban on Korean Grocery Protest. *United Press International,* September 18.

March, James G., and Johan P. Olsen. 1984. The New Institutionalism: Organizational Factors in Political Life. *American Political Science Review* 78 (3): 734–49.

Matthews, Les. 1984. Harlem Pickets Demand Respect for Customers. *Amsterdam News,* October 27, 16.

Mayhew, David R. 1986. *Placing Parties in American Politics: Organization, Electoral Settings, and Government Activity in the Twentieth Century.* Princeton: Princeton University Press.

McAdam, Doug. 1982. *Political Process and the Development of Black Insurgency, 1930–1970.* Chicago: The University of Chicago Press.

McClain, Paula D. 1993. The Changing Dynamics of Urban Politics: Black and Hispanic Municipal Employment—Is There Competition? *The Journal of Politics* 55 (May): 399–414.

McClain, Paula D., and Albert K. Karnig. 1993. Black and Hispanic Socioeconomic and Political Competition. *American Political Science Review* 84: 2 (June): 535–45.

McClain, Paula D., and Steven C. Tauber. 1995. *We Win! You Lose! Implications of Black, Latino, and Asian Socioeconomic and Political Resources for the Other Groups' Electoral Success in Urban Politics.* Paper read at Annual Meeting of the American Political Science Association, at Chicago.

McFadden, Robert P. 1990. Police Now Say Flatbush Attack Wasn't Planned. *New York Times,* May 15, 1.

McQueen, M. P. 1990. Clashes with Koreans Spark B'klyn March. *New York Newsday,* January 28, 19.

McQuillan, Michael. 1995. Interview by author. October 17, New York.

McRae, F. Finley. 1987. Crenshaw Merchants Launch Asian Protest. *Los Angeles Sentinel,* May 14, A1.

———. 1988. Girls Attacked; NAACP Hits Korean Cafe. *Los Angeles Sentinel,* September 22, A1.

Medoff, Peter, and Holly Sklar. 1994. *Streets of Hope.* Boston: South End Press.

Min, Pyong Gap. 1996. *Caught in the Middle: Korean Communities in New York and Los Angeles.* Berkeley: University of California Press.

Mintz, Jerome R. 1992. *Hasidic People: A Place in the New World.* Cambridge, Mass.: Harvard University Press.

Mitchell, Marsha. 1991a. Bakewell Returns: Selective Buying Campaign Continues. *Los Angeles Sentinel,* September 25, A1.

———. 1991b. Black Man Killed by Korean Merchant; No Charges Filed. *Los Angeles Sentinel,* June 13, A1.

———. 1991c. Teenager's Slaying Heightens Black-Korean Tensions. *Los Angeles Sentinel,* April 3, A1.

———. 1991d. Truce Is Called in Black-Korean Conflict. *Los Angeles Sentinel,* October 10, A1.

Moffat, Susan. 1992. Shopkeepers Fight Back; Blacks Join with Koreans in a Battle to Rebuild Their Liquor Stores. *Los Angeles Times,* May 15, D1.

Mollenkopf, John H. 1974. *Community Organization and City Politics.* Ph.D. dissertation, Harvard University.

———. 1990. New York: The Great Anomaly. In *Racial Politics in American Cities,* edited by R. P. Browning, D. R. Marshall, and D. H. Tabb. New York: Longman.

———. 1992. *A Phoenix in the Ashes: The Rise and Fall of the Koch Coalition in New York City Politics.* Princeton: Princeton University Press.

Moore, Patricia. 1992. Seeking Justice in Compton. *Los Angeles Sentinel,* January 30, A7.

Mornell, Eugene S. 1983. Letter to the Editor. *Los Angeles Sentinel,* October 20, A6.

Morrison, Peter A., and Ira S. Lowry. 1994. A Riot of Color: The Demographic Setting. In *The Los Angeles Riots: Lessons for the Urban Future,* edited by M. Baldassare. Boulder: Westview Press.

Mosher, James F., and Rose M. Works. 1994. Confronting Sacramento: State Preemption, Community Control, and Alcohol Blight in Two Inner City Communities. San Rafael, Calif.: Marin Institute for the Prevention of Alcohol and Other Drug Problems.

———. 1990. Mayor Defends Store Stance; Brushes off Criticisms of Slow Pace. *New York Newsday,* May 10, 5.

Mwalilino, Walusako. 1988. Angry Protesters Urge Boycott of "Disrespectful" Korean Trader. *Amsterdam News,* October 1, 3.

Mydans, Seth. 1990. For Them, Racial Harmony Is Work. *New York Times,* May 27, A18.

———. 1991a. Shooting Puts Focus on Korean–Black Frictions in Los Angeles. *New York Times,* October 6, A20.

———. 1991b. Two Views of Protest at Korean Shop. *New York Times,* December 24, A20.

New York City Council Committee on General Welfare. 1990. An Analysis of the Report of the Mayor's Committee Investigating the Protest against Two Korean-Owned Groceries on Church Avenue in Brooklyn.

New York City Mayor's Committee. 1990a. Public Hearing on the Boycott on Church Avenue: Erasmus High School, Brooklyn, New York.

———. 1990b. Report of the Mayor's Committee Investigating the Protest against Two Korean-Owned Groceries on Church Avenue in Brooklyn.

New York State Advisory Committee to the U.S. Commission on Civil Rights. 1994. Resolving Intergroup Conflicts in New York City.

New York Times. 1991. Minister Asks End to Protest at Queens Store. *New York Times,* February 14, B7.

Njeri, Itabari. 1989. Cultural Conflict: Blacks and Korean Americans Have Become Antagonists Instead of Allies. *Los Angeles Times,* November 8, E1.

———. 1997. *The Last Plantation: Color, Conflict, and Identity: Reflections of a New World Black.* Boston: Houghton Mifflin.

Noel, Peter. 1981a. Koreans Vie for Harlem Dollars. *Amsterdam News,* July 4, 26, 39, 56.

———. 1981b. Will Black Merchants Drive Koreans from Harlem? *Amsterdam News,* 3, 16.

———. 1992. Death of a Movement: How New York's Black Activists Won and Lost the Struggle for a United Front. *Village Voice,* August 18, 23–32.

———. 2001. What Black Vote? *Village Voice,* September 5.

Noonan, Deputy Inspector Robert. 1990. Chronology of Events Surrounding Haitian Demonstrations on Church Avenue. New York City Human Rights Commission files.

Olzak, Susan. 1992. *The Dynamics of Ethnic Competition and Conflict.* Stanford: Stanford University Press.

Olzak, Susan, and Suzanne Shanahan. 1996. Deprivation and Race Riots: An Extension of Spilerman's Analysis. *Social Forces* 74 (3): 931–61.

Ong, Paul, Kye Young Park, and Yasmin Tong. 1994. The Korean–Black Conflict and the State. In *The New Asian Immigration in Los Angeles and Global Restructuring,* edited by P. Ong, E. Bonacich, and L. Cheng. Philadelphia: Temple University Press.

Ong, Paul M., and Suzanne Hee. 1993a. The L.A. Riot/Rebellion and Korean Merchants: Analysis and Comments. In *Losses in the Los Angeles Civil Unrest, April 29–May 1, 1992.* Los Angeles: University of California–Los Angeles, Center for Pacific Rim Studies.

———. 1993b. *Losses in the Los Angeles Civil Unrest, April 29–May 1, 1992: Lists of the Damaged Properties and the L.A. Riot/Rebellion and Korean Merchants.* Los Angeles: University of California–Los Angeles, Center for Pacific Rim Studies.

Palmer, Gene, and Joseph W. Queen. 1990. 600 Stage Noisy Protest at Korean Grocery Store. *New York Newsday,* May 13, 4.

Papajohn, George. 1993. Boycott Targets Korean Stores: African-American Group Angry with Policies, Goods. *Chicago Tribune,* December 19, 3.

Park, Kyeyoung. 1991. Conceptions of Ethnicities by Koreans: Workplace Encounters. In *Asian Americans: Comparative and Global Perspectives,* edited by S. Hune, H.-c. Kim, S. S. Fugita and A. Ling. Pullman, Wash.: Washington State University Press.

———. 1992. The Question of Culture in the Black/Korean American Conflict. In *Black-Korean Encounter: Toward Understanding and Alliance,* edited by E.-Y. Yu. Los Angeles: Institute for Asian American and Pacific Asian Studies, California State University, Los Angeles.

Pear, Robert. 2002. Number of People Living in Poverty Increases. *New York Times,* September 25, 1.

Perry, Jan. 1996. Interview by author. December 12, Los Angeles.

Peterson, Paul E. 1981. *City Limits.* Chicago: University of Chicago Press.

——. 1995. Who Should Do What? Divided Responsibility in the Federal System. *Brookings Review* 13 (2): 6–11.

Pryce, Vinette K. 1991. Blacks Declare "Day of Outrage" on Flatbush Board 14. *Amsterdam News,* March 16, 9.

Purdum, Todd S. 1990a. Angry Dinkins Defends Role in Race Cases. *New York Times,* May 9, B1.

——. 1990b. Dinkins Asks for Racial Unity and Offers to Mediate Boycott. *New York Times,* May 12, 1.

——. 1990c. Dinkins Presses for Stiffer Law in Gang Attacks. *New York Times,* May 15, B3.

——. 1990d. Dinkins Supports Shunned Grocers. *New York Times,* September 22, A1.

Reed, Adolph L. 1986. *The Jesse Jackson Phenomenon.* New Haven: Yale University Press.

——. 1991. False Prophet II: All for One and None for All. *Nation,* January 29, 86–92.

——. 1997. Yackety-Yak about Race. *Progressive* (December): 18–19.

Regalado, James A. 1994. Community Coalition-Building. In *The Los Angeles Riots: Lessons for the Urban Future,* edited by M. Baldassare. Boulder: Westview Press.

Rieder, Jonathan. 1985. *Canarsie: The Jews and Italians of Brooklyn against Liberalism.* Cambridge: Harvard University Press.

Roberts, Sam. 1990. Which Mayor Knows Best on the Boycott? *New York Times,* July 30, B1.

——. 1993. The Tide Turns on Voter Turnout: Small Shifts in Voting Blocs Make the Difference for Giuliani. *New York Times,* November 4, B6.

Robinson, Reginald Leamon. 1993. "The Other against Itself": Deconstructing the Violent Discourse between Korean and African Americans. *Southern California Law Review* 67: 17–115.

Rohrlich, Ted. 1997. City Council: L.A.'s Micro-Managers. *Los Angeles Times,* November 3, 1.

Rutten, Tim. 1992. A New Kind of Riot. *New York Review of Books,* June 11, 52–54.

Sa, B. J. 1995. Interview by author. October 19, New York.

Saltzstein, Alan, Raphael Sonenshein, and Irving Ostrow. 1986. Federal Grants and the City of Los Angeles: Implementing a More Centralized Local Political System. *Research in Urban Policy* 2: 55–76.

Sauerzopf, Marty. 1991a. Officials Work to Ease Black-Korean Tension. *Los Angeles Sentinel,* August 15, A1.

——. 1991b. Prayer Vigil in L.A.; Protest in Compton. *Los Angeles Sentinel,* December 11, A1.

Schattschneider, E. E. 1957. Intensity, Visibility, Direction and Scope. *American Political Science Review* 51 (4): 933–42.

Schatzman, Dennis. 1991a. Harlins' Supporters: Mayor Is Insensitive. *Los Angeles Sentinel,* September 18, A1.

———. 1991b. Protesting Continues at the La Fiesta Market. *Los Angeles Sentinel,* August 1, A1.

Schmitt, Eric. 2001. Whites in Minority in Largest Cities, the Census Shows. *New York Times,* April 30.

Schockman, H. Eric. 1996. Is Los Angeles Governable? Revisiting the City Charter. In *Rethinking Los Angeles,* edited by M. J. Dear, H. E. Schockman, and G. Hise. Thousand Oaks, Calif.: Sage Publications.

Sears, David O. 1994. Urban Rioting in Los Angeles: A Comparison of 1965 with 1992. In *The Los Angeles Riots: Lessons for the Urban Future,* edited by M. Baldassare. Boulder: Westview Press.

Seo, Diane. 1993. Korean American Business Owners Hit Hard by Riots and Other Violence, Ponder the Grim Trade-offs as They Debate Whether to Rebuild, Sell, or Move. *Los Angeles Times,* December 12, 14.

Shanahan, Suzanne, and Susan Olzak. 1999. The Effects of Immigration Diversity and Ethnic Competition on Collective Action in Urban America: An Assessment of Two Moments of Mass Migration, 1869–1924 and 1965–1993. *Journal of American Ethnic History* (Spring): 40–64.

Shannon, Edward. 1988. Let's Tone Down Anti-Korean Rhetoric. *Amsterdam News,* October 8, 15.

Shiver, Jube. 1991. Inner City Firms Can Make It: A Look at 3 Entrepreneurs Who Serve Urban Clients. *Los Angeles Times,* November 27, D1.

Sims, Calvin. 1992. Dinkins Thanks New Yorkers for Remaining Cool Last Week. *New York Times,* May 8, B3.

Sinclair, Tom. 1990. Korean Deli Boycott: Will Mayoral Committee Run into A Stone Wall? *New York Voice,* May 5, 2, 22.

Skerry, Peter. 1993. *Mexican Americans: The Ambivalent Minority.* New York: The Free Press.

Skerry, Peter. 2000. Do We Really Want Immigrants to Assimilate? *Society* (March/April): 57–62.

Skocpol, Theda. 1992. *Protecting Soldiers and Mothers: The Political Origins of Social Policy in the United States.* Cambridge: Harvard University Press.

Sleeper, Jim. 1990. *The Closest of Strangers: Liberalism and the Politics of Race in New York.* New York: W. W. Norton.

Smith, Leef, and Lou Cannon. 1992. 24 Dead, 900 Injured in L.A. Rioting. *Washington Post,* May 1, A1.

Sonenshein, Raphael. 1990. Biracial Coalitions in Big Cities: Why They Succeed, Why They Fail. In *Racial Politics in American Cities,* edited by R. P. Browning, D. R. Marshall, and D. H. Tabb. New York: Longman.

———. 1993. *Politics in Black and White: Race and Power in Los Angeles.* Princeton: Princeton University Press.

———. 1996. The Battle over Liquor Stores in South Central Los Angeles: The Management of an Interminority Conflict. *Urban Affairs Review* 31 (July): 710–37.

Song, Ryan. 1996. Interview by author. May 7, Cambridge, Mass.

Starr, Kevin. 1999a. L.A. Is Refounded, and Secessionism Lives. *Los Angeles Times,* June 13, M1.

——. 1999b. A Tale of Three Mayors. *Los Angeles Times,* August 22, M1.

Steinmo, Sven. 1989. Political Institutions and Tax Policy in the United States, Sweden, and Britain. *World Politics* 41 (4): 500–35.

Stolberg, Sheryl, and Frank Clifford. 1991. Black-Korean Truce Termed "Very Fragile." *Los Angeles Times,* October 5, B1.

Stone, Clarence N. 1976. *Economic Growth and Neighborhood Discontent: System Bias in the Urban Renewal Program of Atlanta.* Chapel Hill: University of North Carolina Press.

——. 1989. *Regime Politics: Governing Atlanta, 1964–1988.* Lawrence: University Press of Kansas.

Stone, Sherry. 1993. Blacks and Koreans: The Conflicts—What It All Means. *Philadelphia Tribune,* November 19, 1A.

Tait, George Edward. 1988. ANPM Responds to "Buy Black" Critics. *Amsterdam News,* October 29, 15.

Tarrow, Sidney G. 1994. *Power in Movement: Social Movements, Collective Action and Politics.* Cambridge: Cambridge University Press.

Tate, Katherine. 1993. *From Protest to Politics: The New Black Voters in American Elections.* Cambridge: Harvard University Press.

Terry, Don. 1990a. Dinkins to Ask State Inquiry on 2d Boycott. *New York Times,* August 29, B1.

——. 1990b. Top Legislator Attacks Boycott of Korean Store. *New York Times,* September 13, B2.

Thom, Stephen. 1996. Interview by author. December 10, Los Angeles.

Tierney, Kathleen J. 1994. Property Damage and Violence: A Collective Behavior Analysis. In *The Los Angeles Riots: Lessons for the Urban Future,* edited by M. Baldassare. Boulder: Westview Press.

Tilly, Charles. 1984. Social Movements and National Politics. In *Statemaking and Social Movements: Essays in History and Theory,* edited by C. Bright and S. Harding. Ann Arbor: University of Michigan Press.

Tomz, Michael, Jason Wittenberg, and Gary King. 2001. *CLARIFY: Software for Interpreting and Presenting Statistical Results 2.0.* Harvard University, Cambridge.

Tumulty, Karen. 1990. Tensions Put Pressure on Dinkins to Live up to Campaign Image. *Los Angeles Times,* May 15, A21.

U.S. Bureau of the Census. 1980a. *Characteristics for SMSAs, U.S. Census of Population.* Washington, D.C.: Government Printing Office.

——. 1980b. *General Social and Economic Characteristics, U.S. Census of Population.* Washington, D.C.

——. 1987. *Survey of Minority-Owned Business Enterprises.* Washington, D.C.

——. 1990. *Metropolitan Areas, U.S. Census of Population.* Washington, D.C.

——. 2001. *Projections of the Resident Population by Race, Hispanic Origin, and Nativity: Middle Series, 2050 to 2070.* Washington, D.C.: Population Projections Program, Population Division, U.S. Census Bureau.

Umemoto, Karen. 1994. Blacks and Koreans in Los Angeles: The Case of LaTasha Harlins and Soon Ja Du. In *Blacks, Latinos, and Asians in Urban America: Status and Prospects for Politics and Activism,* edited by J. Jennings. Westport, Conn.: Praeger Publishers.

Useem, Bert. 1997. The State and Collective Disorders: The Los Angeles Riot/ Protest of April 1992. *Social Forces* 76 (December): 357–77.

Verhovek, Sam Howe. 1997. Gloves Come Off in Houston's Election. *New York Times,* December 3.

Wagner, Holly J. 1992. Black-Korean Alliance Blames the System. *Los Angeles Sentinel,* April 30, 1992, A1.

Waldie, D. J. 1999. The City's Future Is in Its Neighborhoods. *Los Angeles Times,* June 6, M1.

White, Douglas H. 1988. Black-Korean Problems and Progress. *Amsterdam News,* November 12, 15.

White House. 2002a. *Building One America for the 21st Century.* National Archives and Records Administration, November 16, 2000 [cited May 14 2002]. Available from http://clinton3.nara.gov/Initiatives/OneAmerica/america.html.

——. 2002b. *One American Dialogue Guide.* National Archives and Records Administration, November 16, 2000 [cited May 14 2002]. Available from http://clinton3.nara.gov/Initiatives/OneAmerica/ch1.html.

Wickham, DeWayne. 1997. Clinton Race Panel Needs More Voices. *USA Today,* December 2, A15.

Wilkinson, Tracy, and Frank Clifford. 1991. Korean Grocer Who Killed Black Teen Gets Probation. *Los Angeles Times,* November 16, A1.

Wilson, James Q. 1998. The Closing of the American City. *New Republic,* May 11, 30–38.

Wilson, William J. 1999. *The Bridge over the Racial Divide: Rising Inequality and Coalition Politics.* Berkeley: University of California Press.

Wolfinger, Raymond E. 1972. Why Political Machines Have Not Withered Away and Other Revisionist Thoughts. *The Journal of Politics* 34 (May): 377–78.

Yamada, Ken. 1990. Boycotters March, but Avoid Groceries. *New York Newsday,* September 30, 18.

Yates, Douglas. 1973. *Neighborhood Democracy.* Lexington, Mass.: Lexington Books.

——. 1977. *The Ungovernable City: The Politics of Urban Problems and Policy Making.* Cambridge, Mass.: MIT Press.

Yoo, Y. S. 1995. Telephone interview by author. September 20, New York.

Yoon, In-Jin. 1997. *On My Own: Korean Businesses and Race Relations in America.* Chicago: University of Chicago Press.

Yu, Eui-Young, ed. 1992. *Black-Korean Encounter: Toward Understanding and Alliance.* Los Angeles: Institute for Asian American and Pacific Asian Studies, University of California-Los Angeles.

Yu, Jerry. 1996. Interview by author. December 9, Los Angeles.

Index

www.ingramcontent.com/pod-product-compliance
Lightning Source LLC
Chambersburg PA
CBHW022311280326
41932CB00010B/1066